ERIC BENTLEY'S
DRAMATIC REPERTOIRE
VOLUME TWO

LIFE IS A DREAM
AND OTHER
SPANISH CLASSICS

Edited by Eric Bentley
Translated by Roy Campbell

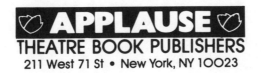
APPLAUSE
THEATRE BOOK PUBLISHERS
211 West 71 St • New York, NY 10023

LIFE IS A DREAM
AND OTHER SPANISH CLASSICS

Library of Congress Cataloging-in-Publication Data
Main entry under title:

Life is a dream, and other Spanish classics.

    (Eric Bentley's dramatic repertoire ; v. 2)
    These 4 plays (with 2 additional plays) previously published as v. 3 of The classic theatre under title: Six Spanish plays.
    Contents: The siege of Numantia / Miguel de Cervantes—Fuente ovejuna / Lope de Vega—The trickster of Seville and his guest of stone / Tirso de Molina—[etc.]
    1. Spanish drama—Classical period, 1500-1700—Translations into English. 2. English drama—Translations from Spanish. 3. Numantia (Ancient city)—Drama. 4. Fuente Ovejuna (Spain)—History—Drama. 5. Don Juan—Drama.
I. Bentley, Eric, 1916- . II. Campbell, Roy, 1901-1957.
III. Series.
PQ6267.E6L5   1985   862'.3'08   85-15671

ISBN 0-87910-248-9
ISBN 0-87910-244-6 (pbk.)

Applause Theatre Book Titles are distributed to the trade by Harper & Row.

First Applause Printing, 1985

CONTENTS

FOREWORD

SIEGE OF NUMANTIA
Miguel de Cervantes
1

FUENTE OVEJUNA
Lope de Vega
65

THE TRICKSTER OF SEVILLE
Tirso de Molina
137

LIFE IS A DREAM
Calderon de la Barca
219

NOTES
293

FOREWORD

Probably there is no body of World Literature so little known to the world as the classic Spanish drama. This is not entirely the world's fault, for few of the translations are readable, let alone impressive. The only collection of Lope de Vega ever published in English is, it seems, *Four Plays*, in English versions by John Garrett Underhill. I defy anyone to read it through. In the nineteenth century Denis Florence MacCarthy spent many years of his life translating Calderón. In trying to reproduce the sound of the Spanish, he effectively prevented himself from writing English. Edward Fitzgerald had much greater success with Calderón, but went to the other extreme of excessive freedom. For a while the effect must have seemed to be one of brilliance: today one is depressed by the persistent feeling that one is reading Victorian poetry of the second class. In ranging pretty widely over the field of Spanish classics in English, I found most enjoyable a volume entitled *Three Comedies from the Spanish,* published anonymously in London in 1807 and known to be the work of Lord Holland. Unfortunately, Lord Holland did not choose to include a single major play.

What was needed, I thought, was fresh air, such as flooded into the translated Greek drama a generation ago when Cocteau and Yeats applied themselves to it. I got hold of some translations which Roy Campbell had recently made for the B.B.C. Third Programme. *Fuente Ovejuna* and *The Trickster of Seville,* flat and even absurd in the earlier translations I had read, came alive. Campbell was in love with old Spain and was one of the few poets writing English in our day who had a touch of bravado, a vein of bravura. Even qualities I had disliked in certain poems of his own were turned to account in the translations. And he also had a straightforward lyrical gift, invaluable for the rendering of Lope's tenderness and charm. When Roy Campbell came to America for a lecture tour in the autumn of 1955, Jason Epstein and I arranged with him to bring out the B.B.C. translations—plus a couple we ourselves commissioned—in this country.

Campbell was killed, with all the sudden, sprawling violence of Spanish life and literature, some 18 months later. The translations were done, but, as they were not revised, let alone polished and fully prepared for the press, the responsibility devolved upon me of editing manuscripts without being able to consult their author. Should research students ever compare the manuscripts with the texts here published, some of them will wish, I imagine, that I had meddled more, others will conclude that I have already meddled too much. The task being impossible, the solutions found were at best partial and questionable. But in human affairs this is not an unusual situation.

The volumes of the present series represent only a small selection from an enormous repertoire. There will always be a case against the particular selection made, and there will always be a case against the particular translations used. I am very willing to concede that such a volume as the present one is only a beginning, if my critics will grant that it *is* a beginning. "Spanish drama of the golden age" has been a phrase only, referring to we knew not what. If this volume communicates something of the spirit of that drama to modern readers (and, who knows? also to theatre audiences) it will have succeeded where many worthy efforts in the past have failed. In any event I shall not be ashamed to have played even a modest part in the enterprise.

E.B.

THE SIEGE OF NUMANTIA

Miguel de Cervantes

English Version by Roy Campbell

When the Roman Senate resolved to destroy Carthage—
"Delenda est Carthago!"—the general to whom the operation
was entrusted was Scipio, thereupon surnamed Africanus. A
second surname—Numantinus—was accorded him by the Senate when in the year 134 B.C. he wrought the downfall of
Numantia in Spain.

E.B.

DRAMATIS PERSONAE

SCIPIO ⎫
JUGURTHA ⎪
CAIUS MARIUS ⎬ *Romans*
QUINTUS FABIUS ⎭
CAIUS, *Roman soldier*
TWO NUMANTINES, *ambassadors*
FOUR ROMAN SOLDIERS
SPAIN
THE RIVER DUERO, CALLED ALSO THE DOURO
THREE BOYS REPRESENTING TRIBUTARY STREAMS
THEOGENES ⎫
⎬ *Numantines*
CARAVINO ⎭
TWO NUMANTINE GOVERNORS
MARQUINO, *a Numantine magician*
MARANDRO ⎫
⎬ *Numantines*
LEONICIO ⎭
TWO NUMANTINE PRIESTS
A NUMANTINE PAGE
SIX NUMANTINE PAGES
A NUMANTINE MAN
MILBIO, *a Numantine*
A DEVIL
A CORPSE
FOUR NUMANTINE WOMEN
LIRA, *a maiden*
TWO NUMANTINE CITIZENS
A NUMANTINE WOMAN
HER SON
A BOY, LIRA'S BROTHER
A NUMANTINE SOLDIER
WAR
PESTILENCE
HUNGER

WIFE OF THEOGENES

HIS SON

ANOTHER SON, AND A DAUGHTER, OF THEOGENES

SERVIUS, *a boy*

BARIATUS, *a boy, who throws himself from a tower*

A NUMANTINE

ERMILIUS, *a Roman soldier*

LIMPIUS, *a Roman soldier*

FAME, *personified*

ACT I

Enter SCIPIO, JUGURTHA, CAIUS MARIUS, QUINTUS FABIUS, *the brother of* SCIPIO, *and other Romans.*

SCIPIO. This difficult and heavy task with which
The Roman Senate charged me weighs me down
And wearies me till my attention almost
Becomes unhinged. Who would not long to finish
The course of such a long and monstrous war
That cost so many Roman lives? Alas!
Who would not tremble, having to renew it?

JUGURTHA. Why, Scipio, you yourself! For you contain
Both luck and peerless valour in your person,
And both will make your victory secure.

SCIPIO. Force, when applied with prudent moderation,
Humbles the steepest mountains to the earth,
But, when it's fiercely plied with a mad hand,
Trenches the smoothest plains to rugged wastes.
From what I see, it seems there's no repressing
The frenzy of our present army here,
Which, careless both of glory and of spoils,
Lies drunk in burning lust. Here's what I plan,
This is my only wish: to turn our troops
To new and better conduct and, by mending
That which is friendly to us first, the sooner
To subjugate our enemy. Ho! Marius!

CAIUS MARIUS. My lord?

SCIPIO.   Give orders for a general muster
Of the whole army without more delay
Or hindrance. Everybody on parade
Together must immediately appear.
I have a short harangue to give the troops.

CAIUS MARIUS. At once, sir!

SCIPIO.   It is right that they should know
My new designs and their past errors. Go!

Exit CAIUS MARIUS.

JUGURTHA. Sir, I can tell you there's no soldier here
  Who does not love you or who does not fear
  You too, because your matchless valour's known
  From the far south up to the Boreal zone.
  Not one of them, but with fierce, daring zeal
  Will serve you once he hears the trumpet peal
  And eagerly looks forward to the day
  Fabulous deeds of valour to display.

SCIPIO. But first we need to bridle and to quiet
  The vice that seems amongst them to run riot.
  While *that* disgrace continues, to their shame,
  How can they hope to win a glorious name?
  If this most harmful plague is left unchecked
  To root its burning flame and to infect
  The camp—then Vice will work us far more harms
  Than could the fiercest enemy in arms.

*The fall-in for the muster is sounded: and these orders are
heard off-stage:*

  "Our general orders every soldier here
  Upon the main parade-ground to appear,
  This instant, fully armed. Whoever's missed
  Will have his name struck from the army-list."

JUGURTHA. I do not doubt but that with a strong bit
  This evil must be curbed, and that it's fit
  The soldier should be jerked on the short rein
  When justice is a name he takes in vain.
  An army's strength is bloodsucked from within
  When not supported by just discipline
  In spite of all the squadrons that it brags
  And the display of many-coloured flags.

*Soldiers enter and fall in on parade. They are equipped in
the ancient style, without arquebuses. SCIPIO gets on a boul-
der, which should be handy nearby, and harangues the
troops.*

SCIPIO. From your fierce mien, and from your sprightly show,
  Comrades, that you are Romans, well I know—
  Romans both strong and lusty for the fight—
  But in your hands so delicate and white,
  And in that pink that's on your faces written,

Why, anyone would think you reared in Britain,
Or that by Flemish sires you'd been begot!
Now, comrades! your joint negligence in not
Heeding what most concerned your good revives
A fallen enemy to seek your lives,
Despising both your prowess and your fame.
For you are Romans, now, only in name.
My sons! does it seem good in your opinion
That the whole world should bend to the dominion
Of Rome, but that you here in Spain, of all
Her subjects, would precipitate her fall?
What a strange flabbiness has laid you low,
A flabbiness, which, in my mind, I know
Is due to Indolence—that deadly foe
To martial strength! Soft Venus does not mate
With Mars, for whole months to cohabitate:
She studies fleeting pleasures, he—the foe,
Conning the art of havoc, blow for blow.
The Cyprian goddess from the camp of Rome
Must leave her quarters, and set out for home.
Her son must leave the barracks, too, who thinks
Of nothing more than banquetings and drinks.
Do you think that mere spears and helms alone
Can raze these mighty battlements of stone?
Or that mere numbers, joined in arms, can crush
And trample down a fortress in one rush?
If no attempt at prudence has been made,
And all things with due foresight are not weighed,
Small profit from vast multitudes can stem,
And far less, from vast armaments, than them.
Now: if in martial unity we stand
It matters not how small may be the band,
You'll see it shine in glory like the sun,
And all its fights will certainly be won;
But if in flabby slothfulness it lies,
Though it should dwarf the whole world with its size,
One moment will suffice to rout it, if
The hand is disciplined, the chest is stiff.
Shame on you, lusty fellows! Shame, I say!
That to our grief, with arrogant display,

A few surrounded Spaniards, in this wall,
Can keep Numantia's eyrie from us all.
Sixteen long tedious years, and more, have passed
Since they have waged us war, up to the last
Holding the vantage still, our ranks dismaying,
And tens of thousands of our kinsmen slaying.
Conquer yourselves! Conquered by vice, you wallow
In base effeminate lust, lewdly to follow
Venus and Bacchus with their trivial charms—
And never reach a hand to take up arms!
Run off, then! If you don't run mad with pain
To see this little country-town of Spain
Defy Rome's might, her own and sole defender,
Offensive most when nearest to surrender!
I'll have your filthy strumpets, at the double,
Run out of camp—the cause of all this trouble!
No man must have more than one eating-bowl.
Your beds, whereon with whores you loved to roll,
Must all be broken up. Let none be found!
And all must sleep on straw, strewn on the ground.
The only perfumes that I will not bar,
Throughout the camp, are those of pitch and tar.
No kitchen pots and pans to fatten greed!
You'll have one mess-can each from which to feed,
For it ill suits with warlike strain and strife
To lead a lounging, plutocratic life.
I'll have no other luxury or scent
Until Numantia to our heel has bent
Than sweat. Men! Let it not appear to you
That you have a rough pathway to pursue
In these just orders! They are what you need
To crown your task, your victory to speed!
It will be difficult at first, I know,
To change your habits at a single blow,
But, if you do not, then this chronic war,
More than it drags behind, will stretch before!
'Twixt wine and dalliance, in soft beds to sport
Suits ill with strenuous Mars. A different sort
Of gear he seeks. He walks in different ways
With different arms his standard to upraise.

I am so sure that, in the end, you'll show
Yourselves true Romans that I now appraise
This beetling wall as naught, which by a foe
Of base, barbarian rebels is defended,
And if your hands can match the zeal you show,
My own to pay you well will be extended,
And with my tongue I'll praise you. Now you know!
The soldiers look at each other, making signs to one of them,
CAIUS, *to answer for them.*

CAIUS. If with attentive eyes you have observed
The changing countenances that surround you
As they were moved by your brief argument,
You've seen how they lost colour, were confused,
And showed the shame and fear that now afflicts
And punishes us all—shame to behold
To what a level they have been reduced
By their own guilt, and that, when chid by you,
They could not find the least excuse to offer
And fear at having made such fatal errors
And having sunk into such drowsy sloth
That they would rather die than do their duty.
But there is still both time and place to spare
For them to make the recompense they owe,
And that's a reason why their grave offences
Should vex you less. Because, from this day on,
With gay and ready zeal, the least of them
Will think of naught but, in your loyal service,
To sacrifice his honour, home, and life.
Accept, my lord, the offer of their saner
And better resolutions, and consider
That in the end they're Romans after all,
In whom there never lacks true, manly fire.
Raise your right hands above your heads, you others,
To show that you approve my vote!

FIRST SOLDIER.   In all
You said, we here confirm you!

SECOND SOLDIER.   And we swear it!

ALL. We swear it: yes!

SCIPIO.   My confidence grows greater

From this day forth, supported by your offer.
For now a new fire kindles in your hearts
With this new change to your old way of life.
I hope the wind will not bear off your vows,
And that you'll make them truthful with your lances.
For my own vows to blossom forth as true,
Yours must as well. It all depends on you.

FIRST SOLDIER. With a safe conduct, two Numantines here
Have come upon an embassy to Scipio.

SCIPIO. Why don't they come? What keeps them?

SOLDIER.   Your permission
Is what they crave.

SCIPIO.   If they're ambassadors
It's theirs already.

SOLDIER.   They're ambassadors.

SCIPIO. Well, let them in then, for, although dissembled,
The enemy will still betray some glint
Of truth. Yes, though he covers it with skill,
You'll always find a little chink through which
You'll get a glimpse of what is wrong with him.
To give an audience to one's enemy
Has always done more good than harm. Experience
In things of war has taught me what I say,
And one acquires sure knowledge in this way.

Enter TWO NUMANTINE AMBASSADORS.

FIRST NUMANTINE. Well, thanks to the safe-conduct that you
        grant
Out of the bounty of your regal greatness,
I'll start upon the reason for our mission.
Numantia, of which I am a burgess,
Illustrious general! has sent me to you,
Being the strongest general of Rome
Whom night has ever hid or daylight seen,
To ask of you, my lord, a friendly hand
To signify an end to all this fierce
And vicious strife that for so many years
Has been so harmful to yourselves and us.
Numantia says that never from the laws
And statutes of the Roman Senate will she

Depart as long as we have not to suffer
Beneath the lawless and insufferable
Weight of one consul's rule after another.
They, with their cruel laws and vicious greed,
Placed such a heavy yoke upon our necks,
We were compelled to shake it off by force.
All through the long duration of this war
We have not found a general till now
Whom we could trust enough to treat of peace.
However, now that Fate has steered our ship
To a good harbour, we have reefed our sails,
And wish at last to come to some agreement.
Do not imagine we were brought by fear
To ask for peace in such an urgent way,
Because a long experience has proved
The stubborn strength and valour of Numantia.
Your virtue and your bravery are the bait
That tempted us and showed how we would gain
If we could count upon you as our friend
And lord. That is the reason why we came.
Answer us now, my lord, what is your pleasure?

SCIPIO. You show these signs of penitence too late.
Your friendship gives me little satisfaction.
Once more go exercise your strong right hand
Because I wish to see what mine can do.
Perhaps Fate has entrusted to its grasp
Our glory and your burial. For the shame
Of these long years, it is small recompense
To sue for peace. Go carry on the war!
And let the valiant ranks be formed once more.

FIRST NUMANTINE. False confidence brings after it a thousand
Deceptions. Study well what you decide,
My lord, since this hard arrogance you show
Strengthens our hands to deal you blow for blow.
And since you grudge that peace which our good will
Demands, our cause will be the juster still,
And long before you tread Numantia's earth
You'll learn what the indignant strength is worth
Of those who, though your foes, to make amends,
Have sought to be your vassals and your friends.

SCIPIO. Have you got more to say?

THE NUMANTINES.   No, but we've more
  To do, since you, my lord, will have it so.
  Not to accept the friendship that we bring
  Ill suits the person that you are. But now
  We'll have to show you what we can perform,
  And you, for your part, show what you can do,
  Since it's another thing to ask for peace
  Than through the armoured ranks to burst in storm.

SCIPIO. That's true. And now, to show you whether I
  Know how to treat of peace or speak of war,
  Learn this: I do not want you for my friends,
  Nor of your country can I pay the score.
  With that, you can return back home once more.

NUMANTINES. So that's your will, my lord?

SCIPIO.   I've told you. Yes.

SECOND NUMANTINE. From words to deeds! Numantines love
    the battle!

  Exeunt NUMANTINES.

QUINTUS FABIUS. Past carelessness on our part caused them thus
  To speak to us, but now the time has come
  When you shall see your glory or your death!

SCIPIO. Vain boasting ill becomes strong, valiant breasts.
  Temper your threats, my Fabius, hold your tongue,
  And keep your courage for the hour of battle!
  And yet I think I can prevent that any
  Numantines come to grips with us, and hope
  To find another way to conquer them
  Which is more profitable, to my mind.
  It will humiliate their pride, astound them,
  And make them turn their fury on themselves.
  I think we'll dig a deep ditch round the town
  And with insufferable famine finish
  Them off. I do not wish the wasted blood
  Of any other Romans to discolour
  This ground again. Enough blood has been shed
  By these cursed Spaniards, in this long, hard war.
  Now let us all exert our hands in breaking

And digging this hard earth. Let friends by friends
Be covered with the dust they raise, no longer
Covered with blood by enemies. None here
Will be excused this task, however high
His rank. Let the Centurion, with the ranker,
Labour alike. I too will ply this heavy
Pick-axe, and easily break up the soil.
Do all of you likewise! To see me work,
All should be satisfied. Let no one shirk!

QUINTUS FABIUS. My valiant lord and brother, you have shown
    us
Your prudence in this labour. It would be
An obvious error and a reckless show
Of folly to contend with the mad rage
Of those poor, luckless desperados there.
Far better wall them up and sap the roots
Of their mad vigour. They can be walled round
On every side, save only by the river.

SCIPIO. To work, then! and may my new plan turn out
Better than the old method. If at last
Heaven should deign to favour me, all Spain
Will then be subject to the Roman Senate:
We've but to humble this mad people's pride.

Exeunt omnes.

SPAIN *enters, crowned with towers and bearing in her hand
a castle (which signifies Spain).*

SPAIN. Lofty, serene, and spacious Heaven above!
Who with your starry influence and love
Enrich the greater part of this, my earth,
And over all the rest exalt its worth,
Be moved to pity by my bitter grief,
You, who to the afflicted bring belief,
O favour me in this, my so-great pain,
Who am the lonely and unlucky Spain!
Let it suffice that once you set on fire
My tender limbs and burned me up entire,
Then through my entrails to the sun displayed
The kingdom of the damned. 'Twas you that made
A thousand tyrants rich with what I paid.

To the Phoenicians and the Greeks you gave me,
Either that your will had to be obeyed,
Or that from my own sins I could not save me.
Must each strange nation in its turn enslave me,
So that, not for the briefest time at least,
My flags to Liberty may be released?
Fierce punishments upon us all do rain
But while all suffer greatest is my pain,
For my courageous sons with one another
Are still at strife and brother envies brother.
While separate schemes and contradicting plans
Upset all unity and split the clans,
Never within one aim can coincide
One man's opinion with another man's;
And all their fury does is to divide
When most they need to battle side by side.
It's thus, with inward discord they invite
Barbarians of voracious appetite,
In search of spoil, to plunder right and left
Till of my riches I am all bereft.
Numantia only had the brave resilience
To draw the sword and flash it with such brilliance.
She only raised her face out of the mud
To suckle Liberty with her own blood,
Belovèd Liberty, her child and heir!
And yet I feel the end is coming there,
Where she will end her life, but not her fame,
And, like a Phoenix, be renewed by flame.
These dreaded Romans by a myriad ways
Rather than front the clansmen face to face,
Although the latter are so few, refuse
Anything else than stratagem and ruse.
Oh, that their subtle webs could be undone,
And all the cunning intrigues they have spun,
That just this one small city could be saved
Because of all the perils she has braved!
But now, alas! the enemy surround,
Not only with their arms the walls that bound
Her limits, but a ditch that hems her hopes
Both from the plain and the surrounding slopes,

And only by the swift Duero's side
This all-encircling stratagem's defied.
The sad Numantines in their walls they hem,
Whence no escape, nor entrance into them:
From all assault they're free, and fear no harm,
Yet cannot reach the foe with their strong arm,
And so I claim for them, in one fierce breath,
Either an open war or speedy death.
And since it's only where the Duero runs
There can come aid or access to my sons,
Whose home's their gaol, I'll ask the grand, proud river
How it were best my people to deliver.
O kindly Duero! in your winding quest,
Who water so much of my ample breast,
So may you ever coil your swirling tides
On golden shingles such as Tagus rides,
So may each fugitive and free wood-nymph
Come with her loveliness to grace the lymph
Of your clear mirrors—though you have to leave
Your joys awhile—O hear me, as I grieve!
I beg you to delay no more, but take
Vengeance upon these Romans for the sake
Of the Numantines in their parlous state.
With endless floods rush headlong down in spate!

Enter the river DUERO, *with three other tributaries repre-*
sented by three boys, dressed as if they were the streams
that join the Duero near Soria (which was called Numantia
in those times) in willows and white poplar leaves.

DUERO. Dear Mother Spain, long have I heard your cry,
And, if I have been tardy to reply,
It is that I have sought, but sought in vain
Some remedy to help you in your pain.
The fatal, sad, black day at length will come!
The stars say that Numantia must succumb.
See Obron, Minuesa, and Tera, here,
Who've swelled my current with their waters clear
To such a height that it has burst its sides:
But with no greater heed of my swelled tides
Than had I been a rill (a thing you never,

Spain, have beheld!) they've spanned my mighty river
With dykes and floating towers. But now I've ended
The worst that Fortune, harsh and adamantine,
Has to inflict upon the doomed Numantine.
Let this console your sorrow: that the splendid
Exploits of the Numantines will not fade
Or wither in oblivion's dusky shade,
But live to be a wonder to all ages!
And since the dire, ferocious Roman rages
Lording it over your dear fertile ground,
The time will come when fate will swivel round
Their two Protean destinies: the Roman
Will be oppressed by his now prostrate foeman.
To the remotest countries will arrive
The folk that on your gentle breast survive.
After they've bent the Romans to their yoke,
Goths[1] they will be, a handsome, comely folk
Whose deeds will fill the whole world with their story.
Here on your breast they'll settle down in glory,
And drink new vigour for new deeds of daring.
These injuries of which you're now despairing
Will be avenged in the great havoc done
To Rome, in times to come, by the fierce Hun,
Attila, whom the world will hold in awe,
For his brave sons and other strangers yet
Even into the Vatican will get,
The pilot of the sacred ship to fright
To foreign lands, an exile, taking flight.
That time will also come when, as the Lord
Of Rome, the Spaniard will uphold his sword
Over the Roman's neck, bent in submission,
Who scarce can breathe except by his permission.
Then the great Alban, dealing blood and fire,
Shall cause the Spanish army to retire,

[1] The allusions in the lines that follow are: Goths, who were in
Spain from the fall of Rome (fifth century A.D.) till the arrival of
the Moors (eighth century). Pilot of the sacred ship, Pope Clement
VII, who had to flee Rome when it was sacked in 1527. The great
Alban, the Duke of Alva (later to be the villain of Schiller's *Don
Carlos*). Philip II reigned from 1556 to 1598. Portugal was incor-
porated in Spain in 1580. [E.B.]

Short, not of courage, but of men and horses,
Since, with them both, he will increase his forces;
And when you reach the peak of your renown
The Maker of the earth and sky above,
Through that Viceroy who represents his crown,
Will give your kings a name of joy and love,
Calling them *Catholic,* with all that own
Rule and allegiance on the Gothic throne.
But he whose hand will raise to greatest height
Your honour, and the general delight,
Making the valour and the name of Spain
Above all other countries show most plain,
Will be a king, whose strong and sane desire
To high and lofty exploits will aspire.
He will be called, by name, Philip the Second,
And nearly all the world as his be reckoned.
Beneath his happy empire he'll combine
Your separate kingdoms, hitherto close-shut,
And in his coat of arms quarter the sign
Of famous Portugal which will be cut
From them, only to be restored again
To famed Castile, and make a part of Spain.
What envy, dear-loved Spain, a thousand lands
Will feel for the sharp sword-thrust of your hands
And your triumphant banners shadowing
The world! Let this some consolation bring
At the sad pass which now you well may mourn!
For we cannot avert the judgment dire
That is already passed and must be borne:
It marks Numantia for her own red pyre.

SPAIN. Your arguments alleviate in part,
Great Duero, the affliction of my heart,
Simply because I trust there's no deception
In what you prophesy.

DUERO.   Without exception,
Though long in coming, Spain, you may be sure
That in the end your triumph is secure.
Farewell! I have a tryst with Neptune's daughters.

SPAIN. May heaven swell your clear, sweet-tasting waters!

ACT II

THEOGENES *and* CARAVINO *enter, with four other* NUMAN-
TINES, *and* MARQUINO, *the magician. They sit down.*

THEOGENES. To me it seems, you vigorous, grown men,
    That dismal omens and contrary fates
    Combine their influences to our harm
    Because our strength is being sapped within us.
    The Romans hold us shut in on all sides
    With craven hands destroying us inchmeal.
    We cannot seek revenge, nor perish killing,
    Nor, without wings, can we escape from here.
    Not only are they likely to subdue us,
    Whom we have put to rout so many times,
    But fellow Spaniards join in league with them
    To cut our throats. Oh, may the heavens prevent
    And with their lightnings strike the fickle feet
    Of friends who run to help the enemy
    To harm their fellow countrymen! Now think
    If you can find some remedy to save us
    From this sad quandary, because this long,
    Laborious siege now threatens to become
    Our funeral. The deep wide trench forbids
    That we should put things to the test of arms
    And hazard an attack, though strength of arms
    Can often burst through such impediments.

CARAVINO. If only it pleased Jupiter supreme
    That our young men alone might reach the full
    Strength of the cruel Roman army, then
    Despising death, they'd open up a road
    To safety for the whole Numantine people,
    But, since within these limits we're confined
    Like women kept inside the house, let's do
    The most we can to show our daring spirit
    By challenging our foes to single combat
    So that, grown weary of this tedious siege,
    We put an end to it, each for himself.

Or, if this remedy proves unsuccessful
In the just measure we expect of it,
There is another path for us to try
Though it is more laborious: by night,
All in one mass, to storm the wall and ditch
That hold us from the foe that lurks beyond them
And rush through to our countrymen for help.

FIRST NUMANTINE. Or through that ditch, or through the gates
    of death,
We have to make an opening for our lives.
Insufferable is the pain of death
If it comes on us when we're most alive,
Yet death's a cure for miseries, when they
Grow with our lives, and all the better, when
It comes with honour, as befits brave men.

SECOND NUMANTINE. With what more honour can our souls
    and bodies
Be parted than by falling on the Romans
To prove the prowess of our strong right hands?
Let any one who wishes to, remain
Here in the city, if he feels afraid.
I find it far more welcome to lie dead
In the closed ditch or in the open field.

THIRD NUMANTINE. This cursèd and insufferable famine
Forces me to agree with all you say
However hazardous and hard it be.
By dying we escape from ignominy.
Let him who does not wish to die of hunger
Plunge down here in the ditch with me, and hack,
To his delivery, a gory track!

FOURTH NUMANTINE. Before you undertake so great a peril
As that which you've resolved, it seems to me
That our fierce enemy should first be summoned
And asked to give permission for one Roman
And one Numantine to have single combat.
The death of one of them will be the verdict,
Thus finishing our differences for good.
The Romans are so proud they must accept,
And if they only do as I expect,

There'll be a speedy end to all our troubles,
Because there's one Numantine with us here
Whose valour and whose strength convince me quite
He'd kill any three Romans in one fight.
Also we should elicit from Marquino,
Who is so famous for his auguries,
What star, what planet, or what constellation
Portends our death or else a glorious ending.
We also should find out if he can tell us
If from this doubtful and oppressive siege
We shall emerge the victors or the conquered.
Next (the first duty that must be performed),
We'll make a solemn sacrifice to Jove
From whom we are entitled to expect
Better rewards than we enjoy today.
Next, our inveterate vices must be cured;
Perhaps our grudging fate would then relent
And to our final happiness consent.
To die? Why, there is always time to die
For any one who's desperate to try.
We'll always be in time for our last breath
With daring hearts to die a hero's death.
But that such time may not be passed in vain
Consider what I've striven to make plain,
And, if you do not find it stands the test,
Let someone else advise us what is best.

MARQUINO. The logic of your reasonings I approve.
Let sacrifices and oblations be
Made to the gods. Then we must launch the challenge.
I shall not lose a chance to show my science
And power. Into the future I shall enter,
And draw what's good or bad from its dark centre.

THEOGENES. I offer myself here to you, who well
May trust in my endeavour, as you know,
To go out and perform the duty offered,
If by good luck, the challenge proves effective.

CARAVINO. Your spotless valour merits greater honours.
Your powers to tasks more difficult than this
Should be devoted, since you are, yourself,

In all things, so much better than the best.
And since you occupy the foremost place
In honour and in valour, with just cause,
And since I come far after you in value,
I wish to be the herald of this joust.

FIRST NUMANTINE. And now, with all my people, I prefer
To do what's pleasing most to Jupiter:
Sacrifice and oblation give delight
To him, if in our hearts we are contrite.

SECOND NUMANTINE. Come, hasten to perform all we proposed
Before this curst, pestiferous hunger slays us,
That Heaven for our death may quash the sentence,
To mercy moved by our sincere repentance!
Exeunt.

Enter MARANDRO *and* LEONICIO, NUMANTINES.

LEONICIO. Whither away, Marandro?

MARANDRO.   If I don't
Know of my own accord, it's very little
You will find out.

LEONICIO.   Your amorous sentiments
Have left you without reason.

MARANDRO.   Tell me rather
That, since I felt them, my wits have increased.

LEONICIO. It has been proved of old that everyone
Who loves, loves to his own discomfiture—
That's the most rational conclusion proved.

MARANDRO. What you have said is tinged with wit and malice.

LEONICIO. You understand my wit, but your stupidity
Is beyond me.

MARANDRO.   It's stupid—to love well?

LEONICIO. Love must be kept within the bounds of reason.
Whom you love, when and how, that is what counts.

MARANDRO. You wish to lay down laws to love?

LEONICIO.   One's reason
Can lay them down.

MARANDRO.   Such laws are rational,
No doubt, but do not daze me with their beauty.

LEONICIO. In love's mad game, reason has got no place.

MARANDRO. Yet love does not oppose our reason though
　　Sometimes it deviates from it.

LEONICIO.　　　　　　　　　And so
　　You think it doesn't go against the reason
　　That soldiers so exemplary as you
　　Should dote with love at such a time as this?
　　When you should be upon your knees to Mars
　　Begging his favour, all that you can do
　　Is worship Love, who deals out milksop pleasures.
　　You see your country half consumed, and by
　　Her enemies shut in, yet tricked and fooled
　　By Love, you must forget her altogether?

MARANDRO. My heart burns in me at your senseless speech.
　　Has loving ever made a man a coward?
　　Have I deserted yet my post as sentry
　　To go and see my girl? Or do I lie
　　Asleep in bed while my commander watches?
　　Have you yet seen me falter in my duty
　　For any vain delight or vicious purpose?
　　Nay, all the less for being so in love!
　　And if you cannot state a single instance
　　What have I to excuse? Why blame me so
　　Because I am enamoured? If I'm shy
　　Of conversation and preoccupied,
　　Put your own hand into your heart, and you
　　Will see I have good reason to be so.
　　Do you not know how many years my heart's
　　Been lost to Lira? And do you not know
　　The time has come to end our suffering
　　Because her father had arranged our marriage
　　And she had found acceptance with my own?
　　You also know that, at this joyful juncture,
　　Came this fierce strife by which my glorious hopes
　　Were slain, and so the wedding was deferred
　　Till after the cessation of the war
　　Because our country's now no place for feasts
　　And happiness, and you can see what small
　　Hope I can have of my delight since now

Victory flies upon the foeman's lance.
We're hunger-stricken, hopeless of a cure.
We're few and prisoners of the wall and dyke,
And all my hopes are scattered to the winds.
That's why I am so sad and discontented.

LEONICIO. Marandro, calm your stormy breast. Return
To the gay vigour you were wont to show.
Perhaps in other ways our luck will turn,
And sovereign Jupiter may find a path
By which to free Numantia from the Romans,
And then in sweetest peace you may enjoy
Your bride and temper the fierce fire of love.
Today Numantia makes sacrifices
To the great thundering Jupiter above:
O Jupiter! look on our plight with love!

They go to the side and TWO NUMANTINES *enter, dressed as
priests of ancient times, pulling in a big ram by its horns:
the ram is crowned with olive and other flowers. There now
follow a* PAGE *with a font of silver and a towel; another
with a jug of water; two more with jars of wine; another
with another font of silver and some incense; others with
fire and wood for fuel. Another* PAGE *lays a table with a
table-cover on which the rest place everything they are carrying. They are all dressed in the Numantine costume. Then
one of the* PRIESTS *leaves the ram in the hands of the other,
begins to speak while* THEOGENES *enters with a crowd of
Numantines.*

FIRST PRIEST. Sure omens of disaster have appeared
Along the way we came, and my white hair
Stands stiff with fright.

SECOND PRIEST.   If I am not a bad
Diviner, we shall never come off well
Out of this plight. Ah! poor Numantine people!

FIRST PRIEST. Let's carry out the rite with all the haste
These dismal presages require of us.
Come, friends, and put a table over here.

SECOND PRIEST. The wine, water, and incense that you bring
Place on the table here, and then go back,
Repenting all the evil you have done.

A spirit cleansed and a sincere good will
Is far the best oblation you can offer.

FIRST PRIEST. The fire must not be kindled on the ground.
Here comes a brazier for it, as religion
And reverence require.

SECOND PRIEST.   Now wash your hands
And clean your neck. Here, bring the water, here!
Will not the fire light?

A NUMANTINE.   Nobody can light it,
My lords.

SECOND PRIEST. O Jupiter, what woe does Fate
Intend to wreak upon us, that the fire
Refuses to be kindled on the torch?

A NUMANTINE. It seems, my lord, at last to come to life.

SECOND PRIEST. Leave it alone and go. Oh, dim, weak flame
What grief I suffer to behold your light!
See how the smoke towards the setting sun
Goes trailing, while the sickly yellow flame
Points to the east. Unhappy sign of woe!
Disastrous portent of our overthrow!

FIRST PRIEST. Although the Romans get the victory
Through our destruction, yet the smoke will turn
To live flames, and our death and glory burn
Forever!

SECOND PRIEST. Then bedew the sacred fire
With wine, and let the incense now be lit!

He sprinkles the fire all round with wine, then throws incense into it.

To the advantage of Numantia's people,
Great Jupiter, reverse and make propitious
The force of their grim fate, and, as this fire
Forces the sacred incense to aspire,
So may the Romans' efforts end in smoke!
And grant (Eternal and Almighty Sire!)
That all Rome's luck and glory be reversed,
For so You can perform it, well I know!
May Heaven hold their cruel strength at bay

As we this victim we're about to slay,
And, like this victim, may it be laid low!

FIRST PRIEST. The omen answers ill. We cannot give
The slightest hope that our unhappy people
May flee from the dread quandary we're in.

*A sound of thunder under the stage made by rolling a tub
full of stores. A rocket is fired.*

SECOND PRIEST. Did you not hear a sound? Did you not see
The fiery thunderbolt fly past us then?
It is a sure presage of all I said.

FIRST PRIEST. I am confounded and I shake with fear!
What ghastly omens! From them I divine
A most disastrous ending to us all.
Do you not see that foul and angry squadron
Of ugly eagles fighting other birds
And wheeling round, embattled, in the sky?

SECOND PRIEST. See! they devote their cruel strength to
          rounding
The other birds into a narrow space,
And, by their skill and cunning, hem them in.

FIRST PRIEST. I curse that omen. I can never praise it.
Imperial eagles are the conquerors?
Farewell, Numantia, then! Your end is nigh.

SECOND PRIEST. Eagles, depart! Announcers of disaster!
For from your augury I can divine
Our hours are numbered.

FIRST PRIEST.   But in spite of all
I'll sacrifice this innocent young ram
So to make less the gods' tremendous ire.

SECOND PRIEST. O mighty Pluto, on whom Fate bestowed
The kingdom of the dark for your abode
And made commander of the realms infernal,
So may the peace and comfort be eternal
Which you derive from loving Ceres' daughter,
And so you may be prosperous in all things
Look upon this sad people, doomed to slaughter,
Who now invoke you! King of shady kings,
Close the great crater at the mouth of hell
From whence emerge the Furies fierce and fell,

The three grim sisters who have wrought our woe,
And make their dire designs as vain, as though
They were these hairs that to the winds I throw.

He pulls some wool from the ram and scatters it in the air.

FIRST PRIEST. With a pure thought and spirit cleansed of sin
Just as I plunge and stain my knife within
This ram's pure blood, so may Numantia stain
Her hard earth with the blood of Romans slain,
And prove a mighty grave to whelm them in!

A DEVIL *emerges to the waist from a hole in the stage. He seizes the ram and carries it off. All kinds of fireworks and rockets go off.*

SECOND PRIEST. But who has reft the victim from my hands?
Ye gods, what's this? What monstrous prodigies
Are these we see? Have our laments not touched
Your hearts, though coming from a tribe afflicted
And full of tears? Have our harped hymns not softened
Your hearts? No! they have hardened them the more
To judge from all these signs of cruel wrath.
The remedies of life are fatal to us:
Neglect of prayer would profit us far more.
Our good is alien, but our ills are native.

A NUMANTINE. Now that the heavens have given out the
                  sentence
Of our most grievous, miserable end,
And do not wish to grant us any mercy,
We'll grieve in such a way for our misfortune
That future ages never will forget.

THEOGENES. Now let Marquino make the final trial
Of his vast science, to find out the sum
Of all the evils that disastrous Fate
Promises us, turning our smiles to tears.

All exeunt, and only MARANDRO *and* LEONICIO *remain.*

MARANDRO. Say, Leonicio, does it seem to you
There's any remedy for our misfortunes
That heaven can afford us? My bad luck
Can only finish when this war is finished
And when the earth becomes my sepulchre.

LEONICIO. Marandro, to a proper soldier, omens
　Should give no pain, because he woos good luck
　With strenuous effort and mistrusts the vain
　Appearances of things from the outside
　Which should not make him lose his common sense.
　Your arm's your lucky star or else your doom.
　Your valour is the talisman in which
　To trust. But if you wish to chase illusions
　And put that sort of thing to further trial,
　Marquino manages it better far
　Than any one who deals in things like that,
　And if you want to know if good or bad
　Will be the net result of all our trouble,
　You'll know quite soon. I think I see him coming—
　But in what strange, extravagant attire!

Here enter MARQUINO *in a huge robe of glazed buckram
with a black wig and bare feet. At his belt are hung three
flasks or phials of water—one black, the second clear, and
the third dyed with saffron. He has a lance in one hand,
stained black; and, in his other hand, a book. Another man
comes along with him,* MILBIO *by name.* MARANDRO *and*
LEONICIO *go to one side.*

MARQUINO. Where, Milbio, did they bury this young man?

MILBIO. Here in this tomb.

MARQUINO. 　　　　　　　You're sure you're not mistaken?

MILBIO. No! with that sprig of ivy that you see
　I marked it, when they buried him with tears.

MARQUINO. What did he die of?

MILBIO. 　　　　　　　Of almighty Famine—
　That cruel sapping pest, born out of hell!

MARQUINO. You're sure it was no wound that cut his thread?
　No cancer is the reason why he's dead?
　I ask you this because I need whole flesh
　To waken and resuscitate afresh.

MILBIO. It's only three hours that I brought him here
　To give him his last rest and burial.
　He died of hunger only, never fear,
　As I declare once more.

MARQUINO.   That's to the good.
Propitious signs favour me at this juncture
From their dark realm to call fierce evil spirits.
Now give attentive hearing to my verse,
You ministers to souls that are perverse!
May luck and fortune bless you! And obey,
Even if you be unwilling, what I say
Upon this dire occasion! No delay!
Do not wait for compulsion harder still.
I wish the body buried in this clay
With its own spirit and new life to thrill
Even though Charon tries to bar the way.
Upon the further bank of the black river,
Though it be hidden in the triple throat
Of Cerberus, I charge you to deliver
His spirit back into this world up here
Soon to return unto your darker sphere.
Since he *must* come, let him bring information
Of this harsh, bitter siege's termination.
Let him hide nought from me, unhappy youth,
But give to me the clear, cold, naked truth.
Let him not speak in riddles to bemuse me
Nor with vague ambiguities confuse me.
Send him at once! Come! Do you dare refuse me,
False ministers? What more do you await?
You will not move the tombstone's massive weight?
How have you dared to make no sign as yet?
A stronger conjuration must I set
Upon you all to soften your hard hearts,
Exerting greater powers in these dark arts?
Crapulous liars! sentenced to the fire,
You know I've but to speak a little higher
To double your fierce rage and torments dire.
Say, you! the faithless husband of a wife
Who for six months of each year of her life
Horns you with countless antlers without doubt—
Why have you dared my dread commands to flout?
This iron, splashed with dew, will search you out,
Which, never having touched the ground this May,
Wounding this stone, will prove that what I say

Is in dead earnest, not in idle play!

*With the clear water from one flask he bedews the point
of his lance and strikes the floor of the stage, beneath which
rockets and crackers and squibs resound with thunder.*

You see, *canaille!* that even from the clear
Water you catch a cruel pang of fear.
What sounds are these, accursèd souls, who though
You've not come yet, were shifted by the blow?
What's this? You'd still delay? Where do you hide?
Are all my threats and menaces defied?
I'll threaten you no more, nor give you quarter,
But with these deadly drops of coal-black water
I'll give just punishment for your delay
And now you'll have a heavy debt to pay!
O water from the fatal black lagoon,
Drawn on a dark, sad night without a moon,
By the great power that lives in you alone,
Against whose power no other power is known,
Now the whole race of devils dire (and thee
Who first became a serpent in the tree!)
I conjure, I constrain you to obey
And all come flying here without delay!

He sprinkles the tomb with black water and it opens.

Unhappy youth! Come out! Return to see
The sun serene and clear! Leave that dark region
Where you need never hope to see a day
Of peace and comfort! Give me, since you can,
The whole relation of what you have learned
In the abyss—what you were sent to say,
And more, if it concerns us, and you can.

The corpse *slowly appears in its shroud and goes on gradually emerging till in the end, when it has finally come out,
it collapses on the stage.*

What's this? No answer? Have you not revived?
What? Have you tasted death a second time?
Then I will cause your pain to wake you up
And you will soon address me with a will!
Since you are of my tribe, come, don't be backward
In speaking and replying. If you're silent,

It will be to your cost that I unloose
That tongue-tied and begrudging voice of yours.

He sprinkles yellow water on the CORPSE *and afterwards begins to thrash it.*

You evil spirits! Will he not learn better?
Then wait! The drops of this enchanted water
Will make him satisfy my will entirely
While he defies and disobeys your own.
Lashed with this whip he will acquire new life,
Though slightly, from the pain that it inflicts.
Rebellious soul, return to your old inn
Where you so lately had your board and lodging!
Now you return. You show it. I can feel you
Entering, though with pain, into yourself.

As he says this the CORPSE *throws itself back into its grave though it remains visible.*

THE CORPSE. Marquino, cease your rigour, fierce and rough!
    The torments I must suffer are enough,
    In the dark realm down there, for me to bear
    Without your adding to my dark despair.
    For you are wrong in thinking that I yearn
    Back to that dismal short life to return
    Which I have lived down there, where I must haste
    Since I am missed. But you cause me far worse pain
    Since now I have to agonise again;
    For death a second time with bitter strife
    Must triumph o'er my spirit and my life.
    My demon foe expects me with clenched hand,
    And with the others of that murky band
    Who serve your pleasure, waits with growing ire
    For me to finish off what you require
    And tell you of the lamentable end
    On which the doomed Numantia can depend,
    Destroyed by that which was her nearest friend—
    The strength of her own hands. Neither the Roman
    Will win the victory, nor o'er her foemen
    Will strong Numantia ever vaunt the glory,
    Friend being good to foe, and foe to friend.
    But do not dream that peace will end the story:

These two conflicting fronts will never bend
Because without assistance from her foes
The sword of friends will deal the fatal blows
And be the murderer of this brave city!
Stay here, Marquino! Let me go, in pity!
The Fates forbid that longer I delay
And though you may not trust in what I say
All will be verified upon the day.

The CORPSE *disappears in the grave.*

MARQUINO. O dismal omens! Lamentable end!
  If this must happen between friend and friend,
  Within this very tomb I'll end my life.

He throws himself into the grave.

MARANDRO. See, Leonicio, if it is not true
  That everything goes dead against my luck.
  The road is blocked that leads to any good
  (Marquino says) save to the tomb and death.

LEONICIO. These things are all delusions and chimeras,
  Fantasies, witcheries, abracadabras,
  Auguries, fortunetellers' whimsies, dreams,
  And things of diabolical invention.
  You have a gift for finding care and trouble.
  The dead don't care for living folks' affairs.

MARANDRO. Marquino never would commit such folly
  Were not our future doom seen in the present.
  Let us announce this to the people. But
  To bring such news, how can one stir a foot?

ACT III

Enter SCIPIO, JUGURTHA, CAIUS MARIUS.

SCIPIO. I'm thoroughly delighted with the way
Good fortune has conformed to my desire,
And to be taming this free, stubborn people
By dint of prudence, without wasting strength.
Seeing occasion for this plan, I chose it,
Since I know that through rushing things in haste,
Especially in the affairs of war,
Much life is lost, and credit runs to waste.
They thought it was an error to surround
The enemy, and that our Roman strength
Lost honour by not conquering the foe
In the outmoded, antiquated way.
I know all that was said, but yet I trust
That all good, practical commanders reckon
That victory the best which costs least blood.
What victory can redound to greater glory,
Judging it from the point of view of war,
Than one that's won without a single sword
Leaving its sheath, and yet can subjugate
And conquer a strong enemy completely?
But when a victory's acquired with loss
Of friendly blood, it spoils the joy of it
To win with blood what might be won without.

They sound a trumpet from Numantia's ramparts.

JUGURTHA. Hark, sir. A trumpet from Numantia sounds,
And I am sure they've got something to tell you
Because the wall prevents their exit here.
There's Caravino on the battlements.
He gives the sign of safety. Let's approach.

SCIPIO. Approach no further. We can hear him here.

CARAVINO *enters on the wall with a flag on a lance.*

CARAVINO. Ho! Romans! can you hear my voice from here?

scipio. If only you don't shout so loud and fast
  Anyone can both hear and understand you.

caravino. Then tell your general to stretch his legs
  Here to the trench because an embassy's
  Coming to him.

scipio.   Out with it, quick! I'm Scipio.

caravino. Well, hear the rest, most prudent generall
  Numantia says, Consider what long years
  Between us and the Romans have endured
  The evils of a long and tedious war,
  And that the pestilence of those same evils
  May not increase, Numantia wishes this—
  If you, too, wish the same—in one brief fight
  To end the war by means of single combat.
  One soldier volunteers out of our ranks
  To fight, in a closed space, with any stout
  Champion of yours, and end this stubborn strife.
  If he whom the harsh Fates condemn to die
  Be ours, we shall deliver up our country:
  If he be yours, then glory to the warl
  For the security of this arrangement
  We'll send you hostages if you require them.
  I know you will accept, since you command
  Soldiers, the least of whom in the open field
  Can make the best of ours break out in sweat,
  And so you can be certain of success.
  So now to expedite the execution
  Of this affair, tell me if you agree.

scipio. You *are* a wit! What quips and jests are these?
  What mad hilarity would you excite?
  Employ the means of humble supplication
  If you still hope to save your scrannel necks
  From the sharp Roman blade and our strong arms!
  The wild beast, once it's shut within a cage
  Because of its ferocity and rage,
  And also because there, by patient wile
  And time, he can be tamed in proper style—
  Why, any fool who lets that creature out
  Not only puts his sanity in doubt

But life in danger! Beasts you are, I say,
And caged as beasts: to learn, the only way
That beasts can learn, their masters to obey.
Numantia will be mine to your vast woe,
Yet not a drop of Roman blood will flow!
Come, let the greatest fighter you can find
Cross this great trench, if so he has the mind;
And if you think there is a little shame
In my refusal, or that I'm to blame,
Why, all that will be whisked off by the wind
When this great victory restores my fame!

SCIPIO *and his companions retire while* CARAVINO *remains.*

CARAVINO. You'll not hear more? You craven! You'll go hide?
    In a fair, equal fight you take no pride?
    Your conduct ill accords with your great name.
    Since all at once a coward you became,
    Answering me. You Romans are all craven!
    In your huge numbers you may find a haven
    But man to man and hand to hand you'll not
    Answer an honest challenge on the spot.
    Disloyal swindlers, sodomites, pernicious,
    Treacherous, lewd, perverse, foul, avaricious
    Tyrants, reducing anyone to slavery,
    Known rather for base cunning than for bravery—
    What glory can you gain from killing us
    By keeping us incarcerated thus?
    In the formed squadron or the skirmish free,
    Out on the open field for all to see,
    Where neither ditch nor dyke impede the jolt
    And shock of death's impetuous thunderbolt,
    It would be well for that so-very-gallant
    Army of yours to show its fighting talent
    Against our weak, starved few, but it's your way
    To fight by unfair means, craft, and delay.
    The straight, fair fight, which valour most concerns,
    Is ill adapted to your twists and turns.
    Rabbits! who go disguised in lions' hide,
    Let your brave deeds by you be magnified!
    But yet I trust great Jupiter, one day,

Will bend you down beneath Numantia's sway,
Her laws and statutes humbly to obey.

CARAVINO *goes out, then returns with* THEOGENES, MAR-
ANDRO, *and others.*

THEOGENES. Our fate now hems us in such narrow limits,
Dear friends, that it would be most fortunate
To finish off our ills with death. You saw
The grievous omen of the sacrifice
And how the grave has swallowed up Marquino.
The challenge was worth nothing. What is left?
One way is to accept our final end.
Let us Numantines show the reckless courage
That burns within our breasts. Let's get to work,
Break through the hostile wall, and rush to die
Out in the open field, not here, like cowards,
As captives. Well I know that such an exploit
Can only change the manner of our death,
Which is a certainty in this case, too.

CARAVINO. With this idea I sympathise. I wish
To die breaching the wall and dealing havoc.
But there's one thing that makes me feel uncertain—
That if our wives get knowledge of this plan
It will prove quite impossible, for sure.
When we had all decided once before
Each one of us to trust in his swift horse
And make a dash for it, learning our drift
They were so vexed, they stole and hid our snaffles
So that we could not find a single one.
If then they could prevent us from a sortie
They'll do it just as easily, I say,
When once they show the tears they showed that day.

MARANDRO. Our plans are evident to all of them.
Each woman knows them. There's not one of them
Who's not complaining bitterly about it.
They say that both in good and evil fortune
They wish to follow us in life or death
Although we find their company a hindrance.

*Enter four women of Numantia, each with a child in her
arms, and* LIRA, *a maiden.*

See, here they come to beg you not to leave them
In such predicaments, and were you made
Of cold, hard steel, the sight of your young children,
Which they so sadly carry in their arms,
Would soften you. Do you not see the loving
Manner in which they bid them their farewell
And give their last embraces and caresses?

FIRST WOMAN. My dearest lords, in hundreds of misfortunes
We've suffered in Numantia up till now
(Death being among the least of those we suffer)
And in the happiness, now gone for good,
We always shared with you as wives and partners,
And you shared with us, too, as loving husbands.
Then why, on this most sinister occasion
With which the angered heavens threaten us,
Do you show us so little of that love?
We've learned, and it is obvious to us all,
You wish to rush into the Roman's hands
To ask a kinder death than that from Hunger,
Who hems us in and from whose clammy hands
Escape is now impossible to hope.
You wish to perish fighting and to leave us,
Shelterless, to dishonour, shame, and death.
First let our necks be severed by your swords
Before we are dishonoured by your foes.
It is my firmly-constituted will,
And I will do the utmost that is in me
To perish with my husband, if I can;
And so would any wife who wished to show
That fear of death can never hinder one
Who loves from loving well, in joy or grief,
In happiness or misery alike.

SECOND WOMAN. What are you thinking of, you men? Do you
Persist in this mad fantasy of leaving
Us women here and absenting yourselves?
Perhaps you want the virgins of Numantia
To fall a prey to the insulting Romans
And your free sons to serve as fettered slaves?
Would it not be far better with your own

Strong arms to strangle them? What! Would you feed
The vaunting Roman's lechery and greed,
To his injustice sacrifice the just,
And leave us as a trophy for his lust?
Must foreign hands destroy our houses? Must
Promised espousals be enjoyed by Romans?
In going forth you'll make a fatal error
Which will give rise to many thousand worse
Because you leave your flock, without its shepherd
And sheepdogs, to the wolf. If you go forth,
Take us along with you because our life
Is to die at your side. Then do not hasten
Your way to death. For Hunger weaves her curtain
Slowly but surely, and its fall is certain.

THIRD WOMAN. Children of these sad mothers—what is this?
What! are you tongue-tied that you do not plead
With tears that your dear fathers will not leave you?
Tell them that they begot you free, and that
You were born free, and that your mothers reared you
In freedom. Tell them, now our fate declines,
That they who gave you life must give you death!
O walls of this sad city, if you can,
Cry out these words, a thousand times repeat them:
"Numantines! free your temples, towers
And these belovèd homes of ours
Which we raised up in love and peace!
The wives and children of your city
Plead that you will be moved to pity,
Their souls from bondage to release.
Let pity move you! Be our friends
Since not in breaking through the wall
Is any remedy at all
For the disaster that impends!"

LIRA. Now the sad maidens as they grieve
Seek your protection, for they know
A cure that's certain to relieve
Their evil plight. What? Will you leave
So rich a plunder to the foe
And our virginities bestow

On those that ruthlessly destroy us?
Must the same hands that lay you low
Be those that strip us and enjoy us?
The Romans are as wolves ferocious,
Rapacious, bloody, and atrocious:
To leave us for them is a crime.
It's desperation and notorious
Folly, to find quick death, though glorious—
Making a sally at this time.
What city in the whole of Spain,
Were you to win, would entertain
Or dare to favour you? Not one.
My poor opinion is, if you
Insist on trying to break through,
You'll give your lives to Rome but none
To poor Numantia, only death—
Her own and yours. Your vital breath
Will animate them. They'll make fun
Of your small number. What can three
To eighty thousand soldiers be
Except a hapless prey? Although
You broke the walls to reach the foe,
You'd reap poor vengeance though good ends.
It's better far that we abide
By Fortune. Let our Fate decide
Whether it worsens or it mends,
And whether life or death betide!

THEOGENES. Dry your eyes, tender women! Know from me
Your anguish has afflicted us so sorely
That it has called forth our most fervent love.
Now grief takes hold of us, now piercing pity
To see how all our happiness has faded.
Never in life or death will we desert you,
Never in life or death will cease to serve you!
We thought to cross the ditch, not to escape,
But to get killed (since it was far more certain)
Because those who avenge themselves while dying
Enjoy a sort of life even in death.
But since our plans have been found out by you

It would be madness now to hazard it.
Belovèd children, and belovèd wives,
From this day forward, our devoted lives
Are yours more than they ever were before.
The one thing we must guard against is this—
The enemy, by our discomfiture,
Must not acquire a single grave of honour,
Profit, or glory. Rather must our foes
Be witnesses to blazon forth *our* glory.
And if you'll all agree to what I say
A hundred thousand years will seem a day
To our immortal fame. This is my plan.
Nothing in all Numantia must remain
That to the enemy could prove a gain.
Right in the central square, we'll make a fire
In which we'll burn all that those swine desire
Of trinkets, even from the poorest penny
Of the poor pauper who has hardly any,
To all that the rich merchant has of worth—
We'll melt it down and hide it in the earth!
This loss seems child's play when each priceless jewel
And heirloom, too, is sentenced to be fuel.
And now for a few hours we must allay
The hungry pangs that gnaw our guts away.
Take out our Roman prisoners and slaughter
The poor devils. Their carcasses we'll quarter
And share together for our final feast.
Sparing neither the grown-up nor the younger,
We'll make our banquet of the Roman beast—
Such is the grim necessity of hunger!

CARAVINO. Friends, how does this strike you? Do you agree?
This project more than satisfies me. Come!
Let's make this strange yet honourable act,
As soon as possible, a living fact!

THEOGENES. Now I'll inform you of my further plans.
When we have done what I have said, each one
Must be a minister of fell destruction
And kindle up the rich, red-blazing fire!

FIRST WOMAN. At once we shall begin with willing hands

To give our ornaments and jewelry
And like them we shall then give up our lives
As we have given up our vain desires.

LIRA. Then let us hurry! Come along, then, come!
And let us pile and burn in one fixed place
Aught that by way of trophy might enrich
The Roman's hands or feed his avarice.

All go out except MARANDRO *who, on the point of departure
takes* LIRA *by the hand. She stays with him. Then* LEONICIO
enters unseen by them and watches them.

MARANDRO. Do not go off at such a speed,
Lira, but let me taste and feed
Upon the only blessing that
Life can provide me ere I die,
And on your beauty feast my eye
For my ill-fortune has grown fat
Feeding upon my care and woe.
O lovely Lira, you that so
Divinely agonise my whole
Continuously thwarted dreams
Till anguish to be glory seems
Since you're the glory of my soul,
What are your thoughts?

LIRA.   Well, I was thinking
How my delight with yours is sinking
And my life, ere war be done,
But not by it cut off and slain,
Is setting like the setting sun
That bleeds to death on yonder plain.

MARANDRO. What's that you say, my soul's delight?

LIRA. That with such hunger I contend
I am near vanquished in the fight
And feel my life is at its end.
What sort of nuptials can you dream
With one whom, in this fierce extreme,
Such agonising pangs devour
That she must perish in an hour?
It was but yesterday my brother
Perished of it. Today my mother

Has died of this same gnawing hunger.
And if against its drawn-out length
And irremediable strength
I still survive, it's that I'm younger
And from my youth I draw some force.
But for some days I've ceased to strive
Against it, let it take its course,
And now I scarcely feel alive.

MARANDRO. O Lira, dry your eyes! Let mine
Like rivers, for these griefs of thine,
Flow forth instead! Though hunger-stricken,
You shall not die! Across the trench
Out of the Romans' hands I'll wrench
The bread for want of which you sicken,
And put the bread between your lips
For your sweet life with death at grips.
For I would die your life to quicken
And it is death to me to see
Your pain. I'll snatch bread from the Roman
And with some damage to the foeman
If my hands are as they used to be.

LIRA. You speak as lovers always speak, Marandro,
But it's unjust that I enjoy the taste
Of something bought of peril to your life.
What you could steal could not sustain me now
And would be likelier fatal than reviving.
Enjoy your youth and health. Your life is of
More value to the city than my own.
You can defend her from the foe's onslaught
But the weak powers of this poor girl here
Are useless. So, my dear love, do not think
Anything more about it. I want nothing
That's won at cost of sweat or blood by you.
Even if for a day you could prolong
My life, you could not end this fearsome hunger.

MARANDRO. In vain you try to shackle me, dear Lira,
From the straight course where both my will and fate
Invite me, nay, compel me. You will pray,
In the meantime, to the great gods on high,

That I may come back safely with the spoils
That will relieve your misery and my pity.

LIRA. Marandro, my sweet friend, oh, do not go!
I would go frantic should the foeman's sword
Be reddened with your blood. Marandro, dearest
Blessing of all my life, if to go out
Is perilous, far worse is the return.
I will placate your ardour: witness heaven!
I dread your peril more than I love life.
But if, belovèd friend, you still persist
Then give me your embrace as a fast pledge
That you will take me with you when you go.

MARANDRO. Lira, may heaven keep you company!
Go! here is Leonicio.

LIRA.   May you thrive,
And nothing happen to endanger you!
Exit LIRA.

LEONICIO. The offer you have made is terrible,
And proves too well, Marandro, as you said,
That in a lover's breast can dwell no coward—
Although from your rare valour and your virtue
One could expect this. But I fear that Fate
Will prove most grudging to our urgent need.
I overheard attentively the piteous
Plight of your Lira, undeserved in one
Of such rare virtue, and I heard you vow
To free her from her present misery
By hurling yourself on the Roman swords.
Well, my good friend, I'm coming with you too.
In such a just and urgent enterprise
It's fit that my small strength should aid your own.

MARANDRO. O friendship of my happy soul! O friendship
That undivided in despair and travail
Endures as in prosperity and pleasure!
Rejoice in your sweet life, my Leonicio!
Stay in the city here! I do not wish
To be the homicide of your green years.
I have to go alone. Alone I wish

To come back with the spoils that should reward
My own inviolable faith and love.

LEONICIO. Well, now you know, Marandro, that my wishes,
In good or in bad luck, still conform
To yours, and that not fear nor death itself
Can swerve them from you by a single hair.
Nothing is stronger than my will to serve you.
I *will* go with you and with you return
If heaven does not bid me to remain,
Killed in defence of you, upon the plain.

MARANDRO. Stay here, my friend, stay here in safety
Because, if in this risky enterprise
I chance to lose my life, you may console
My mother and my most belovèd bride.

LEONICIO. You are so very gracious, my dear friend,
To talk about your death in such a way—
So calmly and so restfully—and say
That I might serve for any consolation
To your sad mother or your grieving bride,
But in your death my own would be accomplished,
And of this doubtful fact I've now made sure.
You see it has to be, my friend Marandro,
So say no more to me about remaining.

MARANDRO. Since I cannot prevent your going with me,
Then, in the silence of this murky night,
We'll leap upon the foemen, lightly armed
And lightly harnessed, since it is to luck
We're trusting in our lofty enterprise
Rather than to the toughness of our armour.

LEONICIO. Come, I will never falter in your service!

Exeunt.

Enter TWO NUMANTINES.

FIRST NUMANTINE. Weep, my dear brother, let your soul flow
out
Of both your eyes and turn to bitter tears!
Let death descend and take the piteous spoils
Of our most sad and miserable lives!

SECOND NUMANTINE. Our miseries can endure but little longer

Because death now is visibly approaching
To carry off in rapid flight the whole
People which treads upon Numantine soil.
I see the grim beginnings which presage
The swift, sad end of our belovèd country,
Without the hostile ministers of war
Taking the slightest part in it at all.
Ourselves it is to whom life has become
So much of an insufferable load,
Who have pronounced the irrevocable sentence,
Though it's a cruel one, of death. Already
Up in the central square they've made a huge
Blazing and hungry conflagration, which,
Fed with our riches, soars to the fourth sphere.
There with sad, fearful haste runs every one,
As with a sacred offering, to feast
The roaring flames with his own goods and chattels,
Sustaining them with households and estates.
There pearls, brought from the rosy Orient,
With gold wrought in a thousand precious vases,
Diamonds and rubies exquisitely cut,
And costly purple robes and rich brocades—
All have been hurled into the midst of this
Raging volcano, to the slightest scrap
Of anything which any Roman could
Stuff in his chest or occupy his hands with.

Here people come in on one side loaded with linen and
clothing, and go out on the other side.

Oh, turn your gaze on this sad spectacle
To see with what wild speed and keen good will
All of Numantia runs in crowds to nourish
The roaring mad inferno of the flames—
And not with green wood or with dried-up straw
Nor with such things as men consign to flames
But with the homes and properties and wealth
They can no longer live with or enjoy.

FIRST NUMANTINE. If in these things our only harm consisted,
With patience we could bear it. But alas!
If I am not deceived, they will decree

That we must all die by a cruel death.
Before the barbarous cruelty of Rome
Severs our necks, ourselves with our own hands
Must be our own fierce butchers, not the Romans!
The orders are that neither women, children,
Nor old folk shall be spared, since in the end
To die of hunger is a death more cruel.
But see! there is a woman coming out
For whose sake once I suffered pangs of love
As fierce as those she's suffering from hunger.

Enter a woman with a child in her arms leading another by the hand, and carrying a bundle of clothes to be burned. Translator's note: *Spanish women still carry all burdens on their heads.*

MOTHER. O woeful life and bitter agony!

SON. Mother! will they give us some bread to eat
For all these clothes?

MOTHER.   What? Bread, my son?
No, neither bread nor anything to eat!

SON. Well, Mother, must I perish in this rage
Of hunger? If you give me just a crumb
I will not ask for more! Dear mother, do!

MOTHER. Son, how you make me suffer!

SON.   Don't you wish
To give me any?

MOTHER.   Yes, of course, I wish
To give you tons, but I don't know where to find it.

SON. Well, you can buy some, then. Or if not you,
Then I can buy it. But to save me trouble
If I can come across some bread I'll trade
All of these clothes for it—just for one piece!

MOTHER, *to the baby.* Poor creature, what is that you're
      sucking
Out of my breast? Can you not taste? It's blood,
Not milk. Come, bite my breasts in pieces
And eat them if it satisfies your hunger.
My thin, tired arms can carry you no more.
My little ones, delighters of my soul,

What more can I provide you than my blood?
O Famine! Terrible and ghastly Famine,
You've swallowed up my life. O useless war!
You came to kill me. I can do no more.

SON. O Mother mine, I'm dying! Come, let's hurry.
It seems that hunger grows the more we walk.

MOTHER. Belovèd son, we're near the square
Where we will throw into the fire
Our pain, our hunger, and despair
And burn our troubles up entire.

The woman staggers out with her children. The TWO
NUMANTINES *remain.*

SECOND NUMANTINE. That woman scarcely now can lift a foot—
Poor piteous, doomed, and desolated mother
On whom her little children still depend!

FIRST NUMANTINE. We all are moving to the same sad end
But now we'd better move along with speed
To find out what the Senate has agreed.

ACT IV

The call to arms is sounded hastily in the Roman camp. At the sound SCIPIO *comes in storming with* JUGURTHA *and* CAIUS MARIUS, *who are also agitated.*

SCIPIO. What is this, captains? Who sounds this alarm?
  Is it, by chance, some lunatics who've come
  To ask for burial here instead of there?
  I hope it's not some mutiny that causes
  This call to arms—because I am so sure
  The foe is finished that I dread much more
  From the curbed-in impatience of my friends.

Enter QUINTUS FABIUS *with his sword drawn.*

QUINTUS FABIUS. Don't be alarmed, my prudent general!
  We know now why this call to arms was sounded:
  But it was at the cost of some of our
  Bravest and strongest soldiers. Two Numantines,
  Whose valour cannot be denied, jumped over
  The gaping ditch, having slid down the rampart,
  And they've put the whole camp in a furore!
  They rushed the outpost guards with such a fury
  That they gave way; then, through a thousand spears,
  They charged with such mad frenzy that these, too,
  Gave way; then charging to Fabricius' tents
  They cut their way, transfixing six more soldiers.
  Not when the red-hot lightning shoots from heaven
  Is it so swift to strike and to return,
  Or when a meteor streaks along the sky
  Is it so swift, as with their rapid pace
  They sliced your ranks and coloured all the place
  Crimson with Roman blood, which right and left
  They drew with peerless skill, they were so deft.
  Fabricius through his chest was pierced clean through.
  Eracius' brains are open to your view.
  Almido had his right arm cut in two,
  And there is little hope that he'll survive

For more than a few hours. Estacio's fleetness
Was little to his profit (nor his valour):
When he caught up with them, they struck him down.
Then rushing round the camp from tent to tent,
They found a few dry biscuits as they went,
And having found them, they turned swiftly back
But could not stem the rage of the attack.
One of them went scot-free, but then his mate
A thousand sword thrusts finished off—too late!
What reason lay behind this valiant deed?
It all was due to hunger and to need.

SCIPIO. If having been starved so, and circled in,
They show such huge excess of valour, what
Would they not do were they in their prime fettle
And free to come and go? O tameless hearts!
But in the end you shall be tamed at last,
For your fierce violence is not in the running
With calculation, industry, and cunning.

Exeunt omnes.

Enter MARANDRO *mortally wounded and bleeding badly,
with a basket full of bread.*

MARANDRO. You have not come with me, ah, Leonicio!
How could I come while you remained behind?
The true friend that you stayed to me through all
Has stayed behind, and yet you never left me,
But I left you. And is it possible
That your hacked limbs bear witness to the price—
And what a price!—this luckless bread has cost?
And is it possible that by the wound
Which laid you dead I am not murdered too?
But cruel Fate denied my death with yours
To do me more and greater harm and prove
Your faithfulness was greater than my own.
You carry off the palm in the contention
As to which of us was the better friend.
Soon, to excuse me, I'll send you my soul,
Yes, soon enough because I'm due to die
At Lira's feet, giving to her this bitter
And costly bread, this bread won from the foe

But at the cost of the unlucky blood
Of two devoted friends.

Enter LIRA *with some clothes to put in the fire.*

LIRA.   What's this I see?

MARANDRO. A thing that very soon you'll see no more,
So rapidly do my misfortunes hasten
My end. Lira, you see I've kept my word
That while I was alive you should not die.
And yet more truly could I say that now
You'll not lack wherewithal to eat: but I,
The wherewithal to live.

LIRA.   What do you say,
Belov'd Marandro?

MARANDRO.   Lira, sate your hunger
While cursèd Fate is severing my thread.
But the salt blood I've lost today, sweet love,
Mingling with it, will make that bread taste bitter.
This is the bread, guarded by eighty thousand
Enemy soldiers, that has cost the lives,
Which each of them loved best, of two good comrades.
And that you know for certain what I'm saying,
Know that I'm dying, and that Leonicio
Died too, to get this bread. Receive my love
Forever and my pure and honest prayers
As a still better banquet—for your soul!
And since you've always been, in calm or tempest,
My lady and my love, receive this body
Now, as you've just received from me my soul!

He falls dead and LIRA *takes his head in her lap.*

LIRA. Marandro: my sweet friend! What's wrong with you?
How do you feel, that suddenly you've lost
Your usual stalwart bearing? Oh, my husband
Is dead—my luckless and unlucky husband!
Oh! The most piteous thing that ever happened!
What cruel Fate, belovèd, made you so
Valiant, so amorous, so excellent,
But so unlucky as a soldier too?
You made a sortie to prevent my death

And by it took away my life! This bread
Stained with the blood that he has shed for me
Is now no longer bread but deadly venom.
My lips shall never touch it, but to kiss
The dear-loved blood that spatters it.

A BOY, *Lira's youngest brother, enters, speaking faintly.*

BOY. Lira, dear sister, Mother's dead already
And, now my father's dying, I must too.
Hunger by now has finished him. My sister,
So you have bread? Oh, bread, you've come too late
Since not a crumb can pass! So tight has hunger
Throttled my throat, that if this bread were water
No drop could pass. You keep the bread, dear sister:
There's bread to spare, when life cannot be spared.

He also falls dead.

LIRA. What, are you dead, dear brother? He has lost
Both breath and life. Ill luck is good
When it comes unaccompanied. Why, Fortune,
Do you still join affliction to affliction
For me to suffer in a single moment,
Making me both a widow and an orphan?
Hardhearted Roman army! Your sharp swords
Keep me surrounded with my dead, a husband
And now a second brother. In this plight
Where can I turn my face, seeing these two
Were the most precious treasures of my soul?
Oh, my sweet husband and my dear young brother,
I shall requite your love, for very soon
I shall be seeing you in heaven or hell.
I'll have to imitate the way you both
Perished, for both by steel and hunger too
My life must end. I'd sooner give a knife
To my throat than this bread. For death is welcome
To those who live like me in anxious care.
What am I waiting for? I am a coward!
My arm, you flinch to strike? My most dear husband
And darling brother, wait for me: I'm coming!

Enter a woman fleeing. Behind her A NUMANTINE SOLDIER
with a dagger to kill her.

WOMAN. Eternal Father Jupiter, protect me
  In this dire strait!

SOLDIER.   However swift you flee
  My hard hand must destroy you!
  Exit the woman.

LIRA.   Turn on me
  The hard steel and your warlike arm! Let life
  Be spared to one who's pleased with hers! Take mine
  For my life is my bane!

SOLDIER.   Although the Senate
  Decreed no woman to remain alive,
  What arm or what impetuous heart would dare
  Bury his falchion in a breast so fair?
  I, lady, am not of such evil fame
  That I can be your homicide. Alas!
  Some other hand, some other sword must do it,
  Since I was born to worship and adore you.

LIRA. O valiant soldier, I can swear by heaven,
  This pity that you have expressed for me
  Is a most harsh misfortune in my eyes.
  I would consider you a friend if, with
  Resolute heart and spirit, you transpierced
  My own sad heart and took my bitter life.
  But since you wish to show me pity, show it,
  Kind author of my comfort, in this plight
  By helping me to give the funeral rites
  Of burial to my unlucky husband,
  Also to him, my brother, lying here,
  Free now from vital breath. My husband died
  To give me life, but hunger slew my brother.

SOLDIER. I'll do what you command me, that is easy,
  Provided that you tell me as we go
  The circumstances that have led to this.

LIRA. My friend, speech is no longer in my power.

SOLDIER. What! have you come to such a pass? You feel
  Truly like that? Well, you can bear your brother:
  He is a lighter burden than your husband
  Whom I shall carry since he weighs the most.

They take out the bodies: and now a woman personifying
WAR *enters with a spear and a shield. She brings with her*
PESTILENCE *and* HUNGER. PESTILENCE *is a woman who is*
supported on a crutch with her head swathed in bandages;
she wears a yellow mask. HUNGER, *wearing a robe of glazed*
buckram and a pale, discoloured mask, carries a figurine of
a naked corpse.

WAR. Hunger and Pestilence, you who administer
  My dread commands, terrific, grand, and sinister,
  Consumers both of life and health, who scorn
  Prayers, pleadings, threats, commands, or tears forlorn,
  Now that you know my plans there is no need
  For me to praise again the willing speed
  With which you have rejoiced me in your mission,
  Obeying orders with such expedition.
  The inexorable Fates, in their design,
  Force me at last my favour to incline
  To the sagacious Romans who must rise,
  By victory exalted, to the skies.
  At the same time these Spaniards must be felled
  And slaughtered wholesale in the town they held.
  But in the end will come a time when I
  Shall change, and, casting down what's proud and high,
  Raise what was once so small and weak before—
  For I am the most powerful Queen of War,
  By mothers so detested, though in vain,
  Since those who wrongly hold me in disdain
  Ignore the valour of my heart and hand.
  I know that through the world in every land
  The valour of the Spaniard will attain
  Triumph at length beneath the happy reign
  Of Philip, Charles the Fifth, and Ferdinand.
PESTILENCE. If Hunger, our dear friend here, had not done
  Her duty in Numantia so quickly
  Killing them all till not a single one
  Will live it out, I, with a doom as sickly,
  Could well have executed your designs
  So that the soldiers in the Roman lines
  Could have reaped easy and great gains which now

Even the partial Fates cannot allow.
But Hunger here has worked at such a rate,
In such a way, on the Numantine folk
That they rush headlong to anticipate
And take the wind out of the sails of Fate.
Now all their riches have gone up in smoke.
What Rome will gain is hardly worth a joke.
For us to go to work now, it's too late.
They on themselves have worked your dread design
So that you need not Hunger's help nor mine.
Fury and Rage (your followers) have taken
Such hold upon their hearts that they awaken
A ruthlessness that, were each friend a foeman,
Could not be worse. As if each were a Roman,
Numantine kills Numantine.

HUNGER.   There's the omen!
Turn to the city! See the high roofs burning!
Hear the sad sighs that, from a thousand yearning
And desolated breasts, groan forth their grief!
Hear the high screams of the most lovely ladies
Whose tender limbs are charring in that Hades
Of fire and blood. No friend can bring relief,
Father, nor lover! Death commands in chief.
As tender lambs and ewes, when by their shepherd
Deserted to the wolves or to the leopards,
Rush bleating here and there in mad career,
So children and their mothers, crazed with fear,
Seeing the drawn sword slash from street to street,
Go rushing round on panic-stricken feet,
Hoping in vain their destiny to cheat.
From his young, newly-wedded bride, the spouse
Cuts with a sword his lately-whispered vows.
Against his mother, whom he once adored,
Unheard-of thing! the son uplifts his sword.
Against the son, his father and his sire,
Whom these contrarious clemencies inspire,
Lifts his strong arm, and what he did beget
Is unbegotten—though with fierce regret
Yet with deep satisfaction. There's no square
Street, alley of that whole great city there

That is not full of corpses. Steel and fire
Rage everywhere, ferocious, fell, and dire,
And soon the highest turret of the town
To match the level earth will topple down,
The sumptuous temple and the richest home
Crumble to dust and ashes—tower and dome!
Come! You will see Theogenes at work
Honing the edges of his sword and dirk
To plunge them in the throat of his dear wife
And rob his tender children of their life,
And now that he has lost them and without
Them does not care to live, he casts about
To seek a death more strange and dread than all
That to a human being may befall.

WAR. Come, then! But let each one in her dire course
Exert the very utmost of her force!
From my commands you must not swerve or flinch
But carry out my orders to the inch!
Exeunt.

Enter THEOGENES *with his two small* SONS. *one* DAUGHTER,
and his WIFE.

THEOGENES. Though my paternal love cannot delay
The execution of my dread design,
Consider, my dear children, ere you die,
The honourable motives of my thought.
Terrible is the pain that must be borne
In dying violent deaths. My fate is worse
Since I am doomed to be your butcher first.
But you must not remain, belovèd children,
To live as slaves, nor by the Roman power
Be led in triumph as a trophy, since
To humble us exalts the Romans' pride.
The least rough path which heaven allows to us—
Nay, offers us and shows us, and instructs us
To take—is this into the arms of death.
Nor must you, dearest wife, remain to see
Your tender breast a prey to the rude hands
And lustful eyes of Rome. My sword must free you
From such an agony, and render vain

The lust and greed which goad them on to gain
The dust and ash which will be all we leave
Of our Numantia. My belovèd wife,
It was myself who first put the suggestion
That all of us should perish rather than
Be subject to the lawless power of Rome,
So I must not be backward to enact it,
Nor must my children be the last to die.

WIFE. Can we escape them by no other means?
Heaven knows I would rejoice, could such be found,
But since it seems impossible to me,
And either way my death is near and certain,
You take the trophy of our lives, my husband,
Rather than leave them to perfidious Rome.
Now, since I have to perish, let it be
Inside Diana's temple. Take us there,
And give us up to lightning, steel, and fire!

THEOGENES. Let it be done! Come, let us not delay!
My sorry fate is calling me away.

SON. Mother, why do you cry? Where are we going?
Wait for me, for I have no strength to walk.
It would be better if we had a meal,
For I am faint with weariness and hunger.

WIFE. Then come into my arms, dear son of mine.
Death is your meal, and it is time to dine.
Exeunt.

Enter two other boys, one of whom is SERVIUS, *and the other*
BARIATUS, *who later throws himself from the tower.*

BARIATUS. Servius, where is it that you wish to flee?

SERVIUS. I? Where you like.

BARIATUS.   Come on! How weak you are!
You sentence us to death by lagging here.
Do you not know two thousand swords are drawn
To kill us?

SERVIUS.   It's not possible to fly.
Where do you think of going? What's your plan?

BARIATUS. To hide myself away inside a tower
Belonging to my father.

SERVIUS.   You can go then,
  My friend. I am too weak and tired with hunger.
  I cannot follow you a single step.

BARIATUS. What? Won't you come along?

SERVIUS.   I would, but cannot.
  If you can't walk you'll have to perish here,
  Either by steel, from hunger, or from fright.

BARIATUS. I'm going. Life is going cheap, I fear,
  And fire or sword must end my short career.
    BARIATUS *goes to the tower.* SERVIUS *remains.* THEOGENES
    enters with a drawn sword and bloody hands. Seeing him,
    SERVIUS *runs off the stage.*

THEOGENES. Spilt blood of my own entrails, since you are
  That of my sons! O hand, impetuous hand,
  That for its honour struck against itself
  So cruelly! O Fortune to my bane
  Ever conspiring! O heavens so devoid
  Of pity and of justice! Grant to me,
  I here beseech you, in my dismal plight,
  An honourable though a speedy death!
  O brave Numantines, take me for a base
  Perfidious Roman, and on him avenge
  The injury and insult you have suffered,
  Dyeing your hands and dagger in my blood.
  In my mad sorrow and my desperate fury,
  It's such a sword I offer to you all—
  Since in a fight to feel the pang of death
  Hurts less than in cold blood. He who deprives
  The other of his life must then consign
  His body to the fire, a pious office!
  Come! What is keeping you? Come on! At once!
  Come, make a sacrifice of me, and turn
  The tender love you had for me as friends
  Into the rage and fury of the foe!

    Enter A NUMANTINE.

NUMANTINE. To whom, stalwart Theogenes, do you
  Address yourself? Say what new way to die
  Are you inventing? Why to such wild and jaggèd

Heights of disaster do you still provoke us,
Inciting us to frenzy?

THEOGENES.   Brave Numantine!
If fear daunt not the vigour of your arm,
Take up your sword, and kill yourself with me
As if you were my enemy! This way
To die I find more pleasing than all others
In such a pass as this.

NUMANTINE.   It satisfies
And suits me too. Let's go to the main square,
For there the great fire burns, and he who wins
Can put the victim on his funeral pyre.

THEOGENES. Well said. Let's hurry. It is getting late
To die the death I anxiously desire.
Honour and glory are in either fate,
Whether by steel it comes, or else by fire.
Exeunt.

Enter SCIPIO, JUGURTHA, QUINTUS FABIUS, CAIUS MARIUS,
ERMILIUS, LIMPIUS, *and other Roman soldiers.*

SCIPIO. If I am not mistaken in my thoughts
And if appearances have not deceived me,
The turmoil you have witnessed in Numantia,
The piteous sounds you've heard, the flames you've seen,
Beyond the slightest doubt proclaim to me
That the barbarian fury of the enemy
Has turned against his own fierce breast at last.
Nobody yet appears upon the walls,
The usual sentinels give out no challenge,
And everything is silent as the grave—
As if these wild Numantines suddenly
Had become tranquillised and lulled to rest.

CAIUS MARIUS. I'll soon resolve you of your doubts, my lord,
Since if you wish it, I will volunteer
To climb the wall, though it is dangerous,
Only to find out what our proud and fierce
Enemies have been doing in Numantia.

SCIPIO. Then, Marius, set a ladder to the wall
And do what you propose.

CAIUS MARIUS.   Go fetch a ladder
At once. Bring, too, my shield and my white-plumed
Helmet, for I will either lose my life
Or else relieve the army of its doubts.

ERMILIUS. Here are your shield and helmet. Limpius
Is coming with the ladder. Here it is.

CAIUS MARIUS. I recommend my soul to Jupiter
For I will now perform the deed I promised.

JUGURTHA. Raise your shield higher, Marius! Crouch lower!
Cover your head! Courage! Now you are there.
What can you see?

CAIUS MARIUS.   You holy gods above!
What do my eyes behold?

JUGURTHA.   What strikes such wonder?

CAIUS MARIUS. A lake of crimson blood! A thousand bodies,
Transfixed upon a thousand points of steel,
Lie stretched in all the streets. Numantia's dead.

SCIPIO. Are any of them living?

CAIUS MARIUS.   Not a soul—
At least not so far as my sight can reach!

SCIPIO. Get down into the town, now, on your life
And look about you. Follow him, my friend,
Jugurtha. But let's all go with him too.

JUGURTHA. It does not suit your rank to go with us
On such a risky enterprise. Be patient,
My general, till Marius or I
Bring back the answer as to what has happened
In the proud city. Hold the ladder firm!
Oh, what a terrible, horrific sight!
What an unheard-of wonder-striking thing!
Warm, steaming blood has flooded all the ground!
Dead bodies populate the streets and squares!
And now I'll go and see the whole of it.
He jumps down into the city.

QUINTUS FABIUS. No doubt the fierce Numantines were incited
To this barbarous fury when they saw
That there was no escape for them, and so
Much rather than surrender up their lives

To our victorious hands (abominated,
In the extreme, by their proud, tameless hearts)
They have preferred to give them up together
To their own swords.

SCIPIO.   If only one of them
　Is left alive, then they will not deny me
　A triumph back in Rome for having tamed
　So proud a nation, so inveterate
　And deadly an antagonist of ours,
　Unbending in opinion, prompt, and daring
　Through greatest perils and the direst trials!
　Indeed no Roman soldier yet can boast
　He ever saw Numantine turn his back.
　Their valour and dexterity in arms
　Force me, with perfect reason, to immure them
　As if they were untamable, wild beasts,
　And conquer them by assiduity
　And wiles—it was impossible by force.
　But look. I think here's Marius returning.

　CAIUS MARIUS *returns to the top of the wall.*

CAIUS MARIUS. Illustrious and most prudent general,
　In vain have we employed our strength, in vain
　Has proved your defence! The victory
　We felt so sure would crown your industry
　And skill has now been turned to wind and smoke.
　The lamentable end and tragic story
　Of the unconquered city of Numantia
　Deserves to live eternally in glory,
　For they have cheated you of all your winnings
　And wrenched your triumph out of your own hands.
　Dying with such great-hearted constancy
　That all our projects have been rendered vain,
　The worn-out people of Numantia have
　(Ending their misery by violence)
　Put a sad ending to a long, long story.
　Numantia is one mighty lake of blood
　Strewn with ten thousand corpses whose own pride
　And stubborn rigour was their homicide.
　Of the unbearable and heavy chain

Of slavery they have escaped the strain
By their audacious and unflinching valour.
Up in the midst of their main square a fierce,
Tremendous blaze of fire is roaring, which
They've fed with their own bodies and possessions.
I was in time to see the furious
Theogenes, a valiant, proud Numantine
(Desiring to have done with life for good,
Cursing his brief and luckless lot on earth)
Hurl himself in the middle of the fire,
Saying these words: "Illustrious Fame, employ
Your tongue and use your eyes on this exploit
Which calls you to recount it! Romans, come!
Come, now, and revel in the promised plunder
Of this dead city, turned to dust and ashes,
With all its fruits and flowers turned to thorns!"
Thence, with my thoughts alert and nimble feet,
I wandered round, searching the most remote
And intricate recesses of the town,
But never one live person did I find
Whom I could fetch with me to bring you word
Of how this huge disaster has occurred.

SCIPIO. Could it have been, by chance, that in my breast
My savage arrogance, pregnant with their doom,
Had left no room for clemency at all?
And is my character, by chance, an alien
To that benignity which every victor
Should use to deal with a defeated foe?
Ill have they judged my heart there in Numantia
Since I was born to conquer and forgive!

QUINTUS FABIUS. Jugurtha now may satisfy you better
In what you want to know. Look, here he comes,
Full of foreboding.

JUGURTHA *appears on the wall.*

JUGURTHA.   Prudent general,
In vain do you employ your valour here.
Turn to some other place the diligence
And skill for which you are so justly famed.
All of them, all, are dead, except, I think,

For one, a boy, who still remains alive
To grace you with a triumph, as I see,
Here in this tower before me. He's well-dressed,
But wears a strange confusion in his looks.

SCIPIO. If this is only true, it will be worth
A triumph over the Numantine nation
In Rome. Why, it's the thing I prayed for most!
Let's go there. Coax him to come down. If only
He falls into my hands alive, that's all
That is important to me at this moment.

BARIATUS *speaks out of the tower.*

BARIATUS. Romans! What do you seek? Where are you going?
If here into Numantia you would enter
By force, you'll find it easy; there's no hindrance.
But I must tell you that I hold the keys,
Though feebly-guarded, of this city here
Over whom death has triumphed.

SCIPIO.   It's for them
That I am coming, and to show you that
Compassion is no stranger to my breast.

BARIATUS. You, cruel man, too late have come to offer
Your clemency, when there is no one left
On whom to use it. I myself intend
To carry out the sentence, too, by which
My own belovèd mother and my father
Met such a cruel and appalling death.

QUINTUS FABIUS. Tell me, boy, if, by chance, you've been struck
    blind
By some rash, headstrong madness, to despise
Your budding youth and hate your sweet, young life?

SCIPIO. Temper, my little man, your reckless courage!
Subject your valour to my glorious power,
Being yourself so little, since from now,
I give my faith and pledge my word on it
You shall be your own master and live free,
Endowed with all the jewels and the treasures
That I can give you or that you desire,
If you surrender to me with good will.

BARIATUS. The whole wild fury of all those who perished
　　Within this town, now turned to dust and ash,
　　Their rage at treaties and agreements broken
　　And offers of submission laughed to scorn,
　　All of their fiery anger and resentment
　　Are here united in my breast alone!
　　I have inherited Numantia's valour—
　　If you think you can conquer me, you're mad!
　　Belovèd country! O unlucky city!
　　Never imagine it, nor fear, that I
　　Would be nonplussed at what I owe to you
　　Being by you engendered, or that I,
　　For promises or fears, would flinch or falter!
　　Now that I have no earth nor heaven nor destiny
　　And the whole world to conquer me conspires,
　　It is impossible that to your valour
　　I should not pay the duty that I owe.
　　If fear enticed me here to hide myself
　　From imminent and terrifying death,
　　Death now will take me forth with greater courage
　　Since I desire to follow in your wake.
　　For my vile fear that now has passed away
　　The reparation will be strong and brave;
　　For the late terror of my tender youth
　　A death of bold resolve will pay in full.
　　And I assure you, my brave citizens,
　　That your resolve within me is not dead—
　　That the perfidious Romans shall not triumph
　　But over our mere ashes. Their designs
　　Are all in vain, whether they strike me down
　　Or tempt me with their doubtful promises
　　To spare my life and ope wide gates to wealth.
　　Hold back, you Romans! Do not waste your strength
　　Or tire yourselves by swarming up the wall!
　　Were you ten times more powerful, your power
　　Could never hope to conquer me at all.
　　Now let me show you my intention. That
　　I loved my dear-belovèd country purely
　　And perfectly, let this fall be the proof!

The BOY *throws himself off the wall. A trumpet sounds.*

SCIPIO. Oh, never in my life have I beheld
    A deed so unforgettable as this!
    Young child with ancient valour in your breast!
    Not only has Numantia but all Spain
    Acquired undying glory by an act
    So spirited, of such heroic virtue!
    You, with this fall, have raised your fame on high,
    And levelled all my victories to the ground!
    If proud Numantia were living yet
    I would rejoice because you lived in her.
    Alone you won this long and famous contest,
    You only! Then, my child, be yours the victory
    And yours the glory with which heaven prepares
    To welcome you, who vanquished by your fall
    Him who, exalted high, you've now brought low.
    Enter FAME *clothed in white.*

FAME. Go forth, my voice, in accents sweet and low,
    From race to race, and kindle as you go,
    In every soul, a burning wish to keep
    Deathless the memory of so brave a leap.
    Raise up your downcast brows, Romans! and bear
    Away this little body that could dare
    Your might and wrest the triumph from your hands.
    For I am Fame, proclaimer to the lands,
    And I shall take great care (while highest heaven
    Towers to the topmost sphere of all the seven
    Pouring its strength and vigour on our earth)
    To publish round the world Numantia's worth
    And peerless valour with a truthful tongue,
    From Bactria to Thule to be sung,
    And reach from Pole to Pole! This peerless deed
    Foretells the valour that the Spanish breed
    Will in the coming centuries inherit
    From ancestors and fathers of such merit.
    Neither the scythe of Death nor course of Time
    Shall make me cease to sing in deathless rhyme
    The glory of Numantia's constant soul
    And her strong arm. In her alone I find

All that can kindle the poetic mind
To fill long ages with sad lamentations,
Praising the bravest of unconquered nations.
And now, remembering her matchless glory,
We give a happy end to our sad story.

FUENTE OVEJUNA

Lope de Vega

English Version by Roy Campbell

In 1476 the peasants of Fuente Ovejuna, a village in Córdoba, rose against their feudal overlords, represented by Fernán Gómez de Guzmán. As Comendador, or Knight Commander, of the Order of Calatrava, Fernán Gómez derived his authority from the Master of that Order, the young Rodrigo Téllez Girón. The larger political background is sketched in Lope's opening scene where the Comendador champions the King of Portugal's claim to the Spanish throne. The rival claimant was Ferdinand of Aragón who had married Isabela of Castile: it is to these "Catholic Princes" that the peasants will later appeal, as to a Supreme Court.

Lope read of the events of 1476 in *A Chronicle of the Three Military Orders* by Rades y Andrada.

E.B.

DRAMATIS PERSONAE

QUEEN ISABEL (ISABELA) OF CASTILE

HER HUSBAND, KING FERNANDO (FERDINAND) OF ARAGÓN

RODRIGO TÉLLEZ GIRÓN, *Master of the Order of Calatrava*

FERNÁN (FERNANDO) GÓMEZ DE GUZMÁN, *Comendador of the Order of Calatrava*

ORTUÑO ⎫
⎬ *his servants*
FLORES ⎭

DON MANRIQUE, *Master of the Order of Santiago*

A JUDGE

TWO ALDERMEN OF CIUDAD REAL

AN ALDERMAN OF FUENTE OVEJUNA[1]

ESTEBAN ⎫
⎬ *mayors of Fuente Ovejuna*
ALONSO ⎭

LAURENCIA ⎫
JACINTA ⎬ *peasant women*
PASCUALA ⎭

JUAN ROJO ⎫
FRONDOSO ⎪
⎬ *peasants*
BARRILDO ⎪
MENGO ⎭

LEONELO, *a student of law*

CIMBRANOS, *a soldier*

MUSICIANS

ATTENDANTS

PEASANTS AND PEASANT WOMEN

SOLDIERS

[1] Fuente Ovejuna should be pronounced in five syllables, thus: Fwént–yov–e–hú–na. It is written as one word on the map today, but the two-word form is less formidable for non-Spanish readers and is not an innovation. *Fuente* means fountain or well; *ovejuna* means pertaining to sheep. [E.B.]

ACT I

The house of the Master of Calatrava in Almagro

Enter the COMENDADOR, FLORES, ORTUÑO.

COMENDADOR. The Master knows I'm here in town?

FLORES.   He knows
Already.

ORTUÑO.   He gets more serious, as he grows.

COMENDADOR. But does he know that it is I, Fernán
Gómez de Guzmán?

FLORES.   He's not yet a man.
Do not be shocked.

COMENDADOR.   My name he may ignore
But not my rank of Grand Comendador!

ORTUÑO. He has advisers who abet his pride
In setting common courtesy aside.

COMENDADOR. Then he will win but little love, for still
Courtesy is the key to men's good will.
Stupid discourtesy's the key to naught
But hate.

ORTUÑO.   If a discourteous man but thought
How all must come to hate him in the end
Although to kiss his shoe they now contend—
He would prefer to die than be like this.

FLORES. How sickening and importunate it is
To suffer such discourtesy! In men
Of equal rank, it's foolishness, but when
Their rank's unequal, it becomes a curse,
And smacks of arrant tyranny or worse.
But you can well ignore a slight like this
From one too young even to've known the kiss
Of women.

COMENDADOR. But the sword he buckled on
The day the cross of Calatrava shone

First on his breast conferred the obligation
Of courtesy.

FLORES. If in his estimation
You have been slandered, you will soon find out.

ORTUÑO. You still can go, if you are still in doubt.

COMENDADOR. It is a question I would fain decide.

Enter the MASTER OF CALATRAVA *with his train of* AT-
TENDANTS.

MASTER. Your pardon, on my life! Fernando Gómez!
I've only just been told you were in town.

COMENDADOR. With much good reason I had cause to frown
Thinking you slighted me, since mutual love
And noble birth should raise us both above
Such wrangling thoughts. You're Master of the Order.
I, Gómez, am your Grand Comendador
And very faithful servant ever more.

MASTER. I little guessed; I had no news of you.
Welcome! Embrace me!

COMENDADOR. It is but my due
That you should honour me: I risked my life
On your behalf so often in the strife
Ere the Pope raised you to this lofty rank,
Waiving your youth.

MASTER. It's you I have to thank,
That's true; and by the holy sign across
Our breasts, I shall repay your toil and loss
With my esteem, and as a father, too,
Shall honour you.

COMENDADOR. I'm now content with you.

MASTER. What tidings of the war?

COMENDADOR. Hear what I say
And learn how much you owe me.

MASTER. Tell me, pray.

COMENDADOR. Grand Master of the cross of Calatrava,
Raised by the valour of a famous father
To that high station! He, eight years ago,
In favour of yourself renounced his Mastership.

This was confirmed and sworn by kings and captains
For greater surety. The most Holy Pontiff,
Pius the Second, sent some Bulls, and others
Were sent thereafter by Pope Paul,[1] appointing
That Juan Pacheco, Master of the Order
Of Santiago, should share equal rank
As your coadjutor. He died; and you,
Despite your tender years, were given sole
Dominion. You must realise your honour
Depends in such a case on serving truly
The cause of your great House. Hear how things stand:
Upon the death of Henry of Castile,[2]
Alfonso, King of Portugal, laid claim
To Henry's title—Joan, Alfonso's wife,
Is Henry's daughter. A like claim is made,
Though with less obvious right to your allegiance,
By Ferdinand of Aragón who cites
His marriage to Castilian Isabel.
Your House, great sir, supports Alfonso's claim.
Your cousin, as it happens, holds this Joan
Fast in his power . . . My advice is this:
To summon all the Knights of Calatrava
With those here of Almagro, and to capture
Ciudad Real, the city on the frontier
Dividing Andalusia from Castile.
Few forces will be needed. As their soldiers
They only have the natives of the place
And some few gentry who support the cause
Of Isabela and King Ferdinand.
It steads you now to make the whole world ring
And stun the misbelief of all beholders
Who deem your cross too broad for the slim shoulders
Of such a child as you are. Think of them—
Urueña's mighty counts from whom you stem
And how from forth their tombs, to urge your quarrel,
They show the garlands of unwithering laurel
They won in life! Think of Villena's lords

---

[1] Pius II (1458–64), Paul II (1467–71).
[2] Henry IV of Castile (1454–74), Alfonso V of Portugal (1438–81), Ferdinand of Aragón (1452–1516). [E.B.]

And other captains famous for their swords,
Too many for the wings of Fame to bear!
Remember them. Your pure, white blade make bare,
Which you must stain the colour of the sign
That spans with crimson cross your chest and mine—
Since Master of the red cross or its knight
No man can be while yet his sword is white!
Both cross and sword in scarlet must be dyed
One on your breast, the other at your side,
And you, the sovereign of your deathless line,
Must as the dome upon their temple shine!

MASTER. Fernando Gómez, rest assured, I'll fight
This quarrel for my lineage and my right,
And, when the city to my conquest falls,
Like forked, red lightning, scorch its battered walls.
So, though my uncle's dead, the world may know
That in my veins his deeds of valour flow,
And, when I draw my sword, its silver flare
Shall flush as crimson as the cross I wear!
But tell me how you're settled now, and where,
And have you any soldiers quartered there?

COMENDADOR. But few; yet trained by me. Inured to battle,
They'll fight like lions. But, as for the village,
Fuente Ovejuna's folk think more of tillage,
And care more for their humble crops and cattle
Than about martial glories. They know naught
Of war.

MASTER. You live there?

COMENDADOR. Yes, I've sought
A haven there in these rough times. But, mind,
Let not a single vassal stay behind!

MASTER. No fear of that! My horse I'll mount today,
Couching my lance, and eager for the fray!

Village square in Fuente Ovejuna

Enter PASCUALA *and* LAURENCIA.

LAURENCIA. Never may he return!

PASCUALA.   Why so?
  I thought, when you had heard the news
  Of his departure, you would show
  More sorrow.

LAURENCIA.   May heaven still refuse
  To let him come back here!

PASCUALA.   I've heard
  Oaths angrier far than those you utter,
  But when it came to test the word
  The hearts have proved as soft as butter.

LAURENCIA. D'you think you'll find a holm-oak drier
  Than I am?

PASCUALA.   Get along with you!
  It is the driest cork takes fire.
  Yet when one's talking of desire,
  And when the gentry come to woo,
  What girl can say, and prove no liar,
  "I shall not go the same way too"?

LAURENCIA. By this bright sun, I swear it's true,
  Though the whole world would say I lie!
  Why should I love Fernando who
  Pursues me? Here's the reason why:
  D'you think he'd marry me?

PASCUALA.   Why, no!

LAURENCIA. His infamy I then condemn.
  How many girls have suffered for
  The ruin that was made of them
  All by this same Comendador!

PASCUALA. I'll hold it as a marvel, though,
  If from his clutches you go free.

LAURENCIA. It's nonsense—all that you foresee!
　For ever since a month ago,
　In vain, he has been after me.
　Ortuño, that sly cur, and Flores,
　His pandar, showed me silks and pearls
　And costly headgear for my curls,
　And tried to frighten me with stories
　About his power to do me harm.
　Yet, though they filled me with alarm,
　They could not bait me with their hook.

PASCUALA. Where did they tempt you?

LAURENCIA. 　　　　　　　　　Last weekend,
　While washing linen by the brook.

PASCUALA. I fear they'll trick you in the end.

LAURENCIA. What? Me?

PASCUALA. 　　　　　　Or, if not you, the priest.

LAURENCIA. Though toothsome, I am just too tough
　To serve His Reverence for a feast.
　But of this "love" I've had enough.
　I am more interested far
　In any slice of roasted bacon
　That from the embers I have taken
　And placed between the bread I've kneaded;
　Or from my mother's favourite jar
　To steal a cup of wine unheeded;
　Or watch at noon the simmering broth
　Where beef chunks in the humming froth
　Of greens are somersaulting round;
　Or, if I've come in tired from walking,
　To splice an *aubergine* well-browned
　With a ham-slice; or else be caulking
　The crannies of my appetite
　With a grape-bunch from my own vine
　(Which God preserve from hail or blight)
　Till we on salmagundi dine
　With oil and pepper seasoned fine;
　And then to bed—to my oration
　Of "Lead me not into temptation"—
　And sleep contented with my prayer.

These are the things for which I care
And prize a hundred times above
The foolish, foxy wiles of love
With which these villains weave their snare.
For if you wish to take their measure
Their only aim's to work us harm,
To make us go to bed with pleasure,
Then to awake in dire alarm.

PASCUALA. You're right, Laurencia, and when
They leave off loving us, the men
Deal with us as the thankless sparrows
Deal with the peasant in the winter:
For when the days begin to narrow
And the fields with frosts to splinter,
Then down, as fast as they are able,
They flit from chimney, cave, and gable
With melting voice to croon and coo
"Tweenie-tweenie-tweenie-twoo"
While with the crumbs swept from his table
The fool regales the faithless crew.
But when the cold has ceased to freeze them
And the fields their flowers reveal,
Past delights no longer please them,
Thanklessness is all they feel.
For all the largesse of his table
They miscall the friend they knew
For an unbelieving Jew
Flitting up to cave and gable
No longer chirping "tweeny-tweeny"
But cursing "Sheeny-sheeny-sheeny!"
Such are men with every maiden:
When they need us, then we are
The wealth with which their hearts are laden,
Their life, their soul, their guiding star,
But when their flames die down to embers,
They chirrup, bill, and coo no more:
All the names their faith remembers
Are the names of "bitch" and "whore"!

LAURENCIA. Trust no man that comes to woo!

PASCUALA. So say I, Laurencia, too!

Enter MENGO, BARRILDO, FRONDOSO.

FRONDOSO. Your arguments have got lopsided,
Barrildo.

BARRILDO. Look! Here's one at hand
By whose decision we may stand.

MENGO. But ere the point has been decided,
You both must swear to pay the cost
You've wagered if the verdict's mine.

BARRILDO. I swear we shall! But, if you've lost,
What prize, in turn, have you provided?

MENGO. I'll bet you, then, my flute of box
Worth a lot more than barns or flocks
Were you to value it as I did.

BARRILDO. I'm satisfied.

MENGO.   Then let's proceed.

FRONDOSO. Ladies! Good day!

LAURENCIA.   "Ladies" indeed!

FRONDOSO. Yes, it's the fashion and the law
Which euphemises every flaw.
The fat man's "well-set-up"; the lean
Is "slim" and "graceful in his mien";
The fledgling scholar, still at college,
Is called "a doctor" for his knowledge;
The stone-blind has a "visual failing";
The squint-eyed has a "roving glance";
The cripple "does not like to dance";
The big-mouthed churl who's always railing
Is "fearless"; the potato-eyed
Old blinkard is called "shrewd and sharp";
The ignorant is magnified
For "wisdom"; he who loves to carp
And cavil, why, he's "persevering";
The busybody's "most endearing";
The gasbag's "deep" and "wise"; the shameless
Is "daring"; and the coward's blameless,
Though "falling short"; the domineering,
Insulting ruffian is miscalled

"A martial figure"; he who's bald
For "grave authority's" extolled;
The grudging sulk is praised for "gravity";
There's "wit" in ignorant depravity;
The insolent is "brave and bold";
The madman goes for "free and easy,"
For "humourous" the tout who's broke;
"Companionable, bright, and breezy"
They call the brandy-gozzled soak;
The snuffler and the bulbous-snouted
Are only "suffering from a cold";
Arrogance for "reserve" is doubted,
And grumpiness for "shyness" goes;
The hunchback passes for "well-loaded" . . .
And so, lest I should be outmoded,
I call you "Ladies" I suppose.
But that's enough, for in this way
I could talk nonsense all the day.

LAURENCIA. Up in the cities, those in fashion
Use gentler words to be polite.
But, by my faith, the terms they ration
For human faults, appear more right
Than the rough terms that can be flung
At random by a spiteful tongue.

FRONDOSO. Well, could you let us have a sample?

LAURENCIA. I'll take the opposite example
To each of yours. The man who's serious
Is "grumpy." One who speaks the truth
They call "self-righteous" and "uncouth."
They call the grave man "sad"; "imperious"
And "tiresome"—one who reprehends;
"Importunate"—who counsels youth;
"Officious"—one who helps his friends;
"Cruel" they call the man who's just,
Impartially though he should try us;
"Listless and tame"—the humbly pious;
And one who's constant in his trust
They take for "simple, dull, and dense";
Courtesy is to "cringe and flatter";

Christian behaviour's "all pretence";
Merit that earns is no such matter,
But "merely luck"; misfortune's "shame"—
For which the sufferer is to blame;
A girl who's virtuous is "a fool";
A wife who does not break the rule
Is merely "dull" . . . But that should be
More than enough to bring me level
In answering your philosophy.

MENGO. By heavens, she is the very devil!
The priest who functioned at your christening
Laid on the salt, in handfuls too!

LAURENCIA. But what's your strife (if I've been listening
Correctly)?

FRONDOSO.   Hark, Laurencia, do!

LAURENCIA. Well, what is it you want?

FRONDOSO.   Laurencia,
Lend me your hearing.

LAURENCIA.   Only lend?
To give it you for keeps, I'll venture,
From this day onwards.

FRONDOSO.   I depend
On your discretion.

LAURENCIA.   What's your bet?

FRONDOSO. I and Barrildo both have set
A wager against Mengo here.

LAURENCIA. What does he say?

BARRILDO.   —Denies a fact
That's certain, absolute, and clear.

MENGO. To put it plainly, I've come here
To floor them with the truth exact.

LAURENCIA. What's that?

BARRILDO.   That love does not exist
Is what *he* holds.

LAURENCIA.   But who can doubt it?
Surely there's love.

BARRILDO.   Of course. Without it
  How on this earth could life persist?

MENGO. Philosophy is all a mist
  To me. I know nothing about it.
  The written word is Greek to me.
  But can you watch, and dare to scout it,
  The strife between each element,
  The endless war they represent?
  And it's from them our bodies borrow
  Their nourishment, their wrath and sorrow,
  Their phlegm and blood—you must agree.

FRONDOSO. The worlds around us and above,
  Mengo, are harmony entire.
  Harmony is pure love, and love
  Is harmony.

MENGO.   I state the worth
  Of self-love, native to this earth:
  That is the love which governs all things.
  Affinities in great and small things
  Must regulate all that we see:
  I don't deny *that*. I agree
  That everything is truly fond
  Of what to it may correspond
  In keeping its integrity:
  My hand against a coming blow
  Leaps up to guard my face, and so
  My feet, by running off, forestall
  A danger that might else befall
  My body. My eyes, blinking tight,
  Avoid whatever harms their sight.
  Such love is natural.

PASCUALA.   Then why
  Object? What is it you deny?

MENGO. That anyone in love can fall
  (Except with his own self) at all.

PASCUALA. Your pardon, Mengo, but you're lying,
  Since is it any good denying
  That force is not material

By which men love their womenkind,
Or animals their mates?

MENGO.   It's blind,
Sheer *amour-propre*, self-satisfaction,
Not love. What's love, then? I'll enquire.

LAURENCIA. Why, love is a divine desire
Of beauty.

MENGO.   Why does love pursue
Beauty? Why? Surely, to acquire
It for one's own good self.

LAURENCIA.   That's true.

MENGO. To love one's own self, one must woo
The thing that self does most require.

LAURENCIA. That's so.

MENGO.   Well, there's no love
Except what for one's own delight
One hunts, to feed one's appetite,
For one's own self the prize to grapple,
To be of one's own eye the apple,
And the sole eye of one's potato!

BARRILDO. The preacher in his recent sermons
Mentioned a certain man called Plato
Who, speaking about love, determines
That we should selflessly admire
The soul and virtue of the one
We love—to set our hearts on fire.

PASCUALA. Right off the beaten track you've run
And bogged your axle in the mire
Where only doctors from the colleges
Find foothold.

LAURENCIA.   You are right: our knowledge is
Too shallow. Do not grind too hard
And fine, but thank the heavens above,
Mengo, that you're so lucky-starred
As to be ignorant of love.

MENGO. Are you in love?

LAURENCIA.   With my good name.

FRONDOSO. May God chastise you for the same
　　With jealous pangs!

PASCUALA.　　　　　　　The wisest plan
　　Is to consult the sacristan.
　　He, or the priest, could answer best . . .
　　Laurencia's never loved a man
　　And I have scarcely stood the test.
　　Our judgment would be all in vain.

FRONDOSO. A curse upon your cold disdain!

　　Enter FLORES.

FLORES. God be with you, good people!

PASCUALA.　　　　　　　　　　Look!
　　The page of the Comendador.

LAURENCIA. Rather his carrion-kite and rook.
　　What news abroad, friend?

FLORES.　　　　　　　　From the war
　　I've just returned, as you may see.

LAURENCIA. And what of Don Fernán? Is he
　　Expected back?

FLORES.　　　　The war at last
　　Has ended. Though it cost some lives,
　　Our cause victoriously thrives.

FRONDOSO. Well, señor, tell us how it passed.

FLORES. Why, yes. Although myself I say it,
　　There's no man better could portray it,
　　Since I was there from first to last,
　　And with my own eyes saw it all.
　　Against that city which we call
　　The Royal City, our young Master
　　Of Calatrava raised his troop,
　　Two thousand infantry, to swoop,
　　And carry slaughter and disaster
　　Together with three hundred horse
　　Of seculars and monks and friars—
　　For even priests must join the force
　　When our great Order so requires
　　(Though that is chiefly with the Moors)
　　To take up arms and fight in wars.

The youthful Master of our Order,
In doublet green with gilded border,
Slit at the sleeve-ends to unfold
The bracelets held with links of gold,
On a huge dapple horse was seen
With grey hairs shot with hairs of silver,
Whose underlip the Guadalquivir
Had bathed, and who had grazed its green.
Its tail with deerskin plaits behind,
Its mane, in front, was deftly twined
With many a ribbon, lace, and bow
Whose flattering whiteness, row by row,
Vied with the dots and dancing speckles
That starred his flanks with fiery freckles
And showered his stalwart croup with snow.
Our own Fernando Gómez rode
With him. The horse that he bestrode
Was of the honey-coloured hue
But mane and tail and fetlock, too,
Were jetty-black at each extreme;
The muzzle was as black to view,
Save that it turned as white as cream
From snorting, slavering, and drinking
The froth that from its snaffle clinking
And champing jaws, flaked sud by sud,
The foam of its aspiring blood,
And smoke to which its wrath was flame.
In glittering scales his chain-mail bound him;
Bright plates of armour spanned his frame
And clipped his shoulders. In wide swirls
His orange tunic-fringe around him
Sparkled with gold and orient pearls.
Over his helmet, wreathed in curls,
The cream-white ostrich-plumes were towering
As if 'twere orange-blossom flowering
Out of his orange-coloured lace—
Slung on a white and scarlet brace,
An ash-tree, lifted on his arm,
To threaten all the Moorish race
And fill Granada with alarm!

The city rose in the King's name
Since for the Crown they all proclaim
Their loyalty to the King's succession.
They made resistance worthy fame.
But in the end, their strength to tame,
The Master entered in procession,
And those who had denied his right
He had beheaded upon sight.
As for the common people there,
He had each snaffled with a bit,
And, having stripped their bodies bare,
He flogged them in the public square
Till they could neither stand nor sit.
He made himself so roundly feared,
So popular and so revered,
Who in so short a time could win,
Chastise, and rule, though adolescent!
They augured that the pale blue crescent
Of Islam in eclipse would spin
To ignominy, shame, and loss,
Before the sun of his red cross.
After he'd lightened, struck, and thundered,
Out of the city's wreck, he plundered
Such vast largesse and wealth for all
(But chiefly the Comendador)
It seemed he had flung wide the door
Of his own house and dining-hall
And bade them ransack all the store.
But now I hear the band approaching.
Rejoice! Forget your cares and quarrels!
To win all hearts, with none reproaching,
Is worth a forest full of laurels.

Enter the COMENDADOR *with* ORTUÑO, JUAN ROJO, *and the
mayor and deputy mayor,* ESTEBAN, *and* ALONSO.

MUSICIANS, *singing.*

> You're welcome in our village,
> Comendador, to stop!
> Battlefields are his tillage
> And lives of men his crop!

Long live the Guzmán faction
And the Girones line
Invincible in action
In peace the most benign.

Who stronger than the oak
Against the Moors did sally
And quelled the sturdy folk
Of Ciudad Reále.[3]

Fuente Ovejuna greets him
The village where his home is
Shout, everyone who meets him:
Long live Fernando Gómez!

COMENDADOR. Dear village, let me thank you from my heart,
For all these signs of love that you have shown.

ALONSO. Of what we feel we've only shown a part
Of all the love you merit as your own.

ESTEBAN. Fuente Ovejuna's mayors and corporation
(Whom you've so graced), along with this ovation,
Beg that you will accept, as from our hearts,
The humble gifts that pile these rustic carts.
You'll find as much good will and homely thanks
Borne in the cradle of their creaking planks
As in more wealthy gifts. Here, two glazed jars
Brim with preserves. Here, from the wooden bars
A flock of geese poke forth their heads to cackle
Your valiant fame. Ten fattened hogs, to crackle
Upon your fire, here offer up their loves,
And their smooth hides, as soft as scented gloves.
A hundred pairs of chanticleers and chickens
For whom full many a widow sighs and sickens
And many an orphaned fledgling joins the mourners
Round dunghills, village-greens, and farmyard corners.
We bring no coats of arms nor gold-trapped steeds
But all from rustic loyalty proceeds
Offered by loyal vassals—men who hold
That love's more lasting and more pure than gold.

[3] Mispronounce "Re/álly" as in original. [R.C.]

And (talking about purity) here's wine—
Twelve skins of it! which could defend a breach
In January, if it did but line
Your warriors' skins inside. It's common speech—
For furbishing clean steel, to make it shine
And cut like lightning, there is naught like wine.
Armour without, I say, but wine within,
Against all comers, they will always win!
I will not speak of cheeses and the rest:
Our house is yours, and you, most honoured guest,
Have won your own deserts from every heart.

COMENDADOR. Thanks, councillors, in peace may you depart.

ALONSO. Now rest, thrice welcome to our countryside!
  If these poor rushes that we strew before you
  Were pearls and rubies which we could provide,
  Even then, they would be insufficient for you.

COMENDADOR. I well believe you. Thank you all. Good-bye.

ESTEBAN. Now, singers, raise your voices up on high.

MUSICIANS *sing*.
> You're welcome in our village,
> Comendador, to stop!
> Battlefields are your tillage,
> And slaughtered men your crop!

Exeunt.

Enter COMENDADOR, LAURENCIA, PASCUALA, ORTUÑO, FLORES.

COMENDADOR. Here! Wait, you two!

LAURENCIA.   What does Your Lordship wish?

COMENDADOR. You turned me down the other day. Yes! Me!
  What does this mean?

LAURENCIA.   Pascuala, is he talking
  To you?

PASCUALA. No! Leave me out of it! Not me!

COMENDADOR. It is to you I'm talking, cruel beauty,
  And to this other wench. Are you not mine?

PASCUALA. Your servants, yes. But not for other use.

COMENDADOR. Go in, get in this doorway here. Come on!
  There are a lot of men here. Don't be frightened.

LAURENCIA. I'll go in if the councillors go too
  (One of them is my father) not unless . . .

COMENDADOR. Flores . . .

FLORES.   My lord!

COMENDADOR. What do they mean not to obey my orders?

FLORES. In with you!

LAURENCIA.   Here, don't claw us!

FLORES.   Don't be foolish!
  Go in!

PASCUALA. No! If we do, you'll bolt us in.

FLORES. Go in! He only wants to let you see
  The trophies he's brought back.

COMENDADOR.   Once they're inside,
  Ortuño, bolt the door.

  Exit COMENDADOR.

LAURENCIA. Flores, please let us pass.

ORTUÑO.   What! Don't you know
  That you're included with the other presents?

PASCUALA. Out of my way, or I shall scream for help!

FLORES. That's taking things too far.

LAURENCIA.   Cannot your master
  Be satisfied with all the meat they've brought him?

ORTUÑO. Yours is the sort of meat he likes the best.

LAURENCIA. Well, may it choke his throat and burst his innards!

  The women leave.

FLORES. And now we're in a fix! Think what he'll say!

In the palace of the Catholic kings at Medina del Campo

Enter KING FERDINAND, QUEEN ISABEL, DON MANRIQUE,
Master of Santiago, and ATTENDANTS.

QUEEN. My lord, we must be wary in this matter.
  The King of Portugal has got his army
  Ready to march. So we must pounce at once
  And win outright, or else we'll court defeat.

KING. Aragón and Navarre are sending help
And I can soon reorganise Castile
To bring us swift success.

QUEEN.   Your Majesty,
Our victory is ensured by that, believe me.

DON MANRIQUE. Two aldermen from Ciudad Real
Beg leave of audience. Shall I bid them enter?

KING. Do not deny our presence. Let them in.

Enter TWO ALDERMEN *from Ciudad Real.*

FIRST ALDERMAN. Great Catholic King Ferdinand, whom
    heaven
Sent to Castile from Aragón to bless
And shelter us. From Ciudad Real
We've humbly come to sue for the protection
Of your unrivalled valour. In the past
We have been happy as your subjects; now
Our adverse fate has brought us down from that
High honour. For the famous Don Rodrigo
Téllez Girón (though young to be the Master
Of Calatrava) that fierce thunderbolt
Of reckless valour, both for his own glory
And to extend the frontiers of his rule,
Laid close siege to our city. Though we fought,
Opposing bravery to violent force,
Till the blood ran in streams, we lost the war.
So then he took possession of the town,
Which he could not have done, save for the help,
Tactics, and counsels of Fernando Gómez.
So he remains our ruler, we his vassals,
Against our will, unless some remedy
Is soon applied.

KING.   Where is Fernando Gómez?

FIRST ALDERMAN. He's in Fuente Ovejuna, I believe,
Since that's his fief. He has a house and land there,
And there, more freely than we dare to tell it,
He tyrannises over his poor vassals
Keeping them alien from content and peace.

KING. Have you a captain left among you?

SECOND ALDERMAN.   Sire,
  No one of noble blood escaped from death,
  Capture, or wounds.

QUEEN.   This case brooks no delay.
  We must strike quickly without losing strength
  Before our daring enemy can act.
  The King of Portugal, advancing through
  Estremadura, finds a sure, safe gateway
  And may cause far more harm if he's not checked.

KING. Now, Don Manrique, Master of Santiago,
  Go! Take two regiments! Repair these harms
  And grant no respite to the foe! The Count
  Of Cabra can go with you: Córdova
  Can claim in him a captain of world fame.
  This is the most that I can send you now.

DON MANRIQUE. Yes, I think this solution is the best.
  I'll stamp out his disorders, or I'll die.

QUEEN. Since it is you we send, victory's certain!

The countryside near Fuente Ovejuna

Enter LAURENCIA *and* FRONDOSO.

LAURENCIA. I had come back from the river
  Although my washing's hardly wrung
  Lest we should be on every tongue
  Because, Frondoso, you're so reckless
  In what you say, that old and young
  Are spreading rumours through the village
  That I on you and you on me
  Are casting looks for all to see.
  They know that of the farmer people
  You are most bold, and proud, and free
  And wear the finest clothes, and so,
  In all the village, there's no man

Or girl that does not claim to know
That you and I will soon be one
And that the village sacristan
Will leave off playing his bassoon
To see us from the vestry soon.
For my own part I wish them thrift,
Full barns in August, with the gift
Of brimming must in every jar.
Their tittle-tattle's very far
From getting on my nerves. A lot
Of sleep I'll lose on that account!
I do not care one tiny jot.

FRONDOSO. Lovely Laurencia, this disdain
Causes my soul such dreadful pain.
It breaks my heart to see and hear you
And makes me frightened to come near you.
If you but realise that I
For you alone would live and die
Your faithful husband—my reward
Is poor!

LAURENCIA. It's all I can afford.

FRONDOSO. But can you really feel no ruth
To see the pain you cause? Mere thinking
Of you prevents me eating, drinking
Or sleeping, in my prime of youth.
Can savagery so uncouth
And cruelty so fierce, be hid
Behind an angel's face? In truth
I fear I shall go raving mad.

LAURENCIA. Try magic spells, if you feel bad.

FRONDOSO. No! I am begging for my life!
My dear Laurencia, be my wife
And let us both, like turtledoves,
With beaks and hearts in amorous strife
Solemnly consummate our loves
When we come from the church together
To bill and coo through life forever.

LAURENCIA. You ask my uncle, old Juan Rojo!
Even if I'm not mad about you

And very well could do without you—
Yet I could care for you.

FRONDOSO.   Confound!
Here comes the Grand Comendador.

LAURENCIA. He's hunting roebuck, I'll be bound.
Hide in this bush.

FRONDOSO.   I'll hide, but where
Can I escape my jealous care?

Enter the COMENDADOR *with a crossbow.*

COMENDADOR. It's not so bad when hunting buck
To fall in with such damned good luck
In place of *buck* to find a *dear*—
A deer so timorous and shy
And so precisely now and here!

LAURENCIA. I am just resting while I dry
Some linen, and, with your good will,
I shall return now to the rill.

COMENDADOR. This ugly kind of frown and fret
Insults my rank which you forget,
And does great havoc to the grace
Both of the figure and the face
Which heaven gave you. Though chance gave
You, other times, a way to save
Your virtue, now good fortune yields
These hushed, conniving, lonely fields
And you alone cannot deny
Your Master's rights, nor hope to fly
From one who holds you in control
And owns your house, your body, and your soul—
One whom, moreover, you insult by this.
Pedro Redondo's wife granted me bliss,
Sebastiania, too—they never parried
The strong urge of my love, though newly married.
Martin del Pozo's wife, two days a bride,
Gave herself up, and laid her by my side.

LAURENCIA. My lord, those women long were at the game
Before their husbands or Your Lordship came!
Follow your roebuck, sir, by God be blessed!

But for that Christian cross upon your chest
I'd say you were the fiend—

COMENDADOR.   I will not stand it:
I'll fling my bow aside, and like a bandit
Will plunder you with my brute-strength alone,
For you are a mere chattel that I own!

LAURENCIA. What? Are you mad?

COMENDADOR.   Don't struggle!

     FRONDOSO *steals out and takes the crossbow.*

FRONDOSO.   Now I've got
The crossbow. Heaven help us all! If not,
I'll have to shoulder it and shoot.

LAURENCIA.   Heaven be my aid!

COMENDADOR. Look, we are all alone. Don't be afraid!

FRONDOSO. Most generous Comendador, let go
Of this poor girl, or else with your own bow
I shall transfix your body without sparing.
Although I tremble at the cross you're wearing!

COMENDADOR. Villainous dog!

FRONDOSO.   No dog, sir!

LAURENCIA.   Have a care,
Frondoso, what you're doing.

FRONDOSO, *to* LAURENCIA.   Run away!

     Exit LAURENCIA.

COMENDADOR. Oh, what a fool I was to leave my sword,
Thinking that it would frighten her.

FRONDOSO.   My lord,
I've but to press this trigger and you die.

COMENDADOR. She's gone, you lowborn villain. Leave that bow
I tell you, put it down, quick!

FRONDOSO.   How can I
Leave it, when you will kill me if I do?
True love is deaf to reason or to rhyme
When he is on his throne for the first time:
So take good warning.

COMENDADOR.   Shoot me villain, do!

Rather than that upon a clod like you
One nobly born should turn his back and flee,
Shoot me, and see what it will lead you to!
Shoot, dog! I break the laws of chivalry
By speaking to you.

FRONDOSO.   I'll not shoot you. No.
But as I'm forced to save my life, I'll go,
Taking your crossbow.

Takes the bow off with him.

COMENDADOR.   How could I foresee
This danger? But by heaven I shall be
Revenged for this rebellion and attack.
God give me patience till I've paid it back!

ACT II

Village square in Fuente Ovejuna

Enter ESTEBAN *and the* FIRST ALDERMAN.

ESTEBAN. My view is this, good sir: let no more grain
  Be taken from the public granary.
  The year wears on. The harvest augurs badly.
  Let us store up reserves in case of need,
  Whatever voices murmur other views.

FIRST ALDERMAN. That's always been my own idea in ruling
  The village peacefully in its best interests.

ESTEBAN. We must present a plea to Fernán Gómez.
  We don't want these astrologers to make
  Long speeches about things they do not know
  Concerning secrets known to God alone.
  What right have they presumptuously to claim
  Deep theologic knowledge and to find
  The future corresponding with the past?
  The present is the time that counts; the wisest
  Of them is ignorant of all but that.
  You'd think they had the clouds on tap at home!
  You'd think the stars were at their beck and call!
  How can they know the goings-on in heaven
  Which fill us with such anxious hopes and fears?
  They think that they can regulate the seedtime
  And deal out laws to barley, wheat, peas, beans,
  Cucumbers, calabashes, pumpkins, and mustard!
  They are the pumpkin-heads! They prophesy
  A beast will die, and then they say it's happened
  Not here but somewhere else—in Transylvania!
  They say there'll be a shortage in our wine,
  But plenty of good beer in Germany.
  In Gascony the cherries will be frozen
  And there'll be lots of tigers in Hircania,
  But after all, whether we sow or not,

The year is always ended in December!

Enter LEONELO, *the student, and* BARRILDO.

LEONELO. We're not the first to get here for a gossip.

BARRILDO. What's Salamanca like?

LEONELO.   That's a long story.

BARRILDO. You'll be a learnèd doctor.

LEONELO.   Not so learnèd.
There's not much future in my faculty.

BARRILDO. Then some are cleverer than you?

LEONELO.   Of course.

BARRILDO. I'm sure that they must think you a fine scholar.

LEONELO. I've done my best to learn what mattered most.

BARRILDO. Now that the printing press has been invented
Everyone seems to pride himself on knowledge.

LEONELO. In spite of that I think they know far less:
There is a strange confusion in excess
Which always must defeat its own intention
And that is one result of that invention.
Not that I would deny the printing art
Finds genius out, and lifts it far apart
From the base throng, where it would lie neglected,
Raising it up by time to be respected.
We owe the press to Gutenberg, a clever
And worthy man from Mainz whose fame forever
Will fill the world. But some deserve the curse
Of the whole world for printing their own verse.
Some people, till their works were printed, had
Been much revered—but now we find them bad.
Others, in envy, signed an honoured name
To their own works, and brought it evil fame.

BARRILDO. Come, come, I can't think that.

LEONELO.   Oh yes, it's true!
Illiterates still grudge scholarship its due.

BARRILDO. But printing is important all the same.

LEONELO. Long centuries had passed before it came
And yet it has not given us a second
Augustine or Jerome who could be reckoned
As due to it.

BARRILDO.   Don't let us get so heated,
Calm yourself down, and let us both be seated.

Enter JUAN ROJO *and another* PEASANT.

JUAN ROJO. Four farms are not sufficient for a dowry
If gifts be reckoned in the modern way:
Take heed, all you who have enquiring minds,
Opinion in this town has gone astray!

PEASANT. Don't lose your temper. The Comendador—
What news of him?

JUAN ROJO.   He has ill-used Laurencia.

PEASANT. No brute is so lascivious as he.
Would he were hanged upon that olive tree!

Enter the COMENDADOR, ORTUÑO, FLORES.

COMENDADOR. God save you all, good people.

ALDERMAN.   Oh! My lord!

COMENDADOR. Please remain seated everyone.

ESTEBAN.   Your Lordship
Be seated. We are quite contented standing.

COMENDADOR. I say you must sit down.

ESTEBAN.   All decent people
Delight in honouring rank. One can't pay honour
To any one, unless one has it.

COMENDADOR.   Come.
We'll have a talk. Sit down there, all of you.

ESTEBAN. You've seen the greyhound, sir.

COMENDADOR.   Yes, my good mayor,
My servants are enchanted with its speed.

ESTEBAN. It's a rare dog. I think it could keep up
With any gaolbird on the run from justice
Or any coward confessing on the rack.

COMENDADOR. I only wish that you could send it after
A certain bit of game that always beats me
By giving me the slip.

ESTEBAN.   Of course I'll send it.

COMENDADOR. I mean your daughter.

ESTEBAN.   What! My daughter!

COMENDADOR.   Yes!

ESTEBAN. What! Is she worthy to be wooed by you?

COMENDADOR. She's very difficult, my worthy mayor.

ESTEBAN. How do you mean?

COMENDADOR.   She's causing me annoyance!
  Why, there are women of high class, and married
  To some I see around me in the square,
  Who, at the first advance, gave themselves to me.

ESTEBAN. Well, they did wrong, my lord, and you yourself
  Are doing wrong in talking thus so freely.

COMENDADOR. Oh, what an eloquent old country bumpkin!
  Flores, you ought to give him Aristotle's
  Treatise on *Politics*.

ESTEBAN.   My lord, this village
  Would fain live peacefully beneath your rule.
  And surely they include some worthy people.

LEONELO. His shamelessness is surely without equal!

COMENDADOR. Alderman, have I said something to hurt you?

ALDERMAN. Yes. What you say is most unjust. Unsay it,
  And do not try to rob us of our honour.

COMENDADOR. *Honour?* Do such as *you* pretend to *honour?*
  You should be called the Calatrava Friars!

ALDERMAN. And some there are boast of the cross you gave
        them
  Whose blood, for all that, is not all it might be!

COMENDADOR. Do I pollute your blood then if I join
  My blood with it?

ALDERMAN.   Yes! When it's fouled with lust,
  Your blood's unclean.

COMENDADOR.   But surely you'll admit
  I do your wives great honour when I woo them?

ESTEBAN. Your words dishonour you. We can't believe them:
  And what you said at first—forget that too!

COMENDADOR. How dull and stupid is the country peasant!
  It's only in the city life is pleasant,
  Where husbands thank you to attend their wives
  And men of wit can lead amusing lives.

ESTEBAN. That's false. You cannot fob us off with that.

God lives in cities, too, and there are people
Quicker to punish crime than you'll find here.

COMENDADOR. Clear out!

ESTEBAN. Is that from you to me alone?

COMENDADOR. Clear out, the lot of you, let none remain!

ESTEBAN. We'll go, then.

COMENDADOR. Not in that way, in one bunch!

FLORES. My lord, contain yourself, beware!

COMENDADOR. They've banded
Together in my absence to defy me.

ORTUÑO. My lord, for God's sake, have some patience!

COMENDADOR. Patience?
I marvel at the patience I have shown.
Go, separately, each to his own home!

LEONELO. Heavens, do you permit this?

ESTEBAN. I'll go this way.

PEASANTS *go slowly and sullenly.*

COMENDADOR. What do you make of them?

ORTUÑO. They do not know
How to dissimulate; and you refuse
To take the measure of their discontent.

COMENDADOR. What! Would they rank themselves, as equals,
with me?

FLORES. It's not exactly ranking as your equals . . .

COMENDADOR. And that base boor that ran off with my crossbow—
Must he remain unpunished?

FLORES. Last night I thought
I'd caught him by Laurencia's door. I hit
Him hard. But it was someone else.

COMENDADOR. Where is he?

FLORES. Frondoso? Oh, he's slinking round about.

COMENDADOR. What! Does he dare to show himself round
here—
A man who wished to kill me?——

FLORES. Yes, like an unsuspecting bird, or else
A fish that glides towards the baited hook.

COMENDADOR. A man that makes Córdoba and Granada
Tremble on their foundations—to be dared
And daunted by a yokel! Really, Flores,
I think this world is coming to an end!

FLORES. The course of love was never smooth.

ORTUÑO.   He must
Be a good friend of yours to be still living.

COMENDADOR. Ortuño, I have used dissimulation.
Otherwise in two short hours, I'd have put
The whole town to the sword. You wait and see,
The moment that they give me the occasion,
How I shall be revenged. Have you no news
Of Pascuala?

FLORES.   She's getting married soon
She tells me.

COMENDADOR. And till then she asks for credit?

FLORES. As far as I can see, it won't be long
Till the whole debt is paid.

COMENDADOR. What of Olalla?

ORTUÑO.   Why, she showed some humour
In answering.

COMENDADOR.   She is a lively wench!
What did she say?

ORTUÑO.   Her bridegroom's getting jealous,
To see the many messages you send
And how you pay her visits with your servants.
But when he's off his guard, you'll still be welcome.

COMENDADOR. I swear upon my knighthood she's a fine one!
But as for that young whippersnapping husband
Let him beware!

ORTUÑO.   He's scared enough already.

COMENDADOR. What news of Inés?

FLORES.   Which one?

COMENDADOR.   Antón's wife.

FLORES. She's game at any time with all her charms,

I spoke to her outside her stableyard
By which she bids you enter when you like.

COMENDADOR. These easy women I like very well
And yet I pay them poorly. They don't know
The value of a decent reputation.

FLORES. You do not get the necessary setbacks
To contrast with their favours. Quick surrender
Undoes the interest and excitement of
Crowning a hope deferred. But there are women
(So the philosopher relates) who need
Men, just as abstract forms require a substance.
That men become mere habit with such women
Is not so strange.

COMENDADOR.   When a man's mad with love
He's pleased with quick surrender, but he values
The woman less, tires quickly, and forgets her.
For even the most grateful man esteems
At a low value that which cost him least.

Enter CIMBRANOS, *a soldier.*

CIMBRANOS. Where's the Comendador?

FLORES.   You're in his presence.

CIMBRANOS. Valiant Fernando Gómez, change that green
Cap of a hunter for your shining morion
And change this tunic for your bright new arms.
The Master of the Knights of Santiago,
Joined with the Count of Cabra, has laid siege
In Ciudad Real to Don Rodrigo
Girón—and in the name of Isabela
Queen of Castile. And so we are in danger
Of losing that which cost us so much blood
As well you know. At early dawn were sighted,
From the high battlements, the crests and colours,
The lions and the castles of Castile
And the bright bars of Aragón. Although
The King of Portugal would aid Girón,
The best that he can hope for, at this pass,
Is to escape, alive, home to Almagro.
So mount your horse. The sight of you alone
Should send them limping back into Castile.

COMENDADOR. Stop! Say no more! Ortuño, in the square
    Get them to sound the trumpet. Say, how many
    Soldiers are quartered here?

ORTUÑO.   Fifty, I think.

COMENDADOR. Get them all mounted.

CIMBRANOS.   If you are not quick,
    Ciudad Real will be the King's and Queen's.

COMENDADOR. Oh, never fear that such a thing could happen!

Countryside round Fuente Ovejuna

Enter MENGO, PASCUALA, *and* LAURENCIA, *fleeing.*

PASCUALA. Don't go away from us!

MENGO.   Whom do you fear?

LAURENCIA. Mengo, let's all return to town together
    In case we meet with him.

MENGO.   The cruel devil—
    Where will he end?

LAURENCIA.   He never lets us rest
    Either in sun or shade.

MENGO.   Would heaven could send
    A thunderbolt to finish with this madman!

LAURENCIA. A foul bloodthirsty beast, I'd rather call him—
    The pestilence and arsenic of the place!

MENGO. They tell me that in this same very meadow
    Frondoso threatened him with his own arrow
    To rescue you, Laurencia, from his lust.

LAURENCIA. Before that day I hated all men, Mengo.
    But now I see them in another light.
    Frondoso was so valiant! Now, I fear
    That it will cost his life.

MENGO.   That man must leave
    The village.

LAURENCIA. Though I've come to love him dearly

That is what I advised him, too. But he
Receives my loving counsels with disdain
And rage, though the Comendador has sworn
To have him hanged head downwards by the feet.

PASCUALA. May he be throttled!

MENGO.   Stoning would be better.
I wish I had the sling I used when herding—
To lodge one in the cracked shell of his noodle!
Galabalo, the Roman emperor,
Was not so wicked.

LAURENCIA.   Heliogabalus,
You mean, who was a foul inhuman beast.

MENGO. "Pelly, oh, gaballer"? I don't care how
You say it. History's not my strong point!
But his revolting memory is outstunk,
In this Fernando Gómez, by a mile!
Is any man in nature quite so evil?

PASCUALA. No: for he is a tiger in his harshness!

Enter JACINTA.

JACINTA. Help me, for God's sake, if you are my friends!

LAURENCIA. What's wrong, Jacinta dear?

PASCUALA.   We are yours.

JACINTA. The pimps of the Comendador, more strongly
Armed with their native infamy than with
Their weapons, are about to drag me with them
To Ciudad Real, whither they're bound.

LAURENCIA. If that is so, Jacinta, I must flee
Since if with you he takes such liberty
What would he do with me? May God protect you.
Exit.

PASCUALA. Jacinta dear, since I am not a man
I can be of no use.
Exit.

MENGO.   It seems that I'm
Forced now to be a man, bearing the gender
And name of one. Jacinta, come with me!

JACINTA. But have you arms?

MENGO.   The first in all the world.

JACINTA. Oh! if you only had.

MENGO.   Why, here are stones,
Jacinta. Yes, and plenty of them too!

Enter FLORES *and* ORTUÑO.

FLORES. You thought you could escape from us on foot!

JACINTA. Oh, Mengo, I am lost.

MENGO.   Why, gentlemen . . .
You surely don't molest poor countryfolk?

ORTUÑO. Can I believe my eyes? You have the cheek
To try to save this woman?

MENGO.   With my pleadings,
Yes, as a near relation, I would save her!

FLORES. Kill him at once.

MENGO.   I swear by this bright gun
If you get in such tantrums, I shall loosen
This hempen sling—to make it life for life.

Enter COMENDADOR *and* CIMBRANOS.

COMENDADOR. What's this? You two have caused me to
        dismount
For such a vile and trivial cause.

FLORES.   The vile
And common folk of this place are defying
Our arms—it's time you had them massacred—
In nothing do they seem disposed to please you.

MENGO. My lord, if pity lives within your breast to see
This unjust act, chastise these soldiers here
Who have misused your name to rob this woman
From her own husband and her honest parents
And give me leave to take her to her people.

COMENDADOR. I'll give them leave to punish you, vile dog!
Let go that sling!

MENGO.   My lord . . . !

COMENDADOR.   Flores! Ortuño!
Cimbranos! Tie his hands up with that thing!

MENGO. Is that how you protect a woman's honour?

COMENDADOR. What do Fuente Ovejuna and its peasants
   Say about me?

MENGO.   Sir, how have we offended
   You in the slightest thing?

FLORES.   Shall he be killed?

COMENDADOR. No, do not foul your swords upon such dirt,
   Since you must honour them in nobler work.

ORTUÑO. Your orders then?

COMENDADOR.   To flog him. Strip him naked,
   And tie him to that oak, then with the reins . . .

MENGO. Have pity, since you are a noble! Please!

COMENDADOR. And do not cease from flogging him until
   The buckles and the studs jump from the thongs
   And leave the leather naked . . .

MENGO.   Oh, you heavens!
   How long until such evil deeds are punished?

FLORES, ORTUÑO, *and* CIMBRANOS *carry off* MENGO.

COMENDADOR. Why do you run away, you countrywoman,
   Am I not better than a sweaty peasant?

JACINTA. Is that the way that you restore the honour
   My name has lost by being chased out here
   By your paid bloodhounds?

COMENDADOR.   How can it have harmed you?

JACINTA. I have an honourable father, sir,
   Who though he's lower in his rank than you
   Is nobler in his dealings, yes, by far!

COMENDADOR. The troubles and the insolence I get
   From such as you will not appease my anger.
   Come on, this way!

JACINTA.   With whom?

COMENDADOR.   With me!

JACINTA. Take care!

COMENDADOR.   Of course I'll take good care. You're now
   A woman of the commissariat,
   The baggage train, and brothels for the army
   At large, but for myself, no more! Away!

JACINTA. I will not live to let them outrage me!

COMENDADOR. Gee up! You dirty slut! Get on the march!

JACINTA. Have pity on me, sir!

COMENDADOR.   Pity, be damned!

JACINTA. I solemnly appeal to the divine
  Justice of God against your cruelty!

  JACINTA *is dragged off.*

ESTEBAN's *house*

Enter LAURENCIA *and* FRONDOSO.

LAURENCIA. How do you dare to come here, risking death?

FRONDOSO. Only to show how deeply I adore you.
  I saw, from that far slope, the bloody squadron
  Of the Comendador go marching out—
  So trusting in your faith, I lost all fear.
  May he have left us, never to return!

LAURENCIA. Don't curse him, for the ones men curse the most
  Always appear to go on living longest.

FRONDOSO. If that's so, may he live a thousand years!
  That ought to settle him, if wishing well
  Can do him any harm. Laurencia, listen!
  I want to know if my deep loyalty
  Has found the harbour it deserves. All round
  The people think we are already one.
  And that we're not united yet they wonder.
  Leave off your coyness. Tell me yes or no.

LAURENCIA. To you, and all the village, I'll say yes.

FRONDOSO. Then let me kiss your feet for this great mercy
  It's like receiving a new life, I swear.

LAURENCIA. Enough of compliments. Talk to my father,
  That's the important part. He's coming here
  Now with my uncle. And I'm sure that I shall be
  Your wife. Good luck.

FRONDOSO.   I trust it all to God!

  Exit LAURENCIA. FRONDOSO *hides.*

Enter ESTEBAN *and the* ALDERMAN.

ESTEBAN. It finished up like this. In the town square
There was almost a riot. His behaviour
Passed all belief or toleration. All
Are stunned by his excesses. Poor Jacinta
Has had to pay the cost of his last madness.

ALDERMAN. All Spain will soon be for the Catholic Princes
(As now they call Queen Isabela and
King Ferdinand) and their just laws obey.
The Master of the Knights of Santiago,
Now as the captain general of their armies,
Sweeps on his way to Ciudad Real
Where still Rodrigo Girón holds the town.
But I am sick to think of poor Jacinta;
She was a well-bred girl, so good and honest.

ESTEBAN. The way they flogged poor Mengo too!

ALDERMAN.   His skin
Was black with weals as ink or pitch or tar!

ESTEBAN. Don't speak about it. Why, it burns me up
To see and suffer this most fiendish treatment
And live beneath the stench of his bad name.
I'd like to know what use is this damned bauble,
A mayor's staff of office? It's a mockery!

ALDERMAN. These dastard crimes were done by his own men,
Not yours. Why should you feel so sore at it?

ESTEBAN. And there's another thing. Redondo's wife—
After he'd finished with her in the valley,
He gave her to his flunkeys after him!

ALDERMAN. But someone's lurking here. Who can it be?

FRONDOSO. It's only I. I hope you do not mind.

ESTEBAN. Frondoso, to my house you're always welcome.
You owe your father one life, but to me
You owe another since I reared you up
And loved you as a son.

FRONDOSO.   Trusting in that
I'll ask a favour. Sir, you know full well
Whose son I am.

ESTEBAN.   Has mad Fernando Gómez
  Done you some foul injustice?

FRONDOSO.   Yes. A great one.

ESTEBAN. The heart within me warned me that was so!

FRONDOSO. Well sir, taking advantage of your kindness,
  I came to beg the hand of your Laurencia,
  With whom I am in love. Forgive my haste
  If I have spoken it too soon, for others
  There are who would opine that I'm too daring.

ESTEBAN. Frondoso, from your words I draw new life
  Because great dread was growing in my soul.
  Thank heaven, my dear son, that for the honour
  Of me and mine, you venture this. I thank
  Your love, and bless the dear, fine zeal you show.
  First now, consult your father, since I'd like
  To know how it strikes him. As for myself
  I could not have been happier about it.

ALDERMAN. But you should know the girl's opinion first.

ESTEBAN. Don't worry about that. The bargain's made.
  I'll bet they had it settled long ago.
  As for the dowry, we can deal with that
  Now, on the spot. I've got a little hoard
  Which I'll be pleased to settle on you both.

FRONDOSO. I don't want any dowry, sir, at all:
  Don't let's get saddened about such affairs.

ALDERMAN. You should be glad he doesn't ask for her
  Stark naked.

ESTEBAN.   Well, we'll ask *her* what she thinks
  If you don't mind.

FRONDOSO.   Yes, that is just. You ask her.
  Opinions should be studied, not ignored.

ESTEBAN, *calling.* Daughter! Laurencia!

  LAURENCIA, *entering to them.*

LAURENCIA.   Yes, my lord and father?

ESTEBAN, *to the* ALDERMAN.

  See if I told you right! You see how quickly
  She answered me.

To LAURENCIA.

                Laurencia, my darling,
I've sent to know your mind about this question.
Come over here. D'you think that your friend, Gila,
Should be the wife of young Frondoso? He
Seems to be quite as upright a young man
As any in the village.

LAURENCIA.   Gila's marrying?

ESTEBAN. If any one deserves him, she's his equal.

LAURENCIA. I say so too.

ESTEBAN.   Yes, but I say she's ugly
And that Frondoso would be better mated
With you.

LAURENCIA. Why, Father, haven't you forgotten
In your old age this scurvy jesting habit?

ESTEBAN. Well, do you love him?

LAURENCIA.   Yes, I am his. He's mine
But there is this affair . . .

ESTEBAN.   Shall I agree?

LAURENCIA. You say the word for me.

ESTEBAN.   The keys are mine
And it is done.

To the ALDERMAN.

           Let's go and find his father
Down in the village square.

ALDERMAN.   Yes, come, let's go.

ESTEBAN, *to* FRONDOSO. What shall I say to him about the
    dowry?
I can well spare for you a cool four thousand
Maravedis.

FRONDOSO.   Why, sir, discuss it now?
It's wounding to my honour.

ESTEBAN.   Don't talk nonsense.
That is a thing you will get over quickly.
To lose a dowry, why, you'll miss a lot.

Exeunt ESTEBAN *and* ALDERMAN.

LAURENCIA. Frondoso, are you glad?

FRONDOSO.   What! Am I glad?
I think I shall go mad with all the joy
And the good feeling in my heart. Laurencia,
My heart seems darting laughter from my eyes
To see you at long last in my possession.

The country near Ciudad Real

Enter the MASTER OF CALATRAVA, *the* COMENDADOR, FLORES, *and* ORTUÑO.

COMENDADOR. Fly, Master, now there is no other way!

MASTER. It was the weakness of the rampart caused it
And the great strength of the invading army.

COMENDADOR. It cost them blood and many thousand lives.

MASTER. But they can never boast it to their glory
The flag of Calatrava graced their spoils
With other captured standards.

COMENDADOR.   None the less,
Girón, your proudest hopes are in the dust.

MASTER. It's not my fault if fortune blindly heaves me
Aloft today, and then tomorrow leaves me.

VOICES *within.* Victory for the monarchs of Castile!

MASTER. The battlements are crowned with lights, the windows
Of all the highest towers are hung with banners
And with victorious flags.

COMENDADOR.   It cost them dear,
Rather a funeral than a feast, I fear
For them today.

MASTER.   I'll home to Calatrava,
Fernando Gómez.

COMENDADOR.   I to Fuente Ovejuna
While you continue following your cause
Or yield yourself up to the Catholic King.

MASTER. I'll write to you what I intend to do.

COMENDADOR. Yes, time will teach you.

MASTER.   Though so young, yet time
   With his deceitful rigour proves my master.

The country near Fuente Ovejuna

Enter, in a crowd, MUSICIANS, MENGO, FRONDOSO, LAUREN-
CIA, PASCUALA, BARRILDO, ESTEBAN, *and* JUAN ROJO.

MUSICIANS, *singing.*
          Long live the bridegroom
          Long live the bride.

MENGO. Your singing must be difficult.

BARRILDO. D'you think that music made by you
   Would have a happier result?

FRONDOSO. Poor Mengo, you're so black and blue,
   You know far more of blows and curses
   Than notes and tremolos and verses.

MENGO. There is one in this place knows how
   To stop your junketing I vow,
   And that's the grim Comendador!

BARRILDO. That's enough, Mengo! Say no more!
   That foul, barbarian, murderous stot
   Has of our honour robbed the lot.

MENGO. He had me beaten by a hundred
   Men in turn. Is it to be wondered,
   When I had nothing but a sling,
   That I submitted to this thing?
   It was both heathen and herètic
   To force so powerful an emetic
   Upon a man of such good fame
   Though modesty conceals his name . . .
   How can you bear with it? For shame!

BARRILDO. Why, for a joke!

MENGO.   There is no laughter

In such a dose. It feels like flame,
And makes you wish to die thereafter.

FRONDOSO. I ask you if your rhyme's in season—
Too coarse either for rhyme or reason!

MENGO. Well, listen. "May the bride together
With her bridegroom make good weather,
Nor ever feel the need to quarrel,
Nor jealousy at things immoral,
And may they in this way behave
Till, tired of living, to the grave
They're trundled off in the same hearse!
Long live the pair!"

FRONDOSO.   May heaven curse
The poet who spawns such a verse.

BARRILDO. He made it quickly on the spot.

MENGO. Talking of poets, have you not
Seen doughnut-bakers at their toil
Chuck chunks of dough into the oil
To fill their cauldron on the boil?
Some come out cooked, some come out charred,
Some come out soft, some come out hard.
Well, that's how poets (I suppose)
Deal with the poems they compose.
Choosing one's matter, just like duff,
In different shapes one kneads the stuff
Then flings it in his paper pot
Hoping to make a lucky shot
And smother up with treacle thick
Such thoughts as might make people sick.
But when he touts the things for sale
On nobody can he prevail.
At last then (without praise or pelf)
He must digest them by himself.

BARRILDO. Hush! let the lovers speak, quit fooling, Mengo.

LAURENCIA. Give us your hands to kiss.

JUAN ROJO.   Yes, my dear niece,
After you and Frondoso kiss your father's.

ESTEBAN. Rojo, to her and her good man, may heaven
　　Grant deepest blessings!

FRONDOSO.　　　　　　　You two, bless us both.

JUAN ROJO. Now all together sing, since they are one!

MUSICIANS *sing*.

> Through Fuente Ovejuna's valleys
> A long-haired girl goes light of foot
> A knight of Calatrava sallies,
> With his red cross, in her pursuit.
> So she hides in bushes green
> To conceal her wrath and shame,
> Feigning that she has not seen
> That running on her tracks he came.
> 　*O why do you hide there*
> 　*My lovely girl, alone?*
> 　*For my desires can fare*
> 　*Through walls and see through stone.*
>
> The nobleman comes near her now
> And, she confused and frightened, tries
> Closer to pull each sheltering bough
> To hide her beauty from his eyes.
> But since, for one who is in love,
> No obstacle was ever met
> On seas beneath or peaks above,
> He goes on singing to her yet:
> 　*O why do you hide there,*
> 　*My lovely girl, alone?*
> 　*For my desires can fare*
> 　*Through walls and see through stone.*

Enter the COMENDADOR, FLORES, ORTUÑO, CIMBRANOS.

COMENDADOR. On with the wedding! Don't let *me* disturb you.

JUAN ROJO. This is no game, my lord; we're glad to take
　　Your orders. May we find a seat for you?
　　What tidings of your warlike enterprise?
　　I'll wager that you conquered.

FRONDOSO.　　　　　　　I am lost!
　　May heaven save me!

LAURENCIA.　　　　　　Fly from here, Frondoso!

COMENDADOR. Don't let him go. Arrest him. Tie him up.

JUAN ROJO. Obey, my lad.

FRONDOSO.   You want them, then, to kill me?

COMENDADOR. I'm not the sort of man to kill a fellow
Who's guiltless. If I were, these soldiers here
Would have already riddled you clean through.
I order him to gaol where his own father
Will have to judge and sentence him, as mayor.

PASCUALA. Why, sir, he's getting married.

COMENDADOR.   Getting married?
What's that to me? Are there no more young men?

PASCUALA. If he offended you, you should forgive him
Being who you are.

COMENDADOR.   Pascuala, I don't count
For anything in this affair at all.
It was that he insulted the Grand Master,
Téllez Girón, whom God preserve; he raised
His arm against the Order; aimed a crossbow
At its most holy symbol; and must suffer
Due punishment to stand as an example
Because it touches on the Master's honour.
Some others might rebel against his rule
Elsewhere, and raise their standards in the field.
It would not do to pardon one who threatened
The Master's Grand Comendador with death
As you all know he did the other day.
What loyal subjects!

ESTEBAN.   As his father-in-law
I'll plead for him. Surely it is not much
That a young man in love should lose control
With you since you were ravishing his bride!
Surely he might defend her! That's no crime!

COMENDADOR. Mayor! You are an interfering fool!

ESTEBAN. It's for your virtue's sake, my lord.

COMENDADOR.   I never
Annoyed his bride—since she was not his bride then!

ESTEBAN. Yes, you molested her. Let this suffice you.

There are a pair of monarchs in Castile
Who are giving out new laws and making havoc
Of old abuses. They would do great wrong,
When resting from their victories, to permit
That lords and barons in the villages
Should be allowed to tyrannise and murder
Because they wear big crosses on their breasts!
Let great King Ferdinand put on the cross,
For such a symbol is for true-born princes!

COMENDADOR. Hey! Take away his staff of office from him!

ESTEBAN. Take it! You're welcome to the useless bauble.

COMENDADOR. And now I'm going to batter him with it
As I would any horse that gets too frisky!

Breaks the staff on ESTEBAN's *head.*

ESTEBAN. Being a vassal, I must suffer this.

PASCUALA. How dare you strike an aged man like that?

LAURENCIA. If you thrash him because he is my father—
What is it in me you would take revenge on?

COMENDADOR. Take her and guard her for me with ten soldiers!

Exeunt COMENDADOR *and his followers, dragging* LAURENCIA *and* FRONDOSO.

ESTEBAN. May justice come down from on high!
Exit.

PASCUALA.   The wedding
Has turned into a day of bitter mourning.
Exit.

BARRILDO. Will no man raise his voice?

MENGO.   I've had my flogging
Already, just for raising it a little.
I've got the seven cardinal colours striped
Upon my hide, and yet I never went
To Rome to fetch them.

JUAN ROJO.   All shall raise our voices!

MENGO. Well, sirs, it seems to me all should be silent.
My buttocks are like slices of raw salmon.

ACT III

Council chamber in Fuente Ovejuna

Enter ESTEBAN, ALONSO, BARRILDO.

ESTEBAN. Have they not come yet to the council?

BARRILDO.   No.

ESTEBAN. Unless they're quick, we run a mortal danger.

BARRILDO. Most of the people have been warned already.
   Frondoso is in shackles in the tower.
   Laurencia, my girl's in such a plight
   That unless God comes quickly to our aid . . .
   Enter JUAN ROJO *and the* ALDERMAN. MENGO *after them.*

JUAN ROJO. Why are you shouting, when our enterprise
   Depends on secrecy, Esteban?

ESTEBAN. That I'm so silent should surprise you more
   Considering my wrongs.

MENGO.   I've also come
   To sit on this great council.

ESTEBAN.   An old man
   Whose snow-white beard is watered by his eyes,
   You honourable farmers, asks of you
   What funeral oration should be made
   For our lost country and its trampled honour?
   Yet of what use to mourn our honours now,
   Since which of you has not been vilely injured
   By this barbarian? Answer! Is there one
   Among you who does not feel that his honour
   And life have not been utterly destroyed?
   Are all of you not sick of mere lamenting?
   Then, since you have lost all that is worth while,
   What are you waiting for? What worse misfortune?

JUAN ROJO. We've suffered that already—the world's worst!
   But since it now is manifest and public
   The King and Queen have pacified Castile,

And now, from Córdoba, are on the way.
Let's send two councillors to beg their mercy
And ask them to deliver us from woe.

BARRILDO. While Ferdinand is humbling to the earth
So many stronger enemies far off,
The greater wars absorb his time and strength:
Some other swifter method should be found.

ALDERMAN. If you would hear my voice, my vote should be
That we desert this village, one and all.

JUAN ROJO. There is not time enough for such a move.

MENGO. If anyone should hear this noisy meeting
It would cost several lives amongst the council.

ALDERMAN. But now the mast of patience has been splintered
Our ship drives on beyond the scope of fear
To that of desperation. From her wedding
They take the daughter of an honoured mayor,
Breaking his staff upon his own white head.
What slave has ever suffered such injustice?

JUAN ROJO. What do you think the people should attempt?
Die, or else perish in the bold attempt
Since they are few and we are many.

BARRILDO.   How!
To arm ourselves against our rightful lord?

ESTEBAN. The King alone, after our God in heaven,
Is our true lord. All right of mastership
Is forfeited by inhumanity.
With God to help our zeal, why fear the cost?

MENGO. Look, sirs, be very cautious in such projects.
I came here on the part of simple peasants
Who suffer the worst injuries of all—
And I must also represent their fears.

JUAN ROJO. If what we've suffered far outweighs the loss
Of life that's scarce worth living—why hold back?
They burn our barns, our vineyards, and our farms.
Tyrants they are. To vengeance let us go!

Enter LAURENCIA, *dishevelled and torn.*

LAURENCIA. Let me inside! For well I have the right

To enter into council with the men
Since if I cannot vote, at least I can
Scream out aloud. Do any of you know me?

ESTEBAN. Great God in heaven! Can this be my daughter?

JUAN ROJO. Do you not know Laurencia?

LAURENCIA.   I have come
In such condition, that you well may wonder
Who this is here.

ESTEBAN.   My daughter!

LAURENCIA.   Do not call me
Your daughter!

ESTEBAN.   Why, my dear one, tell me why?

LAURENCIA. For many reasons and of these the weightiest
Is that you neither rescued me from traitors
Nor yet took vengeance on those bestial tyrants
Whom you let kidnap me! I was not yet
Frondoso's, so you can't fob off on him
The duty of avenging me. On you
The duty lies as well. Until the night
When marriage is fulfilled and consummated,
It is the father's duty, not the husband's.
When one has bought a gem, till it's delivered
The buyer does not pay. It is not he
Who has to guard it from the hands of robbers
Till it's been handed over. I was taken
Under your eyes to Fernán Gómez' house
While you looked on like coward shepherds, letting
The wolf escape uninjured with the sheep.
They set their daggers to my breasts! The vileness
And filth of what they said to me! The threats
They made to tear me limb from limb! The foul
And bestial tricks by which they tried to have me!
Do you not see my hair torn out? These cuts
And bruises and the bleeding flesh that shows
Through my torn rags? You call yourselves true men?
Are you my parents and relations, you
Whose entrails do not burst with grief to see me
Reduced to this despair? You're all tame sheep!

Fuente Ovejuna means the fount where sheep drink—
And now I see the reason! Cowards, give
Me weapons! You are stones and bronze and marble
And tigers—tigers? no! for tigers follow
The stealers of their cubs, and kill the hunters
Before they can escape back to their ships.
No, you are craven rabbits, mice, and hares!
You are not Spaniards but barbarian slaves!
Yes, you are hens to suffer that your women
By brutal force should be enjoyed by others.
Put spindles in your belts. Why wear those swords?
As God lives now, I shall make sure that women
Alone redeem our honour from these tyrants,
And make these traitors bleed! And as for you,
You chickenhearted nancy-boys and sissies,
Spinning-wheel gossips and effeminate cowards,
We will throw stones at you and have you dressed
In petticoats and crinolines and bonnets,
With rouge and powder on your pansy faces!
Now the Comendador's about to hang
Frondoso up alive, to starve and die,
Head downwards from the castle's battlements,
And so he'll soon be doing with you all!
But I am glad of it, you half-men, since
The town will thus be ridded of its women,
And thus become a town of Amazons
Like me, to be the wonder of the age.

ESTEBAN. I am not one who suffers such vile titles.
　　I shall rebel, though it should be alone
　　And all the world against me.

JUAN ROJO.　　　　　　　　　So will I!
　　Though frightened by the greatness of our foe.

ALDERMAN. Let us all die, rather than cringe!

BARRILDO.　　　　　　　　　　　　　Unfurl
　　A cloth upon a pole to be our banner!
　　Death and destruction to this breed of monsters!

JUAN ROJO. What order shall we march in?

MENGO.　　　　　　　　　　　　Without order!
　　Let's kill him straight! One cry will join the people

Since they are all agreed upon his death!

ESTEBAN. Then arm yourselves! Grab swords and pikes and
    cudgels,
Crossbows and slings and anything you can!

MENGO. Long live the Catholic Kings, our rightful masters!

ALL. Long live the Kings!

MENGO.   Death to the bloody tyrants!

ALL. Death to the traitor-tyrants one and all!

Exeunt all the men.

LAURENCIA. March on! And may the heavens hear your cry!

Shouting very loudly.

All women of the village, join the ranks!
The time has come now to retrieve our honour!

Enter PASCUALA, JACINTA, *and other women to* LAURENCIA.

PASCUALA. What's this? What are you shouting for so loudly?

LAURENCIA. Can't you see how they've all gone off to kill
Fernando Gómez—dotards, boys, and men,
All furiously rushing to the fray?
And we, the women, must we yield the honour
Of such a noble action to the men,
Since we have suffered far more harm than them?

JACINTA. Well, what do you propose to do?

LAURENCIA.   Line up!
In order! For we'll show the world today
A deed which centuries will hear with awe
When we are dead and gone. Jacinta, here,
Your greater wrongs earn you the higher rank
So you will be the corporal of the band.

JACINTA. Your own wrongs are not less than mine.

LAURENCIA.   Pascuala,
You will be the ensign.

PASCUALA.   Give me the flag
To hoist upon a lance, and you will see
Whether I merited the rank or not.

LAURENCIA. There is no time. Strike while the iron's hot!
Let kerchiefs, shawls, and bonnets be our standards!

PASCUALA. Now we'll elect our captain.

LAURENCIA.   There's no need.

PASCUALA. Why?

LAURENCIA.   Because, when I go into action—watch me!
You will not need the Cid or Rodomont![4]

The hall in the Comendador's castle

Enter FRONDOSO *with his hands tied,* FLORES, ORTUÑO,
CIMBRANOS, *and the* COMENDADOR.

COMENDADOR. Whatever rope's left over from his hands
Will do to hang him from and hurt the worse.

FRONDOSO. Oh, what an evil name your birth retrieves!

COMENDADOR. Now hang him from that nearest battlement.

FRONDOSO. My lord, I never did intend the deed
When shouldering the crossbow.

A great noise is heard.

FLORES.   What's the uproar?

COMENDADOR. What does it mean?

FLORES.   Like thunder from the highest
It breaks in on our judgment.

More noise.

ORTUÑO.   All the doors
Are being crashed and splintered into dust!

A tremendous noise.

COMENDADOR. What? Breaking in the doors of my own house?
And the headquarters of the Order?

FLORES.   Yes!
The whole town has arrived in force together.

JUAN ROJO, *within.* Kill, destroy, burn, crush, and smash them
all!

----

[4] Heroes of rival peoples (Spanish and Saracen) and of rival
literatures (Spanish and Italian). The latter gave a word to the
English language: rodomontade. [E.B.]

ORTUÑO. These mob revolts are nasty to control!

COMENDADOR. You mean they've risen against me?

FLORES.   Not only risen.
Your gates are sprawling headlong to their fury
And they are here on top of you!

COMENDADOR, *pointing to* FRONDOSO. Untie him.
And humour this poor bumpkin of a mayor,
Frondoso, if you can.

FRONDOSO.   I'll go: it's only
Through love they have committed this offence.
He goes out. The voice of MENGO *is heard from within.*

MENGO, *within.* Long live King Ferdinand and Isabel!
Death to the traitors here!

FLORES.   Don't be found here,
My lord, for.God's sake!

COMENDADOR.   Let them try to force it!
This central hall is very strongly walled
And guarded. Soon enough they will slink home.

FLORES. When a whole people which has been outraged
Makes up its mind, it never goes back home
Without its freight of vengeance and red blood.

COMENDADOR. In this great door, as if at a portcullis,
We can defend ourselves against them all.

FRONDOSO, *within.* Long live Fuente Ovejuna!

COMENDADOR, *derisively.*   What a captain!
Set on them, and you'll see their fury fade!

FLORES. By your own fury, sir, I'm more dismayed!

Enter ESTEBAN, FRONDOSO, JUAN ROJO, MENGO, BARRILDO,
and other PEASANTS, *all armed.*

ESTEBAN. Now we confront the tyrant and his flunkeys!
Fuente Ovejuna, let those tyrants die!

COMENDADOR. Wait, my good people.

ALL.   Insults cannot wait!

COMENDADOR. Tell me your injuries, and I'll repair them,
I swear upon my knighthood and my faith.

ALL. Fuente Ovejuna! Long live the Catholic Kings!
  And death to all bad Christians and to traitors!

COMENDADOR. Will you not listen to me? I'm your master!

ALL. The Catholic King and Queen are now our masters!

COMENDADOR. Here, wait a minute!

ALL.   Die, Fernando Gómez!
  Long live Fuente Ovejuna!

  Exeunt fighting, the COMENDADOR *driven back by the insurgents.*

  Enter the women, armed.

LAURENCIA. Halt at this door. You are no longer women
  But desperate legionnaires.

PASCUALA.   Those poor old pansies
  We once called men, it seems, are men once more
  And letting out his blood!

JACINTA.   Throw down his body
  And we'll impale the carcass on our spears.

ESTEBAN, *within.* Die, foul Comendador!

COMENDADOR, *within.*   I'm dying
  And may the Lord have mercy on my soul
  And pity for my monstrous sins.

BARRILDO, *within.*   Here's Flores!

MENGO, *within.* Have at him! He's the very man that sliced me
  Across my back two thousand fiery lashes.

FRONDOSO, *within.* I would not be avenged were I to spare him.

LAURENCIA. We'll enter now.

PASCUALA.   Wait! Let us guard the door!

BARRILDO, w*ithin.*
  What! soften us with tears? You scurvy cowards
  Who were the lords and masters of us all?

LAURENCIA. I can't wait, Pascuala, I must enter.
  My sword is sick of loafing in its sheath.
  Exit.

BARRILDO, *within.* Ortuño too! Ortuño!

FRONDOSO, *within.*   Slash his face!

  Suddenly enter FLORES *from within,* MENGO *pursuing him.*

FLORES. Have mercy, Mengo, it was not my fault:
   I was obeying orders.

MENGO.   If you don't
   Deserve it 'cause you are a filthy pimp
   You more than merit it for flogging me!

PASCUALA. You give him to us women, Mengo, now.
   Stop flogging him. Just hand him over. Lovely!

MENGO. I've given him enough to pay my stripes.

PASCUALA. I shall avenge you more.

MENGO.   Well, fire ahead!

JACINTA. Die, dirty rat!

FLORES.   What, to be killed by women?

JACINTA. Weren't women in your line?

PASCUALA.   What tears are those?

JACINTA. Die, traitor, and the pandar to his vices!

LAURENCIA, *within.* Die, you dirty devil!

FLORES.   Have pity on me, ladies!

   Enter ORTUÑO *fleeing,* LAURENCIA *after him.*

ORTUÑO. Look, but I am not him you mean!

LAURENCIA.   I know
   The creature that you are.
   To the women.
               Go in, you women,
   Kill! Finish off these villains once for all!

PASCUALA. I shall die killing.

ALL THE WOMEN.   Live the Catholic Kings!
   Long live Fuente Ovejuna! Tyrants, die!

             King's palace in Toro

   Enter KING FERDINAND, QUEEN ISABEL, *and* DON MANRIQUE,
   Master of Santiago.

DON MANRIQUE. Having foreseen and calculated well
   We carried out our plans with few obstructions.

There wasn't much resistance. If there had been
It would have fizzled out. Cabra is busy
And well-prepared against a chance attack.

KING. He has done well. The way to help him best
Is to reorganise our force and send
Covering troops. The King of Portugal
Can be checkmated thus. The Count of Cabra
Is in the key position where he is.
That's to the good. He's one who knows his work.

Enter FLORES, *wounded.*

FLORES. Great Catholic King Ferdinand, to whom
God grants, as worthiest of His knights, to wear
The diadem of Castile, I come to tell you
Of the worst cruelty the sun has seen,
From rise to set, among the whole world's peoples!

KING. Come, come, contain yourself.

FLORES.   My sovereign lord,
My wounds prevent me from more lengthy detail,
Since I am near my death and bleeding fast.
I've come from Fuente Ovejuna where
The village people slew their rightful lord
Fernando Gómez who lies mangled by
Disloyal vassals for a trivial cause.
The countryfolk proclaimed him as a "tyrant"
And worked themselves to frenzy with this cry.
They burst his doors in though he made the promise,
Upon his knightly faith, of reparation
To all whom he had injured. Deaf to prayers,
With ruthless fury, they all fell on him
And, with a thousand cruel wounds, destroyed
A breast that bore the cross of Calatrava.
Then, from the topmost windows, down they hurled him
To fall upon the serried pikes and swords
The women held upright to catch his body.
They clawed out all his beard and half his hair
And hacked his face about with fearful gashes
As his poor corpse was carried to the channel.
Their brutal fury raged to such a height,
His very ears were bargained for, as trophies,

And fetched high prices. After this was done
They chipped away with pikes the coat-of-arms
Over his gateway, saying they were hateful,
And that they would supplant them with your own.
They sacked his palace, and they shared the plunder
As though he'd been a foe in open war.
I saw all this from where I hid, for fate
Would not permit my miserable life
To end just then but thus I lay till night
Permitted my escape to tell of it.
Great lord, since you are just, punish the villains
With a just sentence for their barbarous crimes.
Fernando's blood cries out to you for vengeance
And rigorous justice.

KING.   You may rest assured
They'll not remain unpunished. This sad thing
Amazes me. A judge must go forthwith
To verify this case and make examples
Of those who're guilty. Let him take a captain
For his protection. Such barefaced rebellion
As this requires exemplary chastisement.
Attend that soldier's wounds.

Town square in Fuente Ovejuna

*The village people and their women come in with the head
of* FERNANDO GÓMEZ *on a lance.*

MUSICIANS, *singing.*
                    Long life to Ferdinand our King
                    And to Queen Isabel
                    But death to all the tyrants
                    That on this earth may dwell!

BARRILDO. Now it's Frondoso's turn, to say
    His piece of verse.

FRONDOSO.   I have no art.
    Although my lines may limp astray

Forgive them, coming from my heart:
Long live the lovely Isabel
And Ferdinand of Aragón,
In one and other's arms to dwell,
Each with each, and both as one!
Then may the great Archangel Michael
Raise them in glory to the sky!
Long live the Kings for many a cycle
But let all tyrants quickly die!

LAURENCIA. Your turn, Barrildo!

BARRILDO.   I don't mind.
I've thought mine out with studious care.

PASCUALA. Say it with care, too; then you'll find
It will sound even yet more rare!

BARRILDO. Long live the famous Kings, since they
Have been so many times victorious,
And may they come to reign, some day,
As our own masters, great and glorious!
In triumph, over dwarfs and giants,
We wish them power to rise on high
But to all tyrants shout defiance!
Forever may they burst and die!

MUSICIANS, *singing*.
Long life to Ferdinand our King
And to Queen Isabel
But death to all the tyrants
That on this earth may dwell!

LAURENCIA. Now, Mengo, you recite.

FRONDOSO.   Yes, you!

MENGO. I am no "true-blue" as to verse.

PASCUALA. Rather you mean, and it's quite true,
You're black and blue on your *reverse!*

MENGO. Well, here goes, without more verbosity:
That fellow, on a Sunday morning
Had my back thrashed with such ferocity
It put my hide in hues of mourning
But now I feel no animosity.

Long live the Kings of Christianosity
And perish thus all Tyrannosity!

MUSICIANS, *singing*.

Long life to Ferdinand our King
And to Queen Isabel
But death to all the tyrants
That on this earth may dwell!

ESTEBAN. Take out that head.

MENGO.   How horribly it grins!

Enter JUAN ROJO carrying the Royal Arms on a shield.

ALDERMAN. The new Arms have arrived.

ESTEBAN.   Let's look at them!

JUAN ROJO. Where shall we place them?

ALDERMAN.   Here, on the Town Hall.

ESTEBAN. A splendid shield!

BARRILDO.   What happiness it means!

FRONDOSO. With this new sun, our day begins to break.

ESTEBAN. Long live Castile, León, and Aragón!
Die, tyranny, forever! But now heed me,
Fuente Ovejuna! Hear an old man's words,
Whose counsel never harmed a soul among you.
The King will wish to clarify this case
And, since the town lies in his journey's route,
You should agree on what you'll have to say
When they examine you, as well they may.

FRONDOSO. What's your advice?

ESTEBAN.   If they ask who is guilty,
Die saying "Fuente Ovejuna" only.
Not one word more.

FRONDOSO.   Nothing could be more straight!
Fuente Ovejuna did it.

ESTEBAN.   Will you all
Answer thus?

ALL.   Yes.

ESTEBAN.   Now let me just pretend
I'm the examiner, and we'll rehearse

The better, thus, what we must say and do.
Say Mengo, here, is being put to torture.

MENGO. Can you find no one thinner to stretch out?

ESTEBAN. Come, don't be foolish, Mengo! Were you thinking
This was in earnest?

MENGO.   Well, say on, then! Do!

ESTEBAN. Who was it murdered the Comendador?

MENGO. Fuente Ovejuna did it.

ESTEBAN.   Now, you dog!
Do you want to be racked in half?

MENGO.   My lord!
Although I die . . .

ESTEBAN.   Confess, you knave!

MENGO.   I do.

ESTEBAN. Well, who was it?

MENGO.   It was Fuente Ovejuna.

ESTEBAN. Give him an extra turn!

MENGO.   Why, that is nothing!

ESTEBAN. A fig, then, for the worst the judge can do!
Another ALDERMAN *enters.*

SECOND ALDERMAN. What's going on here?

FRONDOSO.   Why, what is the matter,
Cuadrado?

SECOND ALDERMAN. The examining judge has come.

ESTEBAN. Then scatter round the town.

SECOND ALDERMAN.   He is attended,
Too, by a captain and his troops.

ESTEBAN.   Although
The devil came himself, we'll not be daunted.
You know now the one word we all must answer.

SECOND ALDERMAN. They are arresting everyone on sight.

ESTEBAN. Don't fear. Who murdered the Comendador,
Eh, Mengo?

MENGO.   Who? Why, Fuente Ovejuna!

Palace of the Master of Calatrava in Almagro

Enter the MASTER *and a soldier.*

MASTER. That such a thing could happen! What a fate!
  I almost feel like putting you to death
  For bringing such black news.

SOLDIER.   I only brought it
  As messenger, not to arouse your anger.

MASTER. To think an angry mob could dare so much!
  I'll take five hundred men to raze the village
  That not one person's name shall be remembered!

SOLDIER. Contain your rage, my lord. They have declared
  Their loyalty to the King. Your one last hope
  Is not to anger him more than you've done.

MASTER. How can they give their village to the King
  Since they are of my Order?

SOLDIER.   That will be
  A legal matter to discuss with him.

MASTER. No legal powers affect the papal tenure,
  Yet I must recognise the King and Queen
  And pay them homage; so I'll curb my rage
  Till I have come to some accommodation.
  For though they hold me heavily to blame,
  My youth will plead for me. I go with shame—
  Compelled to go that I may save my honour,
  For one must not be careless in that cause.

The square in Fuente Ovejuna

Enter LAURENCIA, *alone.*

LAURENCIA. Loving, to know the loved one is in danger
  Doubles the pangs of love; foreseeing harms

Adds fears to fears and multiplies alarms.
The firm untroubled mind, to tears a stranger,
Melts at the touch of fear. The steadfast faith,
If fear comes near it, flickers like a wraith,
Imagining the dear one snatched away.
I love my husband. Yet when he is near,
Fearing his harm, I am a prey to fear;
And when he's absent, I am in worse dismay.

Enter FRONDOSO.

FRONDOSO. Laurencia!

LAURENCIA.   My beloved husband, how
Dare you be seen round here?

FRONDOSO.   Is this the way
You welcome my most loving care?

LAURENCIA.   My dearest,
Seek safety. You're in deadly peril here!

FRONDOSO. May heaven forbid that you're not glad to see me!

LAURENCIA. Do you not fear the cruelty of the judge?
And how he's treated others? Save your life
And do not court worse danger!

FRONDOSO.   Save a life
So ill-received? Should I desert my friends
And lose the sight of you in this great danger?
Do not tell *me* to fly. It is unthinkable
That I should make an alien of my blood
On such a terrible occasion.

Cries within.

                              Listen
I can hear cries—of someone being tortured,
If my ears tell me truly. Listen hard.

The voice of the JUDGE *can now be heard from within with
the replies of the* PEASANTS.

JUDGE, *within.* Now, good old man, speak nothing but the
    truth!

FRONDOSO. It's an old man they're putting on the rack.

LAURENCIA. How dastardly!

ESTEBAN, *within.*   Can they leave off?

JUDGE, *within*.   Relax him.
Now speak! Who was it killed Fernando Gómez?
ESTEBAN, *within*. Fuente Ovejuna did it.
LAURENCIA.   Oh, my father!
Your name be praised forever to the skies!
FRONDOSO. Oh, grand example!
JUDGE, *within*.   Now let's rack that boy there.
You, puppy! Yes, I know you've got the answer!
Who was it? Are you silent? Give more turns,
You bungling torturer!
BOY, *within*.   Fuente Ovejuna!
JUDGE, *within*. I'd have you hanged, you riffraff, were I able.
Now on the King's life, tell me who it was!
Who murdered the Comendador?
FRONDOSO.   That they
Could torture a child thus, and he resist them!
LAURENCIA. Oh, valiant people!
FRONDOSO.   Very brave and strong!
JUDGE, *within*. Let's have that woman on the rack at once.
To torturer.
And get that lever working there, come on!
LAURENCIA. He's blind with rage!
JUDGE, *within*.   I'll kill the lot of you
Upon this rack here, on my word, you wretches!
Who murdered him?
PASCUALA, *within*.   My lord, Fuente Ovejuna!
JUDGE, *within, to torturer*. Tighter!
FRONDOSO.   In vain!
LAURENCIA.   Pascuala lasted out.
FRONDOSO. When children last, how can you be surprised?
JUDGE, *within, to torturer*.
Give her some more. It seems that you enchant them.
PASCUALA, *within*. Oh, pitying heaven!
JUDGE, *within, to torturer*. You swine, can you be deaf?
Stretch her, I said!
PASCUALA, *within*.   Fuente Ovejuna did it!

JUDGE, *within, to torturer.*
 Now let's have that half-naked bag of guts,
 That fattest one of all, him, over there!

LAURENCIA. Mengo, no doubt!

FRONDOSO.   He will break down, I fear.

MENGO, *within.* Ay! Ay!

JUDGE, *within.* Now turn the lever of the screw!

MENGO, *within.* Ay!

JUDGE, *within, to torturer.*
 Turn! More! Are you in need of help?

MENGO, *within.*   Ay! Ay!

JUDGE, *within.* Who murdered the Comendador, base villain?

MENGO, *within.* Ay! Ay! I'll tell Your Lordship.

JUDGE, *within, to torturer.*   Now relax it.

FRONDOSO. He will confess!

 A pause—no answer from MENGO.

JUDGE, *within, to torturer.* Put your shoulder this time
 Against the lever!

MENGO, *within.*   Wait! I've had enough.
 I'll tell you all, if you'll but let me free.

JUDGE, *within.* Who was it?

MENGO, *within.*   Why, my lord, to tell the truth . . .
 Little old Fuente Ovejunita did it!

JUDGE, *within.* Was ever such a stubborn villainy?
 They seem to make a jest of agony,
 And he from whom I hoped the most results
 Was far more strongly stubborn than the rest.
 Leave them. I am exhausted. Let them go!

FRONDOSO. Oh, Mengo, may God bless your honest soul!
 With fear enough for two I trembled here
 But fear for you had quite effaced that fear!

 Enter MENGO, BARRILDO, *and the* ALDERMAN.

BARRILDO. Mengo has conquered!

ALDERMAN.   As you see!

BARRILDO. Mengo's the victor!

FRONDOSO.   I agree!

MENGO. Ay! Ay! Ay! Ay!

BARRILDO.   Come drink and eat!
  Here, take this bowl, this stuff's a treat!

MENGO. Ay! Ay!

FRONDOSO.   Pour him another jug!

BARRILDO. The way it gurgles down his mug!

FRONDOSO. It does him good. He soaks it neat.

LAURENCIA. Now give him something more to eat.

MENGO. Ay! Ay!

BARRILDO.   This other is with me!

LAURENCIA. Just look how solemnly he's drinking.

FRONDOSO. One who defies the rack, I'm thinking,
  Needs a good drink!

ALDERMAN.   The next, with me?

MENGO. Ay! Ay! Yes! Yes!

FRONDOSO.   Drink! You deserve it!

LAURENCIA. He soaks as fast as one can serve it.

FRONDOSO. Arrange his clothes: he's getting frozen.

BARRILDO. Some more to drink?

MENGO.   Yes, three rounds more!

FRONDOSO. He needs more wine.

BARRILDO.   There's lots in store.
  Come drink, man, drink! for you're our chosen!
  To be so brave a rack-defier
  Must give a thirst like raging fire.
  What's wrong?

MENGO.   It has a tang of rosin,
  And also I've a cold in store.

FRONDOSO. Why, here's some sweet wine, if you'd sooner.
  But: who killed the Comendador?

MENGO. Why! little old Fuente Ovejunita!

  Exeunt all but FRONDOSO *and* LAURENCIA.

FRONDOSO. It's right that they should do him greatest honour
  But who killed the Comendador, my darling?

LAURENCIA. Fuente Ovejuna killed him, dearest love.

FRONDOSO. Who really killed him? Between you and me?

LAURENCIA. Fuente Ovejuna! Do not terrify me!

FRONDOSO. And how did *I* kill *you*, then? Tell me that.

LAURENCIA. You made me die of loving you so much!

Palace of the King at Tordesillas

Enter KING FERDINAND *and* QUEEN ISABEL.

QUEEN. I did not know I'd meet with the good fortune
    To find you here, my lord.

KING.   The sight of you
    Brings me new glory. I was on the way
    To Portugal, and had to come past here.

QUEEN. Your Majesty did well indeed to come
    Since it was convenient.

KING.   What of Castile?

QUEEN. All peaceful, quiet, and smooth.

KING.   Since it was you
    Who did the smoothing, I don't marvel at it.

Enter DON MANRIQUE, *Master of Santiago.*

DON MANRIQUE. Seeking an audience with Your Majesties
    The Master of the Calatrava Order
    Has just arrived.

QUEEN.   I've always longed to see him.

DON MANRIQUE. I swear it by my faith, Your Majesty,
    Though very young, he is a valiant soldier.
    Exit.

Enter the MASTER OF CALATRAVA.

MASTER. Rodrigo Téllez Girón is my name,
    Grand Master of the cross of Calatrava,
    Who never stints your praises. I have come
    To sue your royal pardons. Ill-advised
    By those around me, I broke all just bounds,
    In rash excess to brave your royal wills.

It was Fernando's counsel that deceived me,
And then my own self-interest. I was wrong.
So humbly now I beg forgiveness of you,
Which, if my supplication can deserve,
Amidst the foremost of your ranks I'll serve
And, in your next crusade against Granada,
No man shall draw his sword with fiercer verve,
For I shall plant my crimson crosses farther
Than any, on the topmost battlements!
Five hundred men I'll bring to join your tents
And I shall sign and seal a solemn oath—
Never to discontent you—to you both!

KING. Rise up then, Master, from the ground, for since
You've come to me, you shall be well received.

MASTER. You are the comforter of the afflicted.

QUEEN. You're quite as good at talking as at fighting.

MASTER. You are the lovely Esther of our age;
And you its godlike Xerxes, Majesty.

Re-enter DON MANRIQUE.

DON MANRIQUE. My lord, the judge examiner is here,
The one who went to Fuente Ovejuna.

KING, *to the* QUEEN.
Now you must judge these riotous aggressors.

MASTER, *thinking erroneously the* KING *addressed him.*
Had I not learned the lesson of your mercy,
I would have served them all a bloody lesson
In how to kill Comendadors.

KING, *to the* MASTER.   Not you.
The days when you gave judgments are no more.

MASTER *falls back rebuked.*

QUEEN, *to the* KING. Would but to God this military might
Were subject to your orders or put down.

Enter the JUDGE.

JUDGE. I went to Fuente Ovejuna, sire,
As I was bid. With all my diligence
And special care, your orders were obeyed.
But as to finding out who did the crime,

No scrap of writing can I bring in proof
Because, with one accord and single valour,
When to the question racked, they all reply:
"Fuente Ovejuna did it" and no more.
Three hundred of them, tortured on the rack
With terrible severity, replied
No other answer. Little boys of ten
Were stretched yet it was useless. Quite as vain
Were flatteries and promises and tricks.
It is so hard to verify the truth
That you must either hang the whole mad village
Or pardon every man-jack of them all.
All of them now are coming here before you
To certify the truth of all I say.

KING. Let them come in, then.

Enter the TWO MAYORS, FRONDOSO, *all the* WOMEN *and the rest of the villagers.*

LAURENCIA.   Are these two the Kings?

FRONDOSO. And very powerful ones!

LAURENCIA.   How beautiful
They are, by my faith! Saint Anthony bless them!

QUEEN. Are these the fierce aggressors we were told of?

ESTEBAN. Fuente Ovejuna greets you here, my lady,
Wishing to serve you. The dire cruelty
And most unsufferable tyranny
Of the Comendador caused all these troubles.
A thousand vile insults were showered upon us.
Our farms were robbed, our daughters forced and raped,
Because he was a man who had no pity.

FRONDOSO. So much was this the case that this young farm girl,
By heaven granted for my wife, with whom
I am by far the happiest man on earth,
Even at our wedding feast, on the first night,
Was forced into his house for his own pleasure
And if she hadn't fought with desperation . . .
There is no need to tell you any more.

MENGO. Is it not time I also had a word
If you will give me leave. You'll be astounded

At how they treated me for once defending
A girl of ours. Seeing his pimp and pandar
About to do her violence, I protested—
When that perverted Nero ordered them
To thrash my back into red salmon slices!
My bum still trembles to remember it
And I have had to spend more cash on balm
Than on my farm.

ESTEBAN.   All that we wish, my lord,
Is to become your own, whom we acknowledge
As our most natural sovereign. And your arms
Are hoisted on our village hall. Before you
We sue for mercy and yield up ourselves
As pledges of our innocence. Have mercy!

KING. Since what has happened is not verified
In writing (and it was a dreadful crime
Worthy of direst punishment), you're pardoned.
As to the town I'll keep it in my name
Until, or if, we find a rightful heir.

FRONDOSO. The King spoke grandly as one would expect
From one who such great wonders could effect.
Good night, discreet spectators, all be friends!
And with this line FUENTE OVEJUNA ends.

THE TRICKSTER OF SEVILLE AND HIS GUEST OF STONE

Tirso de Molina

English Version by Roy Campbell

DRAMATIS PERSONAE

DON DIEGO TENORIO

DON JUAN TENORIO, *his son*

CATALINÓN, *Don Juan's lackey*

THE KING OF NAPLES

DUKE OCTAVIO

DON PEDRO TENORIO, *Don Juan's uncle and Spanish Ambassador in Naples*

THE MARQUIS OF LA MOTA

DON GONZALO DE ULLOA, *father of Doña Ana*

THE KING OF CASTILE [Alfonso XI, 1312–50]

DOÑA ANA

DUCHESS ISABEL

TIIISBE ⎫
ANFRISO ⎪
CORIDÓN ⎬ *fisherfolk*
BELISA ⎭

BATRICIO ⎫
GASENO ⎪
AMINTA ⎬ *farmfolk*
BELISA ⎭

RIPIO ⎫
FABIO ⎭ *servants*

Servants, guards, musicians, etc.

The scene is laid in Naples, Tarragona, Seville, and Dos Hermanas.

The time is the 14th Century but not consistently so.

ACT I

A room in the palace of the KING OF NAPLES

Enter DON JUAN, *with muffled face, and* ISABEL.

ISABEL. Here, Duke Octavio, here's a safe way through.

DON JUAN. Once more, dear Duchess, let me swear my troth!

ISABEL. Then may I glory in each promise, oath,
Flattery, gift, and wish—when they come true!

DON JUAN. You shall, my love.

ISABEL.   Wait while I fetch a light.

DON JUAN. Why?

ISABEL.   To convince my soul of this delight.

DON JUAN. I'll crush the lamp in pieces if you do!

ISABEL. Heavens above, what man are you? For shame!

DON JUAN. Who, I? I am a man without a name.

ISABEL. You're not the duke?

DON JUAN.   No.

ISABEL.   Help! the palace guard!

DON JUAN. Come, Duchess, give your hand. Don't shout so
hard!

ISABEL. Let go, you beast! I'll make the palace ring.
Help, soldiers, guards, and servants of the king!

Enter the KING OF NAPLES *with a lighted candle in a candle-
stick.*

KING OF NAPLES. Who's there?

ISABEL, *aside.*   The king, alas!

DON JUAN.   Why, can't you see—
A man here with a woman? Her and me.

KING OF NAPLES, *aside.* Prudence in this would seem the better
plan.

He runs back so as not to recognize ISABEL.
Aloud.

Call out the palace guard! Arrest this man!

ISABEL, *covering her face.* Oh, my lost honour!

Enter DON PEDRO TENORIO, *ambassador of Spain, and guards.*

DON PEDRO.   From the king's rooms, cries
    And shouting? Sire, from what did this arise?

KING OF NAPLES. Don Pedro, you take charge of this arrest.
    Be shrewd and yet be prudent in your quest.
    Seize and identify this muffled pair
    In secret. Harm may come of this affair.
    But if it proves as it appears to me,
    The scandal will be less, the less I see.
    Exit.

DON PEDRO. Seize him at once!

DON JUAN.   Come, which of you will dare?
    I'm due to lose my life and much I care!
    But I shall sell it dear and some will pay!

DON PEDRO. Kill him at once!

DON JUAN.   Now, don't be led astray.
    I'm resolute to die. For not in vain
    Am I a noble cavalier of Spain
    And of her embassy. That being known,
    Each one of you must fight with me alone:
    Such is the law.

DON PEDRO.   Go, all of you, in there;
    And take the woman. Leave him to my care.

The guards take ISABEL *into the next room.*

DON PEDRO. And now that we two are alone at length
    Let's test this vaunted valour and this strength.

DON JUAN. Although, dear uncle, I've enough of both,
    To use them on yourself I'm something loth.

DON PEDRO. Say who you are!

DON JUAN, *unmasking himself.* I shall. Your nephew, sir.

DON PEDRO, *aside.* My heart! I fear some treason is astir.
    Aloud, to DON JUAN.
    What's this you've done, base enemy? How is it
    That in this guise you come to such a visit?

Tell me at once, since I must kill you here.
Quick! Out with it at once! And be sincere!

DON JUAN. My uncle and my lord, I'm still a lad,
As you were once. Such youthful loves you had.
Then don't blame me that I too feel for beauty.
But since you bid me tell it as a duty:
In this disguise I cheated Isabel
(Who took me for another man) and, well,
Enjoyed her——

DON PEDRO.   How could you so?
If you can lower your voice, sir, let me know.

DON JUAN, *in a lower voice.*
Pretending I was Duke Octavio.

DON PEDRO. What? Say no more! Enough!
    Aside.   If the king learns
The truth, I'm lost. Oh, by what twists and turns
Can I escape so dangerous a maze?
    Aloud.

Say, villain, was it not enough to raise,
With treachery and violence, such shame,
And with another great and noble dame
Back home in Spain but you repeat the crime,
With one that is of princely rank this time,
In the king's palace? May God punish you!
Your father from Castile had shipped you through
Safely to Naples' hospitable strand,
Who might have hoped for better at your hand
Than in return have such shame heaped upon her—
The greatest of her ladies to dishonour!
But here we're wasting time with this delay.
Think what to do and how to get away.

DON JUAN. Pardon for this offence I can't implore.
It would be insincere and, what is more,
Unmanly. My blood's yours—for you to take.
Come, let it out, and let me pay my stake!
Here at your feet, my uncle and my lord,
I offer you my lifeblood and my sword.

DON PEDRO. Curse you! Get up and fight! Prove you're a man!

This meek humility has spoilt my plan.
To slaughter in cold blood I never would.
Would you dare jump that balcony? You could?

DON JUAN. Your favour gives me wings. I surely can.

DON PEDRO. Then down you go! Seek hiding in Milan
Or Sicily!

DON JUAN.   Why, soon enough!

DON PEDRO.   You swear?

DON JUAN. Oh, surely!

DON PEDRO.   You'll be hearing from me there
The consequences of this sad affair.

DON JUAN. A pleasant one for me, you must consent.
Though I may be to blame, I'm well content.

DON PEDRO. You're led astray by youth. Quick, jump the railing!

DON JUAN. And now for Spain how happily I'm sailing!
Exit.

Enter KING OF NAPLES.

DON PEDRO. I tried to execute your orders, sire,
As well as your strict justice would require.
The man . . .

KING OF NAPLES. Is dead?

DON PEDRO.   No, he escaped the sword
And the fierce thrusts of it.

KING OF NAPLES.   How?

DON PEDRO.   Thus, my lord.
You'd hardly told your orders, when, without
More said, he gripped his sword and wheeled about,
Winding his cape around his arm, and so,
Ready to deal the soldiers blow for blow
And seeing death too near for hope of pardon,
Leaped desperately down into the garden
Over this balcony. Followed by all
They found him agonizing from his fall,
Contorted like a dying snake. But, when
They shouted "Kill him!" turning on the men
With such heroic swiftness he upstarted
As left me in confusion; and departed.

Isabel, whom I name to your surprise,
Says it was Duke Octavio in disguise
Who by this treachery enjoyed her.

KING OF NAPLES.   What?

DON PEDRO. I say what she confessed upon the spot.

KING OF NAPLES. Poor Honour! If by you our value stands
Why are you always placed in women's hands
Who are all fickleness and lightness?
Calls.   Here!

Enter a servant, and, after, ISABEL *with guards.*

Bring me the woman now! Let her appear!

DON PEDRO. The guards are bringing her already, sire.

ISABEL, *aside.* How shall I dare to face the king?

KING OF NAPLES.   Retire,
And see the doors are guarded.
Servant and guards retire.

                                Woman, say,
What force of fate, what angry planet, pray,
Makes you defile my palace and my board
With your lascivious beauty?

ISABEL.   Oh, my lord——

KING OF NAPLES. Be silent! For your tongue can never cleanse
Or gild the glaring fact of your offence.
Was it the Duke Octavio?

ISABEL.   My lord——

KING OF NAPLES. Can nothing cope with Love—guards within
        call,
Locks, bolts, and bars, and battlemented wall—
That he, a babe, can penetrate all these?
Don Pedro, on this very instant, seize
That woman! Place her prisoner in some tower!
Arrest the duke as well. Once in my power
I'll have him make amends for this disgrace.

ISABEL. My lord, but once upon me turn your face!

KING OF NAPLES. For your offences when my back was turned,
By the same back you now are justly spurned.

DON PEDRO. Come, Duchess.

ISABEL, *aside.*   Though I know I am to blame
Beyond excuse, it will decrease the shame
If Duke Octavio's forced to save my name.
Exeunt.

Enter OCTAVIO *and his servant* RIPIO.

RIPIO. You're bright and early, sir!

OCTAVIO.   No sleep or rest
With love so fiercely burning in my breast!
For since Love is a child, he is not eased
With softest sheets, nor yet with ermine pleased.
He lies down sleepless, long before the day,
Already longing to be up and play;
And like a child he plays and keeps on playing.
The thoughts of Isabela keep me straying,
Ripio, in the doldrums of despair,
For, since she lives within my soul, my body
Goes suffering with a load of anxious care
To keep her honour safe whether I'm present
Or absent.

RIPIO.   Sir, I find your love unpleasant.

OCTAVIO. What's that, you dolt?

RIPIO.   I find it very wrong
To love as you do. Would you like to learn
The reason why I do?

OCTAVIO.   Yes: come along!

RIPIO. You're certain that she loves you in return?

OCTAVIO. Of course, you idiot!

RIPIO.   *You* love *her?*

OCTAVIO.   I burn!

RIPIO. Why, what an idiot would I be
To lose my reason for the dame,
If I loved her and she loved me.
Now, did she not return your flame,
Then you might well keep such a coil
Adore and flatter her and spoil
And wait till she rewards your toil;
But when you mutually adore

And neither in your faith miscarry,
What difficulty is there more,
What is preventing that you marry?

OCTAVIO. Such weddings are for lackeys, slaves,
And laundry wenches.

RIPIO.   Well, what's wrong
With a fine laundry girl who laves
And sings and washes all day long?
She who defends and then offends
And spreads her linen out to see
And is obliging to her friends
Is good enough for such as me.
There are no kinder people living
Than those who give for giving's sake.
If Isabel is not for *giving*
Then see if she knows how to *take*.

Enter a servant. After him, DON PEDRO.

SERVANT. The ambassador of Spain has even now
Dismounted here. He wears a stormy brow,
Insisting, with a fierce and angry zest,
To speak to you. I fear it means arrest.

OCTAVIO. Arrest? For what? Go, show his lordship in.

DON PEDRO, *entering.*
His conscience must be clear who so can win
So late a sleep.

OCTAVIO.   But when such men as you,
Your Excellency, come, as now you do,
To honour and to favour such as me,
It's wrong to sleep at all. My life should be
An endless vigil. But what could befall
To bring you at such hours on such a call?

DON PEDRO. The king sent me.

OCTAVIO.   Well if the king's kind thought
Bend to me thus, I reck my life as naught
To serve my liege, and would not count the cost
If in the cause of honour it were lost.
Tell me, my lord, what planet of good cheer,

What stroke of goodly fortune, brought you here
To say I am remembered by the king?

DON PEDRO. For you, Your Grace, a most unhappy thing!
I am the king's ambassador. I've brought
An embassy from him.

OCTAVIO.   Yes, so I thought.
That doesn't worry me. Say on. What is it?

DON PEDRO. It is for your arrest I make this visit,
Sent from the king: do not resist the laws.

OCTAVIO. For my arrest he sent you? For what cause?
Tell me my crime!

DON PEDRO.   You ought to know far more
Than I do, for I'm not entirely sure.
Though I may be mistaken, here's my thought,
If not my own belief, why you are sought.
Just when the giant Negroes fold their tents
Of darkness like funereal cerements,
And furtively before the dusky glow
Run jostling one another as they go,
I with His Majesty, while talking late
Of certain treaties and affairs of state
(Arch-enemies of sunlight are the great)
Heard then a woman's scream ("Help! Help!") resound
Through all the halls and corridors around,
And, as we all rushed forth to these alarms,
Found Isabel there, clasped with all her charms
By some most powerful man in lustful arms.
Whoever it could be aspired so high,
Giant, or monster of ambition, I
Was ordered to arrest him. Held at bay
I vainly strove to wrest his arms away
And well I could believe it was the Fiend
Taking a human form, for, ably screened
In dust and smoke, the balcony he lept
Down to the roots of the vast elms that swept
The palace roof. The duchess I assisted,
Who, in the presence of us all, attested
It was yourself who, husband-like, had known her.

OCTAVIO. What's that you say?

DON PEDRO.   Why, man, the whole world over
It is notorious to the public gaze
That Isabel, yes, in a thousand ways
Has . . .

OCTAVIO.   Say no more! Have mercy! Do not tell
So vile a treachery of Isabel.

Aside.

But say this were but caution on her part.

Aloud.

Go on. Say more! Speak out! But if the dart
Is poisoned that you're shooting at my heart,
Impervious to the scandal may I prove—
Unlike those gossips whom their own ears move,
Conceiving there, to give birth through their lips.
Could it be true my lady could eclipse
The memory of me, to deal me doom?
Yes: those who dream too brightly wake in gloom.
Yet in my heart I have no doubt: it seems
These happenings are naught but evil dreams
That, so to give more impulse to my sighs,
Entered my understanding in disguise.
Sir Marquis, could it be that Isabel
Deceived me? that my heart in ambush fell
And so my love was cheated? That can't be . . .
Why, the whole thing's impossible . . . that she . . .
Oh, woman! What a dreadful law is cloaked
In that word honour! Whom have I provoked
To this foul trick? Am I not honour-bound?
A man in Isabela's arms was found
Within the palace . . . Have I lost my mind?

DON PEDRO. Just as it's true that birds live in the wind,
Fish in the wave in keeping with their kind,
That all things have five elements to share,
That blessèd souls in glory know no care,
That staunchness is in friends, in foes is treason,
In night is gloom, in day is light—so reason
And truth are in the very words I say.

OCTAVIO. Marquis! My own belief will scarce obey,

And there's no thing that could astound me more!
That she, whom I as constant did adore,
Should prove no more than woman! More to know
I do not want, since it disgusts me so.

DON PEDRO. Well, since you seem so prudent. Take your pick
Of the best means . . .

OCTAVIO.   I would escape: and quick!
That's my best remedy.

DON PEDRO.   Then go with speed——

OCTAVIO. Spain then will be my harbour in my need.

DON PEDRO. —And slip out by this door while you are able.

OCTAVIO. O bending reed! O weathercock unstable!
Upon yourself alone you've turned the table
Inducing me to flee my native land
And seek my fortunes on a foreign strand!
Farewell, my country!
Aside.

                    Madness, death, and hell,
Another in the arms of Isabel!

Seashore near Tarragona

Enter THISBE, *with a fishing rod.*

THISBE. Of all whose feet the fleeting waters
Kiss (as the breezes kiss the rose
And jasmine), of the fishers' daughters
And longshore maidens, of all those
I am the only one exempt
From Love, the only one who rules
In sole, tyrannical contempt
The prisons which he stocks with fools.
Here where the slumbrous suns tread, light
And lazy, on the blue waves' trance,
And wake the sapphires with delight
To scare the shadows as they glance;

Here by white sands, so finely spun
They seem like seeded pearls to shine,
Or else like atoms of the sun
Gilded in heaven; by this brine,
Listening to the birds, I quarter,
And hear their amorous, plaintive moans
And the sweet battles which the water
Is waging with the rocks and stones.
With supple rod that bends and swishes
And seems to stoop with its own weight
I snare the little, silly fishes
That lash the sea and scarce can wait.
Or else with casting-net, deep down,
I catch as many as may live
Within the many-steepled town
Of conch-shells. I could not be gladder
Than with this freedom I enjoy,
I, whom the poison-darting adder
Of Love did never yet annoy.
And when a thousand lovelorn hearts
Pour forth their bitter plaints forlorn
I am the envy of these parts
Whose tragedies I laugh to scorn.
A thousand times, then, am I blest,
Love, since you never were my lot
But left me tranquil in my nest
And scatheless in my humble cot.
It's just an obelisk of thatch
That crowns my dwelling with its cone,
Though no cicadas it may catch,
Attracting turtledoves alone.
My virtue is preserved in straw
Like ripening fruit, or glass, that's packed
In hay (as by the selfsame law)
In order to arrive intact.
As for the fisherfolk around
Whom Tarragona's lights defend
From pirates in the Silver Sound
I am the one they most commend.
But I their soft approaches mock:

I am as granite to the wave,
To their implorings I'm a rock.
Anfriso to whom Heaven gave,
In soul and body, wondrous gifts,
Measured in speech, in action brave
Resourceful in the direst shifts,
Modest, long suffering of disdain,
Generous, valiant, tough as leather,
Has hung around my hut in vain
Haunting my caves in every weather,
Night after night, in wind or rain,
Till with his health and youth together
He gave the dawn its blush again.
Then also, with the fresh green boughs
Which he had hacked from elm-trees down,
He loves to deck my straw-built house
Which wears his flattery like a crown,
And then beneath the midnight stars
Each evening he would come to woo me
With tambourines and soft guitars.
But all of that meant nothing to me
Because in tyrannous dominion
I live, the empress of desire,
And love to clip love's rosy pinion
And of his hell to light the pyre.
The other girls for him go sighing,
Him, whom I murder with disdain.
For such is love—still to be dying
For those who hate and cause you pain.
In such contentment I employ
Without a care, each youthful year,
And any folly that I hear
Serves but to make me loth and coy
And like the wind to disappear.
My only pleasure, care, and wish
Is forth to cast my trace and hook
To every breeze, and give the fish
My baited line. But as I look
Two men have dived from yonder boat
Before the waves can suck it down.

It strikes the reef and keeps afloat
But now its poop begins to drown,
It sinks, releasing to the gale
Its topsail which finds there its home,
A kite upon the winds to sail,
One with the spindrift and the foam,
A lunatic locked in a cage—

A VOICE OUTSIDE. Help, I am drowning! Save my life!

THISBE. A man, caught in the ocean's rage,
    And bravely with the seas at strife,
    Upon his back his comrade saves
    As once Aeneas bore Anchises,
    And, strongly cleaving through the waves,
    Subdues them as he falls and rises.
    But on the beach there's no one standing
    To lend a hand, or pull them clear.
    Anfriso! Here are wrecked men landing!
    Tirseo, Alfredo! Can't you hear?
    But now miraculously come
    Through the white surf, they step ashore
    Quite out of breath the man who swum,
    But still alive the one he bore.

    Enter CATALINÓN *carrying* DON JUAN.

CATALINÓN. Oh, for the gift of Cana's wine!
    The sea with too much salt is flavoured.
    By all who swim to save their lives
    Freely it may be quaffed and savoured
    But deep down there is doom and slaughter
    Where Davy Jones lives soused in brine.
    Strange, that where God put so much water
    He should forget to mix the wine!
    Master! It seems he's frozen quite.
    Master! What if he should be drowned?
    It was the sea that caused the trouble:
    What if with me the fault be found?
    Bad luck to him who planted pine
    As masts upon the sea to grow
    And who its limits would define
    With measures made of wood! Ah, no!

Cursèd be Jason and his Argo,
And Theseus, cursèd may he be,
Forever, under God's embargo!
Catalinón, unhappy me!
What can I do?

THISBE.   Why in such trouble,
Good man? Why is your life so rough?

CATALINÓN. Ah, fishermaid, my ills are double
And my good luck is not enough.
I see, to free me from his service,
My master's lifeless, is he not?

THISBE. Oh no, indeed, he's breathing yet.
Those fishermen in yonder cot—
Go call them here.

CATALINÓN.   Would they agree?

THISBE. At once! This noble—who is he?

CATALINÓN. Son of the king's high chamberlain
Expecting very soon to be
Raised to a count within a week
In Seville by His Majesty.
That's if the king and I agree.

THISBE. What is his name?

CATALINÓN.   Don Juan Tenorio.

THISBE. Then call my people.

CATALINÓN.   Yes, I'll go.

Exit CATALINÓN. THISBE *has* DON JUAN'S *head on her lap.*

THISBE. Noble young man, so handsome, gay,
And exquisite, wake up, I say!

DON JUAN. Where can I be?

THISBE.   Safe from all harms
Encircled by a woman's arms.

DON JUAN. I live, who perished in the sea,
Only and utterly in thee,
And now I lose all doubt to find
Heaven about me is entwined
After the hell that was the ocean.
A frightful whirlwind wrecked my fleet

And swept me with its fierce commotion
To find a harbour at your feet.

THISBE. A lot of breath you have to waste
For one who nearly lost it all
If after such a storm you haste
To raise a tempest and a squall.
Cruel must be the ocean's thunder
The waves most vicious in their hate
If they can pull your limbs asunder
And make you talk at such a rate!
Beyond all doubt you must have taken
Salt water in above your ration,
More than you'd need to salt your bacon;
You talk in such a saucy fashion—
Quite eloquent enough, I'd say,
Lying as dead upon the beach
With all your senses well in reach
And shamming lifeless as you lay.
You seem the wooden horse of Greece
Washed at my feet for vengeance dire
Seemingly full of cold seawater
But pregnant with deceitful fire.
And if, all wet, you can ignite,
What won't you burn when you are dry?
You promise heat and fire and light,
Please God it will not prove a lie!

DON JUAN. Ah, would to God, dear country maid,
I had been swallowed by the main
So in my senses to remain
And not to lunacy betrayed
For love of you! The sea could harm me
Drowned between silver waves and blue
That roll forever out of view,
But with fierce fire it could not char me!
You share the quality that flashes
In the great sun like whom you show,
Though seeming cold and white as snow
Yet you can burn a man to ashes.

THISBE. The frostier seems your desire

All the more flame you seem to hold
That from my own kindles its fire.
Please God, it was not lies you told!

Enter CATALINÓN, ANFRISO, CORIDÓN, *and other fisherfolk.*

CATALINÓN. They have all come.

THISBE.   Your master's living.

DON JUAN. But only by your presence giving
The breath I yielded.

CORIDÓN, *to* THISBE.   What's your will?

THISBE. Anfriso, Coridón, and friends . . .

CORIDÓN. We seek to gratify you still
By every means to all your ends,
And so your orders, Thisbe, tell,
Out of those lips of fresh carnation,
To us who in your adoration
Would see that all for you goes well,
And ask no more than thus to be,
To dig the earth, to plough the sea,
To trample air or wind or fire
To satisfy your least desire.

THISBE, *aside.* How stupid used to seem to me
Their vows, and how they used to jar
But now in very truth I see
How far from flattery they are!

To the fishermen.

My friends, as I was fishing here
Upon this rock, I saw a barque
Sink in the waves. Two men swam clear.
I called for help but none would hark:
It seemed that none of you could hear.
But one of them lay lifeless here—
Brought on the back of this brave fellow—
A nobleman, who, on the yellow
Sands, lay as though upon his bier,
Very near swamped by wave and tide,
And so I sent his man to guide
And call you to revive him here.

ANFRISO. Well now, we've all arrived. You say

Your orders, though it's not the way
I usually expect from you.

THISBE. Now to my hut we'll gently take him
Where, with the gratitude that's due,
His clothing we'll repair, and make him
His rocktorn garments clean and new.
This bread of kindness that we break him
Will please my dear old father too.

CATALINÓN, *aside.* Her beauty is superb indeed.

DON JUAN. Come, listen here!

CATALINÓN.   I am all heed.

DON JUAN. If here they ask you who I am
You do not know—nor care a damn.

CATALINÓN. D'you try to tell me what to do?
Even here have I to learn from you?

DON JUAN. Why, for her love I'm almost dying.
I'll have her now, then scamper flying—

CATALINÓN. But what d'you mean?

DON JUAN.   Be dumb and follow me!

CORIDÓN. Anfriso, in an hour the fête will be.

ANFRISO. Come on, it's an occasion for good wine,
Sliced melons, and slashed bunches from the vine!

DON JUAN. I'm dying, Thisbe.

THISBE.   Yet you talk and talk!

DON JUAN. You see, yourself, I scarce can move or walk.

THISBE. You speak too much!

DON JUAN.   But you perceive my trend.

THISBE. Please God it be not lies from end to end!

The Alcazar at Seville

Enter KING OF CASTILE *with* DON GONZALO DE ULLOA *and attendants.*

KING OF CASTILE. How did your embassy succeed, my lord
Commander?

DON GONZALO.   There I found your cousin king,
Don Juan,[1] preparing, arming, and reviewing
Some thirty vessels of his fleet in Lisbon.

KING OF CASTILE. Bound whither?

DON GONZALO.   They said Goa, but I guess
It is some closer quarry, like Tangiers
Or Ceuta, which they may besiege this summer.

KING OF CASTILE. May God on high reward and help the zeal
With which he arms His glory! You and he—
Upon what general points did you agree?

DON GONZALO. My lord, he asks for Serpa, Olivenza,
Mora, and Toro. In return for these
He'll give you Villaverde, Mértola,
Herrera, and the districts round about
Which lie between Castile and Portugal.

KING OF CASTILE. At once confirm the contract, Don Gonzalo,
But what about your journey? You return
Both tired and out of pocket, I presume?

DON GONZALO. To serve you, sire, no hardship is too much.

KING OF CASTILE. What's Lisbon like? A good place?

DON GONZALO.   In all Spain
It is the largest city.[2] If you'd like it
I'll paint a picture of it in the air.

KING OF CASTILE. I'd like to hear it. Someone fetch a chair.

DON GONZALO. Why, Lisbon is the world's eighth wonder!
Cleaving the heart of her asunder
To travel half the breadth of Spain,
The sumptuous Tagus swirls its train
And through the ranges rolls its thunder
To enter deep into the main
Along the sacred wharves of Lisbon
Of which it laves the southern side.

[1] John I, who became King of Portugal in 1385. He was not in fact a contemporary of this King of Castile (Alfonso XI). [E.B.]

[2] Portugal was united to Spain from 1580 to 1640. The proper nouns that occur in the ensuing paean to Lisbon are commented on in the scholarly editions of which a convenient one for American readers is to be found in *Cuatro Comedias*, ed. Hill and Harlan, W. W. Norton & Co., New York, 1941. [E.B.]

But just before its name it loses
And its own course, into the tide,
It makes a port in the sierras
Where ships of all the navies ride
That can be numbered in this world
Where like the pikes of massed battalions
The masts of caravels and galleons,
Dhows, galleys, schooners, barques, and sloops
Of Indians, Norsemen, or Italians,
In such innumerable troops
Are mustered upon either hand,
They seem to form a pine-wood city
Which Neptune rules for miles inland!
Up on the side where sets the sun,
Guarding the port on either hand
Of where the Tagus makes its entry,
With many a grimly-snouted gun—
One called Cascaes and one Saint John,
Two fearsome fortresses keep sentry
The navies of the world to stun—
The mightiest strongholds on this Earth!
Just half a league along this firth
Is Belén, convent of Jerome—
The saint whose guardian was a lion
And for his emblem chose a stone—
Where Catholic and Christian princes
Are keeping their eternal home.
After this most astounding fabric,
Beyond Alcántara, you sally
A league, to reach Jabregas' convent
Which fills the centre of a valley
That is encircled by three slopes.
Here, with his paintbrush, would Apelles
Have to renounce his proudest hopes
For, seen from afar, there seem to be
Clusters of pearls hung from the sky,
Within whose vast immensity
Ten Romes would seem to multiply
In labyrinths of convents, churches
With streets and pathways winding by

To many a vast estate and mansion,
Extending to the sea and sky,
And on, in infinite expansion,
Through empires, sowing deathless seeds
Wherever thought of man can fly,
In buildings, arts and letters, deeds
Of glory, feats of arms, and high
Impartial rectitude of law.
But reaching nearest to the sky
And towering over all I saw,
Outrivalling the pen and sword,
The summit of her christian pity,
And, most of all to be adored,
The peak of this imperial city
Is in her vast Misericord!
The thing most worthy of amaze
That in this glorious pile I found
Was that, from its high top, the gaze
For seven leagues could sweep its rays
On sixty villages all round,
And each of them the sea, through bays,
Could reach, and at its door was found.
One of these ports is Olivelas
A convent where myself I counted
Eight hundred cells: the blessed nuns
To full twelve hundred souls amounted.
Lisbon just hereabouts contains
Full fifteen hundred parks and halls—
The sort that here in Andalusia
The populace "sortijo" calls,
And each with poplar groves and gardens,
Surrounded, too, with stately walls.
Right in the center of the city
Rucío lies, a noble square,
Well-paved, with statues, lawns, and fountains.
A century ago, just there,
The sea was lapping cold and green
But thirty thousand houses now,
From sea to city, intervene.
Where fishing yawls were wont to plough

A mighty township stands between.
The sea has lost its bearings here
And gone to rage in other parts
For here they call it New Street where
The treasure of the East imparts
Grandeur and wealth in such a wise
That there's one merchant counts his treasure
(So the king told me) not in coins
But in the old two-bushel measure
We use for fodder for our mules.
Terrero, so they call the place
Wherefrom the royal household rules,
Collects a countless shoal of boats
Constantly grounded in its port
From France and England. The royal court
Whose hands the passing Tagus kisses
Derives its name from its foundation
By him who conquered Troy—Ulysses.
And worthy such a derivation
Ulissibona was its name
As spoken by the Roman nation:
Lisbon's a shortening of the same.
The city arms are represented
By a great sphere on which displayed
Are the red wounds that Don Alonso
Got in the terrible Crusade.
In the great arsenal you spy
All kinds of vessels, among which
Those of the Conquest tower so high
That, looked at from the ground below,
Their mastheads seem to touch the sky.
It struck me as most excellent
That citizens, while they're at table,
Can buy great loads of living fish,
And most from their own doors are able
To catch as many as they wish,
And from the nets where salmon flounder
It's scarce a stone's throw to the dish.
Each afternoon a thousand laden
Vessels are docked, each by its shed,

With diverse merchandise and common
Sustenance—oil, and wine, and bread,
Timber, and fruits of all variety,
With ice that's carried on the head
And cried by women through the street.
(They fetch it, from the peaked Estrella's
Remote sierra, for the heat.)
I could go on like this forever
The city's marvels to repeat
But it would be to count the stars,
Number the sands, and grains of wheat . . .
Of citizens two hundred thousand
It boasts, and, what is more, a king
Who kisses both your hands and wishes
You all success in everything!

KING OF CASTILE. I couldn't have enjoyed so much
Seeing the town in all its grandeur
As thus by your creative touch
To have it brought before my eyes.
By the way, have you children?

DON GONZALO.   Sire,
I have one daughter. She is such a beauty
That Nature in her features may admire
And marvel at herself.

KING OF CASTILE.   Then let me give her
In marriage, from my hand endowered.

DON GONZALO.   My lord,
Your will is mine. But who is it you've chosen?

KING OF CASTILE. Although he is not here, he's a Sevillian.
Don Juan Tenorio is the young man's name.

DON GONZALO. I'll go and tell the news to Doña Ana,
My daughter.

KING OF CASTILE. Go at once, Gonzalo. Yes,
And let me have the answer very soon.

Seashore near Tarragona

Enter DON JUAN *and* CATALINÓN.

DON JUAN. Now go and get those horses ready
Since they are stabled close at hand.

CATALINÓN. Although I'm only just your servant
Catalinón, please understand,
Of decencies I am observant.
People don't say before my nose
Nor even yet behind my back:
"Catalinón is one of those . . ."
Bad names don't fit me. That's a fact.

DON JUAN. While these gay fishermen are spending
The hours in revel, fix the horses!
Galloping hoofs, when danger's pending,
Have always been my best recourses.

CATALINÓN. But surely, sir, you won't abuse her,
Who saved your life?

DON JUAN.   As a seducer
You've always known me. Why, then, ask me
And with my own true nature task me?
Not only that: her hut I'll fire
To daze their minds while we retire.

CATALINÓN. Too well I know you are the scourge
Of womankind.

DON JUAN.   I'm on the verge
Of dying for her: she's so good.

CATALINÓN. How generously you repay
Your entertainment!

DON JUAN.   Understood!
Aeneas paid in the same way
The Queen of Carthage, you poor dolt!

CATALINÓN. The way you tempt the thunderbolt!
Those who cheat women with base sham

In the long run their crime will damn
After they're dead. You'll find out when!

DON JUAN. Well on the credit side I am
If you extend my debt till then
You'll wait till death to punish me.

CATALINÓN. Follow your bent. I'd sooner be
Catalinón than you in what
Pertains to cheating women. See!
The poor unhappy soul draws near.

DON JUAN. Saddle those horses, do you hear?
And get them ready, now, for dodging.

CATALINÓN. Poor trustful creature, oh, how dear
We've paid you for our board and lodging!

Exit CATALINÓN.

Enter THISBE.

THISBE. When I am not with you I seem without
Myself.

DON JUAN. Such a pretence I beg to doubt.

THISBE. Why so?

DON JUAN.   If you loved me, you'd ease my soul.

THISBE. I'm yours.

DON JUAN.   If you were truly mine heart-whole,
How could you kill me thus and make me wait?

THISBE. It is love's punishment at last I've found
In you, and that's what makes me hesitate.

DON JUAN. If, my beloved, I live solely in you
And ever so to serve you will continue
And give my life for you, why do you tarry
Since I shall be your husband? Yes, we'll marry!

THISBE. Our birth is too unequal.

DON JUAN.   Love is king
And under him he matches everything:
Silk with sackcloth, lace with corduroy.

THISBE. I almost could believe you in my joy . . .
If men were not such cheats.

DON JUAN.   With your least wish
You trawl me in your tresses like a fish.

THISBE. And I bow down beneath the hand and word
  Of husband.

DON JUAN.   Here I swear, O peerless eyes!
  Where he who looks within them swoons and dies,
  To be your husband. .

THISBE.   Darling, save your breath
  But, oh, remember God exists—and death.

DON JUAN, *aside.* Yes, on the credit side I seem to be
  If it's till death you'll keep on trusting me!
  Aloud.
  While God gives life, I'll be a slave to you,
  And here's my hand and word to prove it's true.

THISBE. Now to repay you I shall not be coy.

DON JUAN. I cannot rest within myself for joy.

THISBE. Come, in my cabin love has built his nest
  And there forever we shall be at rest.
  Come in between these reeds, my love, and hide.

DON JUAN. But how on earth am I to get inside?

THISBE. I'll show you.

DON JUAN.   With your glory, dearest bride,
  You've lit my soul.

THISBE.   May that compel you, love,
  To keep your word. If not, may God above
  Chastise you.

DON JUAN, *aside.* Well in credit I must be
  If not till death my reckoning: lucky me!
  Exeunt.
  Enter CORIDÓN, ANFRISO, BELISA, *and musicians.*

CORIDÓN. Call Thisbe and the other folk
  So that the guest alone may see
  Our retinue.

BELISA.   This is her cot.

ANFRISO. No better piece of ground could be
  For dancing than this very spot.
  Then call her out to join our glee.

CORIDÓN. Now, steady on, for can't you see
  She's occupied with other guests?

There's going to be some jealousy—
Enough to fill a thousand breasts.

ANFRISO. Thisbe is envied far and wide.

BELISA. Let's sing a little to betide
Her coming, since we want to dance.

ANFRISO, *aside*. How can one's cares find peace and quiet
When jealousy within runs riot
And on our revel glares askance?

ALL, *singing*.

>The girl went out to fish, she thought,
>Casting her net among the shoals
>But there instead of fish she caught
>A thousand lovesick souls.

THISBE. Fire, oh, fire! I'm burning, burning!
My cabin burns, my flames and sighs.
Oh, sound the tocsin, friends, I'm turning
The water on from my own eyes!
My poor hut seems another Troy
Since love, eternally at war,
For want of cities to destroy
Must fire the cabins of the poor.
Fire, oh, fire, and water, water!
Have pity, love, don't scorch my spirits!
Oh, wicked cabin, scene of slaughter,
Where honour, vanquished in the fight,
Bled crimson! Vilest robber's den
And shelter of the wrongs I mourn!
O traitor guest, most curst of men,
To leave a girl, betrayed, forlorn!
You were a cloud drawn from the sea
To swamp and deluge me with tears!
Fire, oh, fire! and water, water!
Diminish, love, the flame that sears
My soul! I was the one that ever
Made fun of men and cheated them,
Then came a cavalier to sever
The thread, and by base stratagem
Destroy and kill my honour dead
By swearing marriage as his bait,

Enjoy me and profane my bed
And, heartless, leave me to my fate.
Oh, follow, follow him, and bring
Him back to me. But no, do not!
I'll take it even to the king
And ask him to avenge my lot.
Fire, oh, fire! and water, water!
Have mercy, love, and grant me quarter.
Exit THISBE.

CORIDÓN. Follow that fiendish cavalier!

ANFRISO. In silence I must bear my lot
But I'll avenge me, never fear,
Against this thankless, misbegot,
Impostor of a cavalier.
Come, let us catch him in the rear
Because he flees in desperate plight
And who knows whether, far or near,
He may contrive more harm?

CORIDÓN.   It's right
That pride should finish, thus, in mire
And such proud confidence should bite
The dust at last.

THISBE.   Oh, fire! Oh, fire!

ANFRISO. She's thrown herself into the sea.

CORIDÓN. Thisbe! Don't do it! Stop! Retire!

THISBE. Fire! Oh, fire! and water, water!
O spare me, love, your furnace dire!
Have pity on a poor man's daughter!

ACT II

The Alcazar at Seville

Enter KING OF CASTILE *and* DON DIEGO TENORIO.

KING OF CASTILE. What's that you say?

DON DIEGO.   My lord, I know it's true.
   This letter's just arrived here from my brother,
   Your own ambassador. They caught him with
   A noble beauty in the king's own quarters.

KING OF CASTILE. What sort of lady?

DON DIEGO.   The Duchess Isabel.

KING OF CASTILE. But what temerity! Where is he now?

DON DIEGO. From you my liege I can't disguise the truth:
   He's just arrived in Seville with one servant.

KING OF CASTILE. You know, Tenorio, I esteem you highly.
   I'll get particulars from the King of Naples
   And then we'll match the boy with Isabel
   Relieving Duke Octavio of his woes,
   Who suffers innocently. But, on this instant,
   Exile Don Juan from the town.

DON DIEGO.   My lord,
   Where to?

KING OF CASTILE. He must leave Seville for Lebrija
   Tonight, at once; and let him thank your merit
   His sentence is so light. Meanwhile determine
   What can be told Don Gonzalo de Ulloa.
   For now the thought of marriage with his daughter
   Is quite beyond the question.

DON DIEGO.   Well, my liege,
   I hope that your commands will be to honour
   The lady in some other way as worthy
   The child of such a father.

KING OF CASTILE.   Here's a plan
   That will absolve me from Gonzalo's anger:

I'll make him major-domo of the palace.

Enter a servant; afterwards, OCTAVIO.

SERVANT. A noble, sire, has just come from abroad.
He says he is the Duke Octavio.

KING OF CASTILE. The Duke Octavio?

SERVANT. Yes, my lord.

KING OF CASTILE. Let him enter.

OCTAVIO. A miserable pilgrim and an exile
Offers himself, great monarch, at your feet,
Forgetting all the hardships of his journey
In your great presence.

KING OF CASTILE. Duke Octavio!

OCTAVIO. I have come fleeing from the fierce pursuit
Of a demented woman, the result
Of the unconscious fault of some philanderer—
For which I have to seek your royal feet.

KING OF CASTILE. Already, Duke, I know your innocence.
I've written to the king my vassal, also
Restoring your estate, and any damage
You might have suffered owing to your absence.
I'll marry you in Seville (if you like
And she agrees) to one beside whose beauty
Isabel's would seem ugly, even were she
An angel. Don Gonzalo of Ulloa,
The grand commander of Calatrava
Whom pagan Moors praise highly in their terror
(For always cowards are flatterers and praisers)
Has a young daughter whose outstanding virtue's
A dowry in itself (I count it second
To beauty)—and a living marvel too!
She is the sun, the star of all Castile
And it is she I wish to be your wife.

OCTAVIO. The very undertaking of this voyage
Was worth while, sire, for this one thing alone
That I should know and do what gives you pleasure.

KING OF CASTILE, *to* DON DIEGO.
See that the duke is entertained and lodged
Down to his least requirement.

OCTAVIO.   O my lord,
The man who trusts in you wins every prize.
You're first of the Alfonsos, though eleventh!

Exeunt KING OF CASTILE *and* DON DIEGO.

Enter RIPIO.

RIPIO. What's happened?

OCTAVIO.   All my toil's rewarded well.
I told the king my wrongs. He honoured me.
Caesar was with the Caesar: as you see
I came, I saw, I conquered, and as well
He's going to marry me from his own palace
And make the King of Naples understand
And so repeal the law by which I'm banned.

RIPIO. With real good reason do they call this king
The benefactor of Castile. And so
He's offered you a wife?

OCTAVIO.   Yes, a friend, a wife
And one from Seville. Seville breeds strong men
And bold ones and breeds strapping women too.
A dashing style within a veiling mantle
Which covers a pure sun of dazzling beauty
—Where do you see such things except in Seville?
I am so happy, it was worth my troubles.

Enter DON JUAN *and* CATALINÓN.

CATALINÓN, *aside to his master.*
Wait, sir, there is the injured duke,
Isabel's Sagittarius—
Rather, I'd say, her Capricorn.[3]

DON JUAN. Pretend.

CATALINÓN.   You flatter those you sell.

DON JUAN. I went from Naples in such haste
Upon the summons of the king

---

[3] In this elaborate allusion, Isabel stands to Octavio as Heracles
to Sagittarius, who is also the ninth sign of the zodiac and as such
is followed by Capricorn. Catalinón drags the latter in because of
the connotation of horns—cuckoldom. For a fuller account of such
points, the reader is again referred to the Hill and Harlan edi-
tion. [E.B.]

I had no time to say good-bye,
Octavio.

OCTAVIO.   For such a thing
I hold you blameless.

Aside.

                        So we two
Today have met in Seville.

DON JUAN.   Who
Would think I would see you in Seville
Where I would serve you if I may
At your commands in every way?
You leave good things behind, for Naples
Is good, but only Seville's worth
Exchanging for so fine a city
Of all the cities on this earth.

OCTAVIO. If you had told me that in Naples
Before I ever came this way
I would have laughed the thought to scorn
But now I credit what you say.
In fact you would have said much more:
Why such understatement, pray?
But who's that coming over there?

DON JUAN. The Marquis of la Mota! Now
I'll have to be discourteous . . .

OCTAVIO. If ever you should need my sword
I'm at your service, my good lord.

CATALINÓN, *aside.*
And if he wants another dame,
Too, to dishonour in your name
I suppose you're at his service just the same.

OCTAVIO. I'm very pleased with meeting you.

Exeunt OCTAVIO *and* RIPIO.

Enter the MARQUIS OF LA MOTA *with servant.*

MARQUIS. All day I've been upon your track
But couldn't find you anywhere.
How strange you should be safely back
And your old friend be in despair
Of finding you!

DON JUAN.   For heaven's sake,
That seems a lot of fuss to make.
What news in Seville?

MARQUIS.   The whole court
Has changed.

DON JUAN.   What women? Any sport?

MARQUIS. Of course.

DON JUAN.   Inés?

MARQUIS.   She has retired
To Vejel.

DON JUAN. Oh, she's time-expired!
And Constance?

MARQUIS.   She's in sorry plight—
Moulting—both hair and eyebrows too!
A Portuguese said she was *old*
And she thought he meant *pretty*.

DON JUAN.   True!
Our word for "lovely to behold"
Is like the Portuguese for "old."
And Theodora?

MARQUIS.   Why, this summer
She cured herself of the French ill
That seemed about to overcome her,
Sweating it out in streams, until
She is grown so tender and polite
She pulled a tooth for me and quite
Surrounded me with heaps of flowers.

DON JUAN. And what of Julia Candlelight?
Does she still sell herself for trout?

MARQUIS. For stale salt cod, I have no doubt.

DON JUAN. How's Catarranas, the old slum?

MARQUIS. Why, crawling with the same old scum!

DON JUAN. Are those two sisters still on view?

MARQUIS. Yes, and that monkey of Tolú
The Celestina, their old dame,
Who read them scriptures on the game.

DON JUAN. Oh, her! Beelzebub's old sow!
  How is the elder of them now?

MARQUIS. She's spotless, and reformed at last,
  And has a saint for whom to fast.[4]

DON JUAN. A single lover, and no share?

MARQUIS. She's firm and faithful as she's fair.

DON JUAN. The other?

MARQUIS.   Leads a livelier dance
  And never yet would miss her chance.

DON JUAN. What jokes or scandals have you played?
  What harlots have you left unpaid?

MARQUIS. De Esquival and I both made
  A cruel fraud last night. Tonight
  We've got a better hoax in sight.

DON JUAN. I'll come with you. Tell me: what's brewing
  I' the way of courting, suing, wooing?
  For I already, sir, have got
  My nest eggs hatching out a plot.

MARQUIS. Speak not of territory where
  My heart is buried deep in care!

DON JUAN. How so?

MARQUIS.   I love one that is not
  Attainable.

DON JUAN. The girl, does she
  Reject you?

MARQUIS.   No, she favours me
  And loves me.

DON JUAN.   Who is it?

MARQUIS.   My cousin,
  Ana, who has arrived here newly.

DON JUAN. Where has she been?

MARQUIS.   In Lisbon with
  The embassy.

DON JUAN.   Good-looking?

MARQUIS.   Truly

---

[4] Metaphor for being a kept woman true to one lover. [R.C.]

She's Nature's masterpiece. In her
Nature has strained her powers.

DON JUAN.   Such beauty?
By God, I'd like to see her!

MARQUIS.   Yes,
You'll see in her the greatest beauty
The king has seen in all his state.

DON JUAN. Get married then, since it's your fate.

MARQUIS. The king's betrothed her to some other.

DON JUAN. But she accepts it that you love her?

MARQUIS. Yes, and she writes me daily too.

CATALINÓN, *aside*. Keep your mouth shut or you'll be sorry:
Spain's greatest trickster marks his quarry.

DON JUAN. Who, then, more satisfied than you?

MARQUIS. I've come to see what resolution
Is taken on the lady's fate.

DON JUAN. Yes, go and see, and here I'll wait
For your return.

MARQUIS.   I'll come back soon.

CATALINÓN, *to the servant*.
Mister Round or Mister Square,
Good-bye.

SERVANT.   Good-bye.

Exeunt MARQUIS *and servant.*

DON JUAN, *to* CATALINÓN. Now we're alone.
Shadow the marquis, keep his track,
He went into the palace there.
See where he goes and then come back.

Exit CATALINÓN.

A servant woman at a barred window speaks to DON JUAN.

WOMAN. Who am I speaking to?

DON JUAN.   Who called me?

WOMAN.   Now, sir,
Seeing you are a good friend of the marquis,
Prudent and courteous, take this note, and give it

Into the marquis' hands, for it contains
The happiness and honour of a lady.

DON JUAN. As I'm a gentleman and his good friend
I swear to give it to him.

WOMAN.   Stranger, thanks.
Good-bye.

The servant woman disappears.

DON JUAN.   The voice has gone and I'm alone.
Does it not seem like magic, what has passed
This minute? That this letter should arrive
As if the wind were carrier to my thoughts
And luck my letter-box? Why, this must be
A letter to the marquis from the lady
His speeches so endeared to me. In Seville
I'm called the Trickster; and my greatest pleasure
Is to trick women, leaving them dishonoured.
As soon as I have left this little square
I'll open this and read it. Idle caution!
It makes me want to laugh outright. The paper's
Open already. And it's plain it's hers,
For there's her signature, and here it says:
"My unkind father secretly has forced me
To marry. I cannot resist. I doubt
If I can go on living, since it's death
That he has given me. If you respect
My will and my dear love of you, then show it
This once. For, just to see how I adore you,
Come to my door this evening at eleven
And you will find me waiting, and it open,
So to enjoy the very crown of love.
Wear for a signal (that the maids may know it
And let you in) a cape of crimson colour.
My love, I trust in you; farewell; your own
Unhappy love." Why, it's as good as done!
Oh, I could roar with laughter! I'll enjoy her
By the same trick that limed the other one,
Isabel, back in Naples.

Enter CATALINÓN.

CATALINÓN.   Here's the marquis
  Returning now.

DON JUAN.   Tonight the two of us
  Have lots to do.

CATALINÓN.   You've some new swindle!

DON JUAN. This one's a wonder!

CATALINÓN.   Well, I disapprove.
  You claim that we'll escape being caught out
  But those who live by cheating must be cheated
  In the long run.

DON JUAN.   You've turned a bloody preacher,
  Have you, you cheeky boor?

CATALINÓN.   Right makes men brave!

DON JUAN. Yes, and fear makes men cowards, just like you.
  You earn by serving. If you'd always earn,
  Act always on the spot. He who does most
  Wins most.

CATALINÓN.   And those who say and do the most
  Collide with things the most and come to grief.

DON JUAN. But now I'm warning you! So, for the last
  Time, listen, for I shan't warn you again!

CATALINÓN. Well, yes, from now, whatever you command
  I'll do as if you were flanked on either side
  By a tiger and an elephant, Don Juan!

DON JUAN. Hark! here's the marquis.

CATALINÓN.   Must he be the victim?

  Enter MARQUIS OF LA MOTA.

DON JUAN. Out of this casement, Marquis, someone gave me
  A very courteous message for yourself.
  I could not see who gave it but the voice
  Was of a woman, and she said at twelve
  You are to go in secret to the door,
  Which at that hour will be open to you,
  And you must wear a cape of crimson colour
  So that the maids will know you.

MARQUIS.   What?

DON JUAN.   This message

Was passed me at the window here without
My seeing who it was who whispered it.

MARQUIS. This message has restored my life, dear friend:
May God reward you for it without end!

DON JUAN. I haven't got your cousin here inside
So why should your embraces be applied
To one so worthless?

MARQUIS.   You delight me so
That I am quite outside myself, I know.
O sun, go down!

DON JUAN.   It slopes towards its setting.

MARQUIS. Come, friends. Come, night. My reason I'm for-
    getting.
I'm mad with joy.

DON JUAN.   One sees that quite all right.
You'll reach the peak at twelve o'clock tonight.

MARQUIS. Crown of my very soul! My heart's delight
Who are to crown my loving faith tonight!

CATALINÓN, *aside*. Dear Christ! I would not even bet a dozen
Bad halfpennies on that belovèd cousin.

Exit the MARQUIS *and enter* DON DIEGO.

DON DIEGO. Don Juan!

CATALINÓN.   Your father calls you.

DON JUAN.   At your orders.

DON DIEGO. I'd like to see you far better behaved,
Good-natured, with a better reputation.
Can it be possible you wish to kill me
With your behaviour?

DON JUAN.   Why in such a state?

DON DIEGO. For your behaviour and your madness now
The king has bade me ban you from the city,
For he is justly angered by a crime
Which, though you hid it from me, *he* has heard of
In Seville here—a crime so grave and evil
I scarcely dare to name it. Make a cuckold
Of your best friend and in the royal palace!
May God reward you as your sins deserve:

For though it now appear that God above
Puts up with you, consenting to your crimes,
The punishment is certain—and how fearful
For those who've taken His great name in vain!
His justice is tremendous after death.

DON JUAN. What, after death? How long you give me credit!
A long, long time, before I need repentance!

DON DIEGO. It will seem short when you receive your sentence.

DON JUAN. And now what would His Highness with myself?
Will it be for a long, long time as well?

DON DIEGO. Until you have repaired the august insult
Done to the Duke Octavio, and appeased
The scandals you have caused with Isabel,
You have to live in exile in Lebrija.
The king requires you go there instantly.
The sentence is too slight for such a crime.

CATALINÓN, *aside.* And if he also knew about the case
Of that poor fishergirl the good old man
Would be far angrier.

DON DIEGO.   Since no punishment,
Nor anything I say or do, affects you,
Your chastisement I here confide to God.
Exit.

CATALINÓN. The dear old man was overcome.

DON JUAN. Tears are well suited to old age.
Well now, the night is coming down.
We'll seek the marquis. Come, my page.

CATALINÓN. And now you will enjoy his bride.

DON JUAN. Which promises to be great sport.

CATALINÓN. Pray God that we come out of it
Alive!

DON JUAN. Now, now!

CATALINÓN.   I think the best
Way to describe you, sir, would be
As a locust to whom girls are grass,
And so by public proclamation
Whenever you're about to arrive

Towns should be warned: "Here comes the plague
Of women in a single man
Who is their cheater and betrayer,
The greatest trickster in all Spain."

DON JUAN. You've given me a charming name.

It is night time.

Enter the MARQUIS *with musicians who move up and down
the stage.*

MUSICIANS, *singing.*
> To him who waits a promised pleasure
> Delay is like despair to measure.

MARQUIS. May never break of day destroy
The night in which I take my joy.

DON JUAN. What's this?

CATALINÓN.   Why, music.

MARQUIS, *aside.*   It appears
The poet speaks to me.
Aloud.

>   Who's there?

DON JUAN. Friend!

MARQUIS.   It's Don Juan?

DON JUAN.   The marquis, you?

MARQUIS. Who other would it be?

DON JUAN.   I knew
You by the coloured cape you wear.

MARQUIS, *to the musicians.*
Sing, since Don Juan's come here to.

MUSICIANS, *singing.*
> To him who waits a promised pleasure
> Delay is like despair to measure.

DON JUAN. Whose house is that you gaze at so?

MARQUIS. Why, Don Gonzalo's.

DON JUAN.   Where shall we go?

MARQUIS. To Lisbon.[5]

---

[5] "Evidently refers to a street or district of Seville inhabited by
Portuguese courtesans" [Hill and Harlan, *op. cit.*].

DON JUAN.   How,
  Being in Seville?

MARQUIS.   Don't you know?
  And do you wonder that the worst
  Of Portugal live on the first
  And best of Spain, right here and now?

DON JUAN. Where do they live?

MARQUIS.   Why, in the street
  Called "Of the Serpent." There one sees
  Adam, become a Portuguese,
  Wooing a thousand Eves to eat
  And take a bite out of their pockets.
  And, sure, it's quite a hole they make
  With all those big doubloons and ducats.

DON JUAN. You run along there while you can.
  I have to play a scurvy joke.

MARQUIS. I'm being shadowed by a man
  Some pimp or bravo . . .

DON JUAN.   Leave him to me.[6]
  I shan't let him escape, you'll see.

MARQUIS. Around your arm, then, wrap this cloak
  The better so to deal your stroke.

DON JUAN. A good idea; then come and show
  The house to which I have to go.

MARQUIS. Now, while you carry out the plan,
  Alter your voice and talk as though
  You were indeed some other man.
  D'you see that "jealousy"?

DON JUAN.   I do.

MARQUIS. Then go to it and whisper there:
  "Beatrice." Then pass right through.

DON JUAN. What sort of woman?

MARQUIS.   Soft and pink.

CATALINÓN. Some water-cooling jar, I think.

MARQUIS. I'll wait for you at Gradas Stair.

  [6] Here Don Juan takes on Mota's enterprise, which proved more
dangerous than the latter had bargained for. [R.C.]

DON JUAN. Till then, dear Marquis! I'll be there.

CATALINÓN. Now whither bound?

DON JUAN.   Shut up, you bear!
I go to where my jest is played.

CATALINÓN. Nothing escapes you unbetrayed.

DON JUAN. I adore cheating.

CATALINÓN.   Now to the bull!
Pass me your cape.

DON JUAN.   Not so, the fool
Beast has passed his cape to me.

MUSICIANS. The trick appeals to such as we.

MARQUIS. That is succeeding by mistake.

MUSICIANS. And the whole world doth errors make.

MUSICIANS, *singing*.
        When one awaits a promised pleasure
        Delay is like despair to measure.

Room in the House of DON GONZALO

DOÑA ANA *within, with* DON JUAN *and* CATALINÓN

DOÑA ANA, *within*. False friend, you're not the marquis! You
    have tricked me!

DON JUAN. I tell you who I am.

DOÑA ANA, *within*.   False foe, you lie!
    Enter DON GONZALO *with drawn sword*.

DON GONZALO. I hear my daughter Doña Ana's voice.

DOÑA ANA, *within*. Will nobody kill this false traitor here,
    The murderer of my honour?

DON GONZALO. Can such effrontery exist? She said:
    "My honour murdered." Then alas for me!
    Her giddy tongue is like a bell to clamour
    Our sad disgrace to all.

DOÑA ANA, *within*.   Kill him!

DON JUAN *and* CATALINÓN *enter with drawn swords.*

DON JUAN.   Who's this?

DON GONZALO. The closed and fallen barbican is here
Of the strong fortress of my honour, which,
Base traitor, you have falsely undermined,
Though there my life was warden.

DON JUAN.   Let me pass!

DON GONZALO. Pass? You shall pass the point of this bare sword.

DON JUAN. You'll die for this.

DON GONZALO.   That is no matter.

DON JUAN.   Look,
I'll have to kill you.

DON GONZALO.   Die yourself, base traitor.

DON JUAN, *thrusting with sword.*
This is the way I die.

CATALINÓN, *aside.*   If I get free
Then no more feasts and scurvy tricks for me!

DON GONZALO. He's given me my death.

DON JUAN.   You took your life
By being rash.

DON GONZALO.   What use was it to me?

DON JUAN. Come, let us run.

Exeunt DON JUAN *and* CATALINÓN.

DON GONZALO.   My frozen blood you've swelled
With fury. I am dead. I can expect
No better thing. My fury will pursue you.
You are a traitor, and a traitor is
A traitor, being first of all a coward.

He dies. Servants enter and carry off the corpse.

Enter MARQUIS OF LA MOTA *and musicians.*

MARQUIS. Now midnight will be striking soon:
Don Juan's[7] surely very late.
How hard a thing it is—to wait.

Re-enter DON JUAN *and* CATALINÓN.

[7] R.C. evidently used the traditional, anglicized pronunciation
of Don Juan—Byron rhymed it with "true one." [E.B.]

DON JUAN. Is that the marquis?

MARQUIS. You're Don Juan?

DON JUAN. I am. Here, take your cape.

MARQUIS. Your pranks . . .

DON JUAN. Have had a most funereal end
In death.

CATALINÓN. Oh, flee from the dead man!

MARQUIS. Tell me, whom did you trick, my friend?

CATALINÓN, *aside.* You are the latest victim, thanks
To him.

DON JUAN. This prank has cost most dear.

MARQUIS. Don Juan, the whole debt I'll clear . . .
Because the girl will be complaining
Of me . . .

DON JUAN. The stroke of twelve draws near.

MARQUIS. May never break of day destroy
The night in which I take my joy!

DON JUAN. Farewell then, Marquis!

CATALINÓN. What a treat
Awaits the wretch!

DON JUAN. Let's run!

CATALINÓN. My feet
Than wings of eagles feel more fleet.

Exeunt except the MARQUIS OF LA MOTA *and servants.*

MARQUIS. Now you can all go home. I'll go
Alone.

SERVANTS. God made the night for sleeping.

Exeunt servants.

VOICES *within.* Was ever such a sight of woe?
Alas! How pitiless a blow!

MARQUIS. God shield me! I hear cries and weeping
Resounding from the castle square.
At such an hour what could it be?
Ice freezes all my chest. I see
What seems another Troy aflare,
For torches now come wildly gleaming

With giant flames like comets streaming
And reeking from their pitchy hair,
A mighty horde of tarry hanks.
Fire seems to emulate the stars
Dividing into troops and ranks.
I'll go and find out . . .

Enter DON DIEGO TENORIO *and guards with torches.*

DON DIEGO.   Who goes there?

MARQUIS. One who would know of this affair,
And why there's such a hue and cry.

DON DIEGO, *to the guards.*
Bind him!

MARQUIS, *drawing his sword.*
          What? Me? I'd sooner die!

DON DIEGO. Give me your sword. The greatest valour
Is speech without recourse to steel.

MARQUIS. And is it thus that you would deal
With me, the Marquis of la Mota?

DON DIEGO. Your sword! Whatever you may feel,
The king has ordered your arrest!

MARQUIS. Ye gods!

Enter the KING OF CASTILE *and his attendants.*

KING OF CASTILE. Through Spain from east to west
See that he can't escape. As well
In Italy (for who can tell
If he should get there?) start the quest.

DON DIEGO. He is here.

MARQUIS.   Then, sire, I'm apprehended,
Truly, by your own orders. Why?

KING OF CASTILE. Take him, and have his head suspended
Upon a rampart near the sky.
—Don't linger in my presence, sir.

MARQUIS, *aside.* The ecstasies of am'rous passion
Always so light as they occur
Grow heavy after in this fashion.
"There's many a slip," once said the sage.
But why the king's revengeful rage?

Aloud.

I can't make out what crime I've done.

DON DIEGO. You know as well as anyone.

MARQUIS. Me?

DON DIEGO.   Come!

MARQUIS.   What strange confusion!

KING OF CASTILE.   Try him

And cut his head off before day.
For the commander, don't deny him
Solemnity and grave display
Such as men grant to royal or sacred
Persons. The funeral must be grand.
Statue and tomb of bronze and stone
With Gothic letters see them planned
Proclaiming vengeance is at hand.
And where has Doña Ana gone?

DON DIEGO. To sanctuary swift she ran
In the convent of Our Heavenly Queen.

KING OF CASTILE. This loss is grave, for such a man
Has Calatrava seldom seen.

Countryside near Dos Hermanas

Enter a betrothed couple, BATRICIO *and* AMINTA. *Also*
GASENO, BELISA, *and shepherd musicians.*

MUSICIANS, *singing.*

      Brightly April's sun shines over
      The orange flowers and scented clover
      But though she serve him as a star
      Aminta shines out lovelier far.

BATRICIO. Upon this carpet made of flowers,
When the red earth seems turned to snow,
The sun exhausts his dazzling powers
And freshens to his dawning glow.
Come, let us sit, for such a place
Invites us with its charm and grace.

AMINTA, *to the singers.*
A thousand, thousand favors show
To my betrothed, Batricio.

MUSICIANS, *singing.*
Brightly April's sun shines over
The orange flowers and scented clover
But though she serve him as a star
Aminta shines out lovelier far.

GASENO, *to the singers.*
As well has sung each lad and lass
As sings the choir at Holy Mass!

BATRICIO. Aminta, when the sun sees thee
It is o'erwhelmed with jealousy!

AMINTA. Batricio, when I hear thee,
I hear the voice of flattery!
But take my thanks, good lad, for soon
I'll be content to be the moon
If thou'lt give light to everyone
And be the all-commanding sun.
I'll wax and wane contentedly
Taking my light, dear sun, from thee!
May the dawn ever sing to us
Its subtle salutation, thus:

MUSICIANS, *singing.*
Brightly April's sun shines over
The orange flowers and scented clover
But though she serve him as a star
Aminta shines out lovelier far.

Enter CATALINÓN *in travelling clothes.*

CATALINÓN. Good people all, for your espousal
More guests have come to the carousal.

GASENO. Let everybody be invited.
I hope that all will be delighted.
Who's coming?

CATALINÓN.   Don Juan Tenorio.

GASENO. The old one?

CATALINÓN.   No, I mean the young.

GASENO. He must be something of a rake.

BATRICIO, *aside*. This omen very hard I take.
  For being a cavalier and young,
  It brings on envy, takes off lustre.
  Aloud.
  Who gave him notice of our muster?

CATALINÓN. He heard of it along the road.

BATRICIO, *aside*. That to the devil must be owed.
  But why anticipate the load?
  Aloud.
  Then come to my sweet wedding night
  All those who wish to dance and dine
  Aside.
  Except that one of them's a knight:
  I take this as an evil sign.

GASENO. Let the Colossus be invited
  From Rhodes, the Pope and Prester John
  With Don Alfonso the Eleventh,
  His court, and all who follow on!
  Loaves of bread are piled in mountains
  For this wedding! Wine stands ready
  To overflow in springs, in fountains,
  In Taguses and Guadalquivirs!
  Babels and Babylons of ham,
  Thrushes and quails in timid flocks
  Are here your bulging sides to cram—
  And tender doves and basted cocks!
  To Dos Hermanas, welcome here!
  Bring in the noble cavalier
  To honour these white hairs of mine!

BELISA. Son of the chancellor!

BATRICIO.   A sign
  Of evil is this guest of mine
  For they must place him by my bride.
  To eat and drink I am not zealous
  Since heaven dooms me to be jealous,
  To love, to suffer, and abide.
  Enter DON JUAN.

DON JUAN. I heard by chance there was a marriage-feast
When I was passing by this village here
And so I've come to revel in it too
Being so lucky as to pass just then.

GASENO. Your Lordship comes to honour and ennoble it.

BATRICIO, *aside.* And I, who am the host and master, say,
Within me, that you come in evil hour.

GASENO. Won't you make room there for the cavalier!

DON JUAN. With your permission, I will take this place.
Sits next to the bride.

BATRICIO. If you sit down before me, sir, you'll seem
The bridegroom.

DON JUAN.   If I were, I could choose worse!

GASENO. He *is* the bridegroom.

DON JUAN.   Oh, I beg your pardon
For my mistake.

CATALINÓN, *aside.* Oh, poor unhappy bridegroom!

DON JUAN, *aside to* CATALINÓN.
He seems annoyed.

CATALINÓN.   I'm quite aware of that
But if he has to serve you for a bull
What does it matter if he seems annoyed?
I would not give one horn-toss for his wife
Nor for his honour. Poor unhappy man
To fall into the hands of Lucifer!

DON JUAN. Can it be possible I am so lucky?
I'm almost feeling jealous of your husband.

AMINTA. You seem to flatter me.

BATRICIO, *aside.*   Well is it said:
"A great one at a wedding brings bad luck."

GASENO. Come, let us eat and drink a while
So that your Lordship, while we dine,
May rest himself!

DON JUAN *takes* AMINTA's *hand.*

DON JUAN.   Why hide your hand?

AMINTA. It's mine.

GASENO.   Let's go.

BELISA.   Strike up the song again!

DON JUAN. What do you make of it?

CATALINÓN.   I fear a vile
Death at the hands of those same sturdy peasants.

DON JUAN. What lovely eyes and spotless hands—
They're burning me with flaming torches!

CATALINÓN. It's *you* will brand *her* with your mark
Then put her out to winter-grazing.
Three little lambs, and this makes four.[8]

DON JUAN. How all of them are staring at me!

BATRICIO. It is an evil-boding thing
A noble at my wedding.

GASENO.   Sing![9]

BATRICIO. God! I feel as if I'm dying.

CATALINÓN, *aside.*
They sing now, who will soon be crying.

[8] Isabel, Thisbe, Doña Ana, and now Aminta. As Act II closes,
we have met all of the Don's women as far as this play is concerned; the threads are drawn together in the third and last act.
[E.B.]

[9] Gaseno's trying to keep up appearances. [R.C.]

ACT III

GASENO's house in Dos Hermanas

Enter BATRICIO, pensive.

BATRICIO. Jealousy, timepiece of our cares, who strikes
    Fierce torments and alarms at every hour,
    Torments, with which you kill, although you give
    Disjointed blows, cease from tormenting me,
    Since it's absurd that, if love gives me life,
    You should give death. What do you wish of me,
    Sir Cavalier, that you torment me so?
    Well did I say, seeing him at my wedding:
    "An evil omen." Was it not well done
    That he should sit beside my bride, not letting
    Me even put my hand in my own plate?
    Because each time I tried to do so, he
    Would brush it off exclaiming: "What ill breeding!"
    And when I turned to others and complained
    They answered: "You have nothing to complain of!
    Don't take this thing so hard! And don't get scared!
    At court it's quite the custom. Just keep quiet!"
    The custom! And they laughed! Fine custom this!
    A worse one (in my eyes) than that of Sodom!
    Another man at table with the bride
    While the bridegroom goes hungry! And this other
    Kept saying to me: "Don't you eat that, ha?"
    The scoundrel then would snatch it from my plate
    Saying that I was wrong not to enjoy it.
    I am ashamed. This wedding was a jest
    And not a marriage. None will suffer me,
    Nor let me pass among them. Now he's supped
    With both of us, I suppose he has to come
    To bed with us, and, when I take my wife,
    To chide me: "What ill breeding! What ill breeding!"
    He's coming now. I can't resist. I'll hide.
    But that can't be, since he has seen me now.

Enter DON JUAN.

DON JUAN. Batricio.

BATRICIO.   Yes, my lord.

DON JUAN.   It's just to tell you—

BATRICIO, *aside.* What can it be but more ill luck for me?

DON JUAN. It's just to tell you that I lost my soul
  Some days ago to our Aminta and
  Enjoyed . . .

BATRICIO.   Her honour?

DON JUAN.   Yes.

BATRICIO, *aside.*   A certain proof
  Is all that I've just seen. Did she not love him
  He never would have ventured to her house.
  Aloud, to DON JUAN.
  She's only proved a woman, after all.

DON JUAN. Aminta, in the end, grew jealous, desperate
  In fact, thinking herself forgotten by me,
  And being married to another man,
  And so she wrote this letter sending for me
  And in return I promised to enjoy
  That which our souls had promised long ago.
  Well, that's how things stand. Give your life a chance.
  For ruthlessly I'll kill whoever stops us.

BATRICIO. Why, if you leave it to my choice, I'll further
  Your wishes. For when rumour breathes abroad,
  Honour and woman suffer worst of all,
  And women in the general opinion
  Will always lose more than they gain. For women
  Are tested, just as bells are, by their sound,
  And it is known how reputation suffers
  When in the common speech a woman's name
  Rings with the sound of a cracked bell. Since you
  Subdue me, I no longer want the bliss
  That love commanded me to take. A woman
  Half good, half bad is like a piece of gold
  Seen in the twilight. For a thousand years
  Enjoy her, sir! I'd sooner die un-hoodwinked
  Than live the dupe of others.

Exit.

DON JUAN.   Through his honour
I conquered him, and always, with these peasants
They hold their honour in both hands, and look
To their own honour first. For honour
Was forced, by so much falsity and fraud,
To leave the city for the countryside.
But now, before I work the final damage,
I shall pretend to remedy it too.
I'll go and talk to her old father and get him
To authorise the deed against his will.
O stars of morning, give me luck in this
Deception since you keep the payment, due
In death, for such a long, long time ahead!

Exit.

Enter AMINTA *and* BELISA.[10]

BELISA. See, where your bridegroom comes, Aminta. Come,
Enter and strip.

AMINTA.   Of this unhappy wedding,
I don't know what to think. For my Batricio
All day was bathed in melancholy tears.
All's jealousy and wild confusion. What
A terrible misfortune!

BELISA.   But what young knight
Was that . . . ?[11]

AMINTA.   Leave me, for I am all confusion
Since Shamelessness was made a knight of Spain.
Evil befall the knight that lost me my
Good husband!

BELISA.   Quiet! for I think he's coming.
Let no one tread the floor of so robust
A bridegroom.

AMINTA.   Now farewell, my dear Belisa.

[10] Belisa in the dark mistakes Don Juan for the bridegroom coming. [R.C.]

[11] There are two interpretations of this. I take it that Belisa, who was a snob and formerly proclaimed Don Juan's rank, pretends to be ignorant when he becomes unpopular. [R.C.]

BELISA. You will appease his anger in your arms.

Exit.

AMINTA. May it please Heaven my sighs might seem endearments
And these poor tears appear to him caresses!

Exeunt.

Enter DON JUAN, CATALINÓN, GASENO.

DON JUAN. Good-bye, Gaseno.

GASENO.   Let me keep you company
So that I may congratulate my daughter.

DON JUAN. Oh, there'll be time enough for that tomorrow.

GASENO. Yes, you are right. I offer my own soul
Together with the girl.

DON JUAN.   Rather, my bride.

Exit GASENO.

DON JUAN. Catalinón, go saddle up.

CATALINÓN.   For when?

DON JUAN. For dawn, and when the sun, half-dead with laughter,
Rises to see the hoax.

CATALINÓN.   For in Lebrija
There is another bridal that awaits us.
For God's sake, hasten with the one in hand.

DON JUAN. But this will be the greatest hoax of all.

CATALINÓN. I only hope we come out safely from it.

DON JUAN. Seeing my father is chief justice and
The king's most private friend, what can you fear?

CATALINÓN. God is accustomed to take vengeance on
Those who use privacy just to deprive,
And often, when there's gambling on, spectators
Are apt to lose as badly as the gamblers.
I've long been a spectator of your gambles,
And for this office I would dread to be
Struck by the thunderbolt to dust and cinders
When it gets you.

DON JUAN.   Go saddle up those horses!
Tomorrow night I have to sleep in Seville.

CATALINÓN. In Seville?

DON JUAN. Yes.

CATALINÓN. What are you saying? Look
At what you've done, master, and look how short
Even the longest life is until death!
And there's a hell behind the gates of death.

DON JUAN. If you concede me such a long, long time
You'll be deceived . . .

CATALINÓN. Listen, my lord!

DON JUAN. Get out!
Get out! You bore me with your farfetched fears!

CATALINÓN. How we admire the fearless Scythian
The brave Galician, Persian, Lybian!
But, I confess, for all of me,
They all can keep their bravery.
Exit.

DON JUAN. Night spreads across the world. Silence is black.
The Pleiades now tread the highest pole
'Mid starry clusters. Now I set my trap.
Love guides me to my joy—none can resist him.
I've got to reach her bed. Aminta!

AMINTA. Who
Calls for Aminta? Is it Batricio?
He is at her door. She comes out, as from bed.

DON JUAN. I'm not Batricio. No.

AMINTA. Then, who?

DON JUAN. Look slowly,
And you'll see who I am.

AMINTA. Why, sir, I'm lost,
With you outside my bedroom at these hours!

DON JUAN. Such are the hours that I am wont to keep.

AMINTA. Return, or I shall shout. Please don't exceed
The courtesy you owe to my Batricio.
You'll find, in Dos Hermanas, there are Romans—
Emilias and Lucreces who avenge!

DON JUAN. Just hear two words and hide the blushing scarlet
Of your fair cheeks deep down within your heart!

AMINTA. Go, go! My husband's coming.

DON JUAN.   I'm your husband.
  So what have you to marvel at?

AMINTA.   Since when?

DON JUAN. From now on, and forever, I am he!

AMINTA. But who arranged the marriage?

DON JUAN.   My delight.

AMINTA. And who was it that married us?

DON JUAN.   Your eyes.

AMINTA. By what authority?

DON JUAN.   Why, that of sight!

AMINTA. But does Batricio know?

DON JUAN.   Yes! He forgets you.

AMINTA. Has he forgotten me?

DON JUAN.   Yes. I adore you.

AMINTA. How?

DON JUAN. Thus with all my heart I swoon before you.

AMINTA. Get out!

DON JUAN.   How can I when you see I'm dying
  With love for you alone?

AMINTA.   What shameless lying!

DON JUAN. Aminta, listen and you'll know the truth,
  Since women are the friends of truth. I am
  A noble knight, the heir of the Tenorios,
  The conquerors of Seville. And my father,
  Next to the king, is honoured and esteemed
  Beyond all men in court. Upon his lips
  Hang life or death according to his word.
  Travelling on my road, by merest chance,
  I came and saw you. Love ordains these things
  And guides them, so that even He, Himself,
  Forgets that they were anything but chance.
  I saw you, I adored you, I was kindled
  So that I am determined now to wed you.
  Even though the king forbid it, and my father
  In anger and with threats tries to prevent it,
  I have to be your husband. What's your answer!

AMINTA. I don't know what to say. Your so-called "truths"
Are covered with deceitful rhetoric—
Because if I am married to Batricio
(As is well known) the fact is not annulled
Even if he deserts me.

DON JUAN.   Non-consummation,
Either by malice or deceit, is reason
For an annulment.

AMINTA.   In Batricio all
Was simple truth.

DON JUAN.   Tush! Come, give me your hand,
And let's confirm our vows.

AMINTA.   You're not deceiving?

DON JUAN. I'd be the one deceived.

AMINTA.   Then swear before me
To carry out your promised word.

DON JUAN.   I swear
By this white hand, a winter of pure snow.

AMINTA. Swear then, to God. Pray that he curse your soul
If you should fail!

DON JUAN.   If in my word and faith
I fail, I pray to God that by foul treason
I be murdered by a man!
Aside.

                    I mean a dead one,
For living man, may God forbid!

AMINTA.   This promise
Has made me your own wife.

DON JUAN.   My very soul
I offer you between my outstretched arms.

AMINTA. My life and soul are yours.

DON JUAN.   Ah, my Aminta,
Tomorrow you will walk in silver buskins
Studded with tacks of gold from heel to toe.
Your alabaster throat will be imprisoned
In necklaces of diamonds and rubies,

And your white fingers, in their flashing rings,
Will seem transparent pearls.

AMINTA.   From now to yours
My will bows down, and I am yours alone.

DON JUAN, *aside.* Little you know the Trickster of Seville!

Near Tarragona

Enter ISABEL *and* FABIO *in travelling costume with an oxcart.*

ISABEL. He robbed me of my master—
By treason—of the man whom I adored!
O pitiless disaster
To truth! O night abhorred!
Black mask of day, who aided the deceit,
Antipode of the sun, and spouse of sleep!

FABIO. What serves it, Isabel,
Always upon your sorrows so to dwell?
—If love is naught but cunning,
Always through fields of scorn and anger running,
If he who laughs today
Tomorrow has to weep his woes away?
The sea is swelled with anger
And from this mighty tempest and its clangour,
Out of the foamy welter,
Duchess, the galleys now have sun for shelter
Beneath the towers that crown
This rocky strand.

ISABEL.   Where are we?

FABIO.   At the town
Of Tarragona. Hence,
By land, we'll reach the city of Valence
In very little time,
The palace of the sun, a most sublime
And stately city. There
For several days you may divert your care
And then to Seville sailing

You'll see the world's eighth wonder. What of failing
To win Octavio's hand?
Don Juan is more famous in the land!
Then why so sad? They say
He's made a count already. Anyway,
The king himself is giving
Your hand to him. Of all the nobles living
The nearest to the king,
His father is the first in everything.

ISABEL. My sadness is not due
To marrying Don Juan, since it's true
He is most nobly born
And the world knows it. What makes me forlorn
Is honour which, though wife,
I must lament the years of all my life.

FABIO. A fishermaid appears
Sighing most tenderly and bathed in tears.
Surely she's come to you
Some favour or some sympathy to woo.
So while I fetch your train
You two may all the sweetlier complain
Together.

Exit FABIO *and enter* THISBE.

THISBE.   Sea of Spain,
Rough sea with waves of fire and fleeting foam!
Burned Troy of my poor home!
O fire, conceived and hatched deep in the main,
Which waves brought forth,[12] to turn
Again to running water, though it burn
With flames in these salt tears.
Cursed be the wood that on the wave careers
To work the woe that was Medea's!
Cursèd be those that had the mad ideas
Of twisting hemp or lint
To crucify the canvas on a splint
And be the engines of deceiving—
Serpents of rope their deep enchantments weaving!

[12] Don Juan was the fire who came to her out of the water and
then produced more water in the form of her tears. [E.B.]

ISABEL. Why, lovely fishermaid,
Do you make complaint so sadly of the sea?

THISBE. Why, madam, I have made
A thousand such, and happy must you be
To laugh at such a thing.

ISABEL. I also have such sad complaints to sing.
Where are you from?

THISBE.   Behind
There, where sore-wounded by the wind
You see those huts, the gales
Over them so victoriously rampage
That through their shattered pales
Each bird can find a nesting place, their rage
Forces so many a rift!
Of these great bulls, are you the prize they left,
O beautiful Europa, in this cart?

ISABEL. Though much against my heart,
They're taking me to Seville to be wed.

THISBE. If my sad lot has bred
Some pity in you, and if you as well
Some woes of the injurious sea can tell,
Then take me with you, and I'll be your slave.
I have an audience with the king to crave
For reparation of an evil hoax
Played by a noble on us humble folks.
Lifeless and stranded by the angry wave
Was Don Juan de Tenorio, whom to save
I sheltered until he was out of danger,
When this ungrateful and relentless stranger
Proved to my foot a viper in the grass.
With promises of marriage he confused me
And for his own mere pleasure then abused me.
Woe to the woman who believes man's oath!
He ran away and left me to my woe.
Say have I right to vengeance then, or no?

ISABEL. O cursed woman, hold your tongue,
By which even to death I have been stung!
After reflecting.

But, if it's grief that's actuating you,
It's not your fault. Proceed! But is it true?

THISBE. How happy, were it false!

ISABEL. Woe to the woman who believes man's oath!
Who's coming with you?

THISBE.   One old fisherman,
My father, and the witness of my wrongs.

ISABEL. No vengeance can suffice so great an evil.
Come in my company, and welcome both!

THISBE. Woe to the woman who believes man's oath.

The cloister or nave of a church in Seville. In one of the side chapels is the tomb of the commander Don Gonzalo with a statue of the dead man.[13]

Enter DON JUAN *and* CATALINÓN.

CATALINÓN. I tell you things are looking bad.

DON JUAN.   How so?

CATALINÓN. First, that Octavio has got to know
That hoax in Italy. The marquis, too,
Knows that the message which he got from you
And which you said his cousin gave was faked.
Then Isabela's on the way: she's staked
A marriage claim, and also it is spoken . . .

DON JUAN. Here, hold your tongue!
Hitting him.

CATALINÓN.   Look, master, you have broken
A molar in my mouth.

DON JUAN.   Then hold your jaw.
Who told you all this nonsense?

CATALINÓN.   Nonsense?

DON JUAN.   Yes.

---

13 Fugitives from justice cannot be arrested in a church in Seville. That is why Don Juan goes to one. [R.C.]

CATALINÓN. It's gospel truth!

DON JUAN.   I don't care if it is.
And what if Duke Octavio tries to kill me—
Have I not hands as well? Where is our lodging?

CATALINÓN. Down in the darkest, hidden street.

DON JUAN.   That's good.

CATALINÓN. Here in this church, it's holy ground.

DON JUAN.   Just so.
D'you think they'll kill me here in broad daylight?
And have you seen the groom from Dos Hermanas?

CATALINÓN. I saw him, too, looking both grim and sad.

DON JUAN. For two whole weeks Aminta has not known
How she's been tricked.

CATALINÓN.   So thoroughly she's hoaxed
She goes about calling herself the countess!

DON JUAN. God, what a funny hoax!

CATALINÓN.   Funny enough;
And one for which that girl must weep forever.

They both look at the sepulchre.

DON JUAN. Whose sepulchre is this?

CATALINÓN.   Here Don Gonzalo
Lies buried.

DON JUAN.   What? the same one I killed?
They've done him very nobly for a tomb.

CATALINÓN. This tomb was ordered by the king. What says
That writing there?

DON JUAN, *reads.*   HERE, TRUSTING IN THE LORD
FOR VENGEANCE ON A TRAITOR, THE MOST LOYAL
OF ALL TRUE KNIGHTS LIES BURIED. What a joke!
So you think you'll avenge yourself on me?
Pulling the statue's beard.

So now you sprout a beard of solid stone,
Good gaffer?

CATALINÓN.   There are beards that can't be plucked.
You watch yourself with beards that are too strong.

DON JUAN, *addressing the statue.*

Tonight I will await you at my inn
For supper. There we can arrange a duel
Although it will be difficult to fight;
A granite rapier must be stiff to handle.

CATALINÓN. Come, sir, it's getting dark. We'd better go!

DON JUAN, *to the statue.*

How long this vengeance seems to be in coming
Especially if you are going to wreak it!
You mustn't be so motionless and sleepy!
And if you're willing still to wait till death,
Why, what a lot of chances you are wasting
That for so long a time you give me credit!

A room in an inn

Two servants of DON JUAN *are laying the table.*

FIRST SERVANT. We must prepare the room because Don Juan
Dines here tonight.

SECOND SERVANT.   The tables are prepared.
If he's so late there's nothing one can do
But let the drinks warm and the food grow cold.
But who could order order from Don Juan,
The ace of all disorder?

Enter DON JUAN *and* CATALINÓN.

DON JUAN.   You've locked the doors?

CATALINÓN. I've locked the doors exactly as you ordered.

DON JUAN. Then bring my supper, quick.

FIRST SERVANT.   It's here already.

DON JUAN. Catalinón, sit down.

CATALINÓN.   I sup more slowly.

DON JUAN. Sit down, I tell you.

CATALINÓN.   Well, if you insist.

FIRST SERVANT, *aside.* He must be on a journey, now, as well,
To sup with his own lackey.

DON JUAN.   Come, sit down.

A loud knock is heard on the door.

CATALINÓN. Say, that's some knock!

DON JUAN.   It must be someone calling.
See who it is.

FIRST SERVANT. I fly, sir, to obey you.

CATALINÓN. What if the police have come?

DON JUAN.   What if they have?
No need for fear!

FIRST SERVANT *enters, fleeing in terror.*

                    What's this? You're all atremble.

CATALINÓN. He has seen something evil. One can tell it.

DON JUAN. Don't make me lose my temper. Speak, man, speak!
What have you seen? Some devil's terrified you?
Go, you, and see whatever's at the door.
Go on! Go, quick!

CATALINÓN.   Who, I?

DON JUAN.   Yes, you, at once.
Yes, you, get your feet moving. Aren't you going?

CATALINÓN. Who's got the keys?

SECOND SERVANT.   Only the bolt is slid.

DON JUAN. What's wrong with you then? Move! Why don't
    you go?

CATALINÓN. What if the raped and ravished have arrived
To have their final vengeance?

He goes out to see.

CATALINÓN *rushes back in panic, trips, falls over, and
gets up.*

DON JUAN.   What's all this?

CATALINÓN. God help me! You can kill me if you like.

DON JUAN. Who's killing you? What is it? What have you seen?

CATALINÓN. Master . . . there . . . I saw . . . well, when I
    got there . . .
Aside.
But what has seized me? What has snatched my mind?
Aloud.
I got there to the door . . . then after, I was blind . . .

But there I saw . . . I swear to God . . . I saw it . . .
I spoke and said: "Who are you?" And he answered.
I opened, went ahead, and bumped into—

DON JUAN. Well, who? Bumped into who?

CATALINÓN.   Oh, don't ask *me!*

DON JUAN. How wine confuses people! Here! That candle!
I'll go and see myself who it can be.

DON JUAN *takes the candle and goes towards the door.* DON
GONZALO *walks in to meet him in the form of the statue
that was on the sepulchre.* DON JUAN *staggers backwards
in a state of perturbation, holding his sword by the hilt.
In the other hand he carries a candle.* DON GONZALO
advances towards him with slow, short steps, and DON
JUAN *retreats before him till they reach the middle of the
stage.*

DON JUAN. Who's this?

DON GONZALO.   It's I.

DON JUAN.   But who on earth are you?

DON GONZALO. The person you invited here to dine.

DON JUAN. Why, there's enough for both of us, and more,
If you've brought any friends along with you.
The table's set already. Sit down here.

CATALINÓN. May God be with me now in my sore need
With Saint Panuncio and Saint Antón.
What? Do the dead eat too?
Aside.

                    He nods in answer.

DON JUAN. Catalinón, sit down with us.

CATALINÓN.   Excuse me:
I take it that he's dined.

DON JUAN.   You've lost your head.
Are you afraid of a dead man? What then?
If he were living, how much more you'd fear him!
What an illiterate and rustic fear!

CATALINÓN. Dine with your guest, sir. I have supped already.

DON JUAN. You wish to make me angry?

CATALINÓN.   Sir, I stink

And that's the reason I would not offend you.
I smell too bad.

DON JUAN.   Sit down! I'm waiting for you.

CATALINÓN, *aside.* I'm dead with fear. My bum has mis-
behaved.

The two servants are trembling with fear.

DON JUAN. You others there! What about you? You're trembling?

CATALINÓN. I never liked to eat with foreigners
Who come from other countries. Me, my lord—
You'd have me feasting with a guest of stone?

DON JUAN. What stupid fear! If he is stone, what matter?

CATALINÓN. It knocks me all to pieces all the same!

DON JUAN. Speak to him courteously.

CATALINÓN.   Sir, are you well?
That "other life," is it a pleasant country?
What is it like—all plains? Or steep sierras?
Do they give prizes there for poetry?

FIRST SERVANT. To every question he has nodded: Yes.

CATALINÓN. And are there lots of taverns there? Why, surely,
If Noah lives around there, there must be!

DON JUAN. Fetch wine.

CATALINÓN.   Señor Dead Man, say, in your country,
Do the drinks there have ice in?

DON GONZALO nods.

                              Ah! with ice!
What a good country!

DON JUAN.   If you want a song
I'll make them sing.

DON GONZALO nods.

                    Then sing!

CATALINÓN.   The Señor Dead Man
Has real good taste.

FIRST SERVANT.   He's nobly bred, and so
He is a friend of pleasure, naturally.

They sing within.

If you expect it of us men
That our deserts shall find adjusting
But not till after death, why then,
A long, long time you are for trusting!

CATALINÓN. Either he finds the heat is overpowering
Or else he is a man who eats but little.
I cannot keep from trembling at my dinner.
It seems that they don't drink much over there
And so I'll drink, for both of us

Drinks.

a pledge
Of stone. I feel less terrified already.

They go on singing within.

If that's the date you ladies give
To enjoy all for whom I'm lusting
You grant a long long time to live
And burnish up my joys from rusting.

If you expect it of us men
That our deserts shall find adjusting
But not till after death, why then
A long, long time you are for trusting!

CATALINÓN. Of which of all the ladies you have cheated
Do they make mention?

DON JUAN.   I laugh at them all,
My friend, on this occasion. Why, in Naples
With Isabel . . .

CATALINÓN.   She's not so badly cheated
Since you will have to marry her, quite rightly.
But that poor girl who saved you from the sea,
You treated in a pretty sorry fashion.
You cheated Doña Ana.

DON JUAN.   Hold your jaw!
For here is someone who has suffered for her
And waits for his revenge.

CATALINÓN.   He is a man
Of mighty valour, being made of stone,
And you of flesh. It's not a pleasant problem.

DON GONZALO *makes a sign for the table to be cleared, and for* DON JUAN *and himself to be left alone together.*

DON JUAN. Here, clear this table, since he's making signs
The rest should go and leave us both together.

CATALINÓN. It's bad! For God's sake, master, don't remain!
For here's a dead man that with one sole fist-cuff
Could floor a giant.

DON JUAN.   All of you, get out!
Were I Catalinón, then I might flinch.
But go; for he approaches.

The servants go out, and DON JUAN *and* DON GONZALO *remain alone together.* DON GONZALO *signs to* DON JUAN *to close the door.*

DON JUAN.   The door's shut
And I am at your service. What's your will,
Shade, vision, or phantasma? If your soul
Is travailing in pain, if you await
Some satisfaction or relief, then tell me,
And I will give my word to do whatever
You should command me. Are you in the grace
Of God? Or was it that I killed you recklessly
In a state of mortal sin? Speak! I am anxious.

DON GONZALO, *speaking slowly, as if from another world.*
And as a gentleman you'll keep your word?

DON JUAN. I keep my word with men, being a knight.

DON GONZALO. Then give your hand on it. Don't be afraid!

DON JUAN. What! *Me* afraid? Were you both hell and death,
I'd dare to give my hand.

He gives his hand.

DON GONZALO. Now lower both your hand and voice. To-
morrow
At ten, *I'll* be awaiting *you* for supper.
You'll come?

DON JUAN.   Why, I expected something far
More dangerous than what you ask of me.
Tomorrow I shall be your guest. But where?

DON GONZALO. In my side-chapel, by my tomb.

DON JUAN.   Alone?

DON GONZALO. No, you can bring your servant. And you'll honour
  Your word, as I have done the same to you?

DON JUAN. Of course. I am Tenorio born and bred.

DON GONZALO. And I a born Ulloa.

DON JUAN.   I'll be there,
  And without fail.

DON GONZALO.   I trust your word. Good-bye.

  He goes towards the door.

DON JUAN. Wait, let me get a torch to light your way!

DON GONZALO. My soul requires no light. I am in grace.

  He retires very, very slowly, looking at DON JUAN, *until he
  disappears, leaving* DON JUAN *in a state of panic.*

DON JUAN. God save me, all my body's bathed in sweat!
  My very heart seems frozen here inside.
  For when he took me by the hand and squeezed it
  It seemed I was in hell. Such was the heat.
  And yet his breath and voice were like the blizzard
  Of an infernal frost. But all these things,
  Begot by fear on the imagination,
  Are quite unreal. To fear the dead is baseness.
  If I am not afraid of noble bodies
  With all their powers, alive with wits and reason,
  To fear dead bodies is a stupid thing.
  Tomorrow I will go there to the chapel
  Where it invited me, that all of Seville
  May make a living legend of my valour.

The Alcazar at Seville

Enter the KING OF CASTILE, DON DIEGO TENORIO, *and their
suite.*

KING OF CASTILE. So Isabela has arrived at last.

DON DIEGO. Against her will.

KING OF CASTILE.   She does not like this marriage?

DON DIEGO. She feels the worst at losing her good name.

KING OF CASTILE. It is some other cause that thus torments her.
   Where is she?

DON JUAN.   She has taken up her lodging
   With the Barefooted Nuns.

KING OF CASTILE.   Then fetch her here
   And at her leisure she may serve the queen.

DON DIEGO. And if her marriage must be with Don Juan,
   Then, please, command it, that he may appear.

KING OF CASTILE. Yes, let him come here, full-dressed as a
      bridegroom!
   I'll have this marriage famed throughout the land.
   For from today Don Juan is the Count
   Of Lebrija: to rule it and possess it.
   If Isabel has lost a duke, her equal,
   At least she's won a most outstanding count.

DON DIEGO. For this great kindness I could kiss your feet.

KING OF CASTILE. You have deserved my favours worthily.
   I still am far behindhand in requiting
   Your services. It seems, too, that today
   The Lady Ana should be wedded also.

DON DIEGO. What! with Octavio?

KING OF CASTILE.   Should it not be
   That Duke Octavio must save the shame
   Of this great scandal? Doña Ana and the queen
   Have begged the marquis' life, and now the father
   Is dead, she wants a husband of her choice.
   So now she loses one and wins the other.
   Go to Triana's fort, and tell the marquis
   That for his injured cousin's sake he's pardoned.

DON DIEGO. Now I have seen what most I have desired!

KING OF CASTILE. This evening, then, the weddings will take
      place.

DON DIEGO. All's well that ends well. It should be easy to
   Convince the marquis he was greatly loved
   By his fair cousin.

KING OF CASTILE.   Also, warn Octavio:

The duke is always luckless with his women.
For him they're all appearances and rumours.
They say he's furious against Don Juan.

DON DIEGO. I shouldn't be surprised, since he found out
The truth about that dirty trick he played
Which has done so much damage on all sides.
Here comes the duke.

KING OF CASTILE.   Don't leave my side at all,
For in this crime you, too, are implicated.

Enter OCTAVIO.

OCTAVIO. Give me your feet, unconquered Majesty!

KING OF CASTILE. Rise, Duke. Put on your hat. What is your
trouble?

OCTAVIO. I come to ask a right that should be granted.

KING OF CASTILE. Duke, if it's just, I swear to grant it. Name it.

OCTAVIO. Already, sire, you know by letters from
Your own ambassador, and the whole world
Knows by the tongue of rumour, how Don Juan,
With Spanish arrogance in Naples lately
In my own name defiled the sacred virtue
Of a great lady.

KING OF CASTILE.   Don't go any further!
I know of your misfortune. What's your plea?

OCTAVIO. To fight it out with him in open country
For he's a traitor.

DON DIEGO.   No, his blood's too noble!

KING OF CASTILE. Don Diego!

DON DIEGO.   Sire!

OCTAVIO.   Why, who are you who speak
Before the king in such a fashion?

DON DIEGO.   I
Am one who holds his peace when the king bids it.
Otherwise I would answer with this sword.

OCTAVIO. You're far too old!

DON DIEGO.   I once was young in Italy.
My sword was known from Naples to Milan.

OCTAVIO. Your blood is frozen. "I was once" is nothing
  To: "I am now."

DON DIEGO.   I am both "was" and "am."

KING OF CASTILE. Come, come, restrain yourselves! Enough!
  Be silent, Don Diego. For my person
  You have shown disrespect. As for you, Duke,
  After the marriages are celebrated
  We'll speak of this affair at greater leisure.
  Don Juan's my creation and my henchman,
  And of this trunk a branch. So keep your distance!

OCTAVIO. Your Majesty, I'll do as you command.

KING OF CASTILE. Come, Don Diego.

DON DIEGO, *aside*.   Oh, my son, my son,
  How badly you repay the love I bear you!

KING OF CASTILE. Duke!

OCTAVIO.   Sire!

KING OF CASTILE.   Tomorrow we shall have you
  married.

OCTAVIO. So be it, if it is Your Highness' wish.

  Exeunt KING, DON DIEGO, *and their suite.*

  Enter GASENO *and* AMINTA.

GASENO. This gentleman may tell us where to find
  Don Juan Tenorio. Is he round about?

OCTAVIO. You really mean Don Juan Tenorio?

AMINTA. Yes, that's the one I mean, and no mistake.

OCTAVIO. Oh yes. He's here. What do you want with him?

AMINTA. Why, that young man's my bridegroom. Yes, he is.

OCTAVIO. What's that?

AMINTA.   You, being of the palace, haven't
  Yet heard of it? That's strange.

OCTAVIO.   He didn't tell me.

GASENO. Can that be possible?

OCTAVIO.   Well, so it seems.

GASENO. Lady Aminta is most honourable,
  And now they're marrying. She is by lineage
  One of the ancient Christians, pure Spanish,

And is the heir to our own cattle-farm
Which we rule just like counts or marquises.
Don Juan took her from Batricio
And was betrothed to her.

OCTAVIO, *aside.*   This is another
Of his foul tricks, and for my own revenge
They're giving it away.

To GASENO.

What is your wish?

GASENO. I want to see the marriage celebrated
Because the time is passing. Otherwise
I'll take it to the king.

OCTAVIO.   And very justly too.

GASENO. All I require is reason and just law.

OCTAVIO, *aside.* It just fits in, in keeping with my thoughts.
Aloud.

Today there is a wedding in the palace.

AMINTA. Why then, it must be mine!

OCTAVIO.   To make quite sure,
I have a little plan. You come with me,
Lady, where you'll be dressed in courtly fashion
Then into the king's quarters go with me.

AMINTA. Give me your hand and lead me to Don Juan.

OCTAVIO. This is a wise precaution.

GASENO.   Reason prompts it.

OCTAVIO, *aside.* So these good people give me my revenge
Against that traitor villain, base Don Juan,
And his foul injuries to Isabel.

*A street in full view of the church wherein the commander
is buried*

Enter DON JUAN *and* CATALINÓN.

CATALINÓN. How did the king receive you?

DON JUAN. Lovingly.
As if he were my father.

CATALINÓN. Did you see
The Duchess Isabel?

DON JUAN. Yes. Her also.

CATALINÓN. How did she seem?

DON JUAN. An angel.

CATALINÓN. She received you
Courteously?

DON JUAN. Her face seemed bathed in milk
And blushing with her blood like a white rose
With all its dews lit by the red aurora.

CATALINÓN. And so the wedding is this evening, sir?

DON JUAN. Yes, without fail.

CATALINÓN. If it had been before
Perhaps you'd not have harmed so many women.
But now you take a wife with heavy charges
And grave responsibilities.

DON JUAN. Are you being
Impertinent and stupid once again?

CATALINÓN. You might at least have waited till tomorrow.
Today's unlucky!

DON JUAN. What day is it?

CATALINÓN. Tuesday.
"Never travel or get married on a
Tuesday."

DON JUAN. Oh, to hell with all that nonsense
Which only fools and madmen take to heart!
That day alone's unlucky, cursed, and foul
When I run out of money. Other days,
All other days, are revelry and laughter.

CATALINÓN. Come, let us go, for you must dress in style.
They're waiting for you now and it grows late.

DON JUAN. We have another business first at hand.
So they'll just have to wait.

CATALINÓN. What other business?

DON JUAN. To sup with the Dead Man.

CATALINÓN.   What need for that?

DON JUAN. Well, don't you know I gave my word upon it?

CATALINÓN. And if you broke it, sir, what could it matter?
A jasper figure can't expect so much
From a live man as to insist on vows.

DON JUAN. The Dead Man, then, could say I was a coward.

CATALINÓN. But anyway you see the church is shut.

DON JUAN. Knock, then.

CATALINÓN.   What does it matter if I knock?
There's nobody to open it inside
And all the sacristans are sleeping.

DON JUAN.   Knock!
Here at this postern.

CATALINÓN.   It is open.

DON JUAN.   Enter.

CATALINÓN. Let friars enter with their stoles and hyssops!

DON JUAN. Then follow me and hold your tongue. Be silent.

CATALINÓN. Silent?

DON JUAN.   Yes.

CATALINÓN.   I am silent. Oh, my God,
Please bring me out alive from such a feast!
They go out on one side and will come in on the other.

Interior of the church

Enter DON JUAN *and* CATALINÓN.

CATALINÓN. It's very dark for such a great big church.
Oh, sir, protect me, someone grabbed my cloak!
DON GONZALO *comes in as before in the form of a statue.*

DON JUAN. Who's that?

DON GONZALO.   It is I.

CATALINÓN.   I am dead with fright!

DON GONZALO. I am the Dead Man: do not be afraid.

I did not think that you would keep your word
Since you delight in breaking it so often—

DON JUAN. I suppose that you imagine me a coward!

DON GONZALO. Why, yes! Because, that night, you fled from me
When you killed me.

DON JUAN.   I fled from recognition.
But here I stand before you. What's your will?

DON GONZALO. Why, only to invite you here to supper.

CATALINÓN. Pray let us be excused. Here all the victuals
They serve are cold—cold supper and cold lunches.

DON JUAN. We'll sup then.

DON GONZALO.   Well, to do so, you must lift
The lid, here, off this tomb.

DON JUAN.   Why, if you wish it
I'll lift these pillars too!

DON GONZALO.   You're very willing.

DON JUAN, *lifting by one end the lid of the tomb which
folds back easily, leaving discovered a black table already
laid and set.*

DON JUAN. Yes, I have strength and courage in my body.

CATALINÓN. This table must have come from Guinea's coast
It is so black. Are there none here to wash it?

DON GONZALO. Be seated.

DON JUAN.   Where?

CATALINÓN.   See two black servants come
With stools

Enter two figures in black with stools.

                    So here, too, people go in mourning
With flannel made in Flanders?

DON JUAN.   You! Sit down!

CATALINÓN. What, me, sir? I've already fed this evening.

DON JUAN. Don't answer back!

CATALINÓN.   All right, I will not answer.
Aside.

O God, in safety get me out of this!

Aloud.

What dish is this?

DON GONZALO.   Tarantulas and vipers.

CATALINÓN. Really? How nice!

DON GONZALO.   That is our diet here.
But you're not eating.

DON JUAN.   I shall eat it
Were all the snakes in hell upon one plate.

DON GONZALO. I'd like to have them sing to you a little.

CATALINÓN. What sort of wine do they have here?

DON GONZALO.   There, taste it.

CATALINÓN. Vinegar, frost, and ice. That's what this wine is!

DON GONZALO. Well, that's the sort of wine that we press here.

They sing within.

> Let all those know who judge God's ways
> And treat his punishments with scorn
> There is no debt but that he pays,
> No date but it is bound to dawn.

CATALINÓN. How terrible! I've heard this tune before
And now it is addressed to me.

DON JUAN, *aside.*   My breast
Is frozen, and the ice tears me apart.

They sing.

> While in the world one's flesh is lusting
> It is most wrong for men to say:
> "A long long time in me you're trusting"
> For very shortly dawns the day.

CATALINÓN. What is this: fricassee?

DON GONZALO.   Of fingernails.

CATALINÓN. Then they must be the fingernails of tailors
They are so sharp and claw-like and rapacious.

DON JUAN. Now I have eaten, let them clear the table.

DON GONZALO. Give me your hand. Don't be afraid! Your hand.

DON JUAN. Afraid, you say. *Me* frightened? Here's my hand.

He gives it.

I'm roasting, burning! Do not burn me so
With your fierce fire!

DON GONZALO.   That's nothing to the fire
Which you have sought yourself! The wondrous ways
Of God, Don Juan, are not fathomable.
And so He wishes now for you to pay
Your forfeits straight into the hands of death.
This is God's justice. What you've done, you pay for.

DON JUAN. I'm roasting. Do not grip my hand so hard!
I'll kill you with this dagger. But the blows
Strike only empty air. Look. With your daughter
I did no harm. She saw the hoax in time.

DON GONZALO. That does not matter. It was your intention.

DON JUAN. Then let me send for a confessor quickly,
So to absolve my soul before I die.

DON GONZALO. Impossible. You've thought of it too late.

DON JUAN. Oh, I am burning! Oh, I am roasting, burning!
I'm dying!

He falls dead.

CATALINÓN. There is no escape. I, too,
Must die for having been your companion.

DON GONZALO. Such is God's justice. What is done is paid for.

The tomb sinks with a rumbling thunder, taking DON JUAN
and DON GONZALO *with it.* CATALINÓN *creeps out of the
wreckage.*

CATALINÓN. So help me God! What's this? The chapel's burning
With wondrous light. And I'm left with the corpse
To watch with it and guard it. To his father
I'll creep away now and proclaim the news.
Saint George and Holy Lamb of God protect me
That I may come in safety to the street!

The Alcazar

Enter the KING OF CASTILE, DON DIEGO, *courtiers, and attendants.*

DON DIEGO. The marquis wants to kiss your royal feet.

KING OF CASTILE. Then let him enter. Call the Count Don Juan
As well, that he be kept no longer waiting.

Enter BATRICIO *and* GASENO.

BATRICIO. Where are such foul monstrosities permitted
That your own servants should affront, unpunished,
The humble people?

KING OF CASTILE.   What is that you say?

BATRICIO. Don Juan Tenorio, treacherous, detestable,
Stole my young wife the evening of our marriage,
And here I have the witnesses.

Enter THISBE *and* ISABEL.

THISBE. Sire, if Your Highness will not do me justice
On Don Juan Tenorio, both to God and men
I will complain through all my days to come!
When dying he was swept ashore, I gave him
Both life and hospitality. With lust
And promises of marriage he repaid
This kindness. He abused me and then left me.

KING OF CASTILE. What do you say?

ISABEL.   She's telling you the truth.

Enter AMINTA *and the* DUKE OCTAVIO.

AMINTA. Where is my spouse?

KING OF CASTILE.   Who is he?

AMINTA.   What, you don't
Know, even yet? Don Juan Tenorio,
With whom I've come this evening to be wedded,
Because he owes it to my name and honour
And, being noble, will not break his word.

Enter the MARQUIS OF LA MOTA.

MARQUIS. It's time to drag some truths into the light,
My lord. Know then that of the selfsame crime
For which you sentenced me, Don Juan is guilty
(A cruel fraud to put on a best friend)
And I've the witnesses to prove it here.

KING OF CASTILE. Could any shamelessness compare to this?

DON DIEGO. Sire, to reward my services to you,
Let him be made to expiate his crime
So that the heavens themselves don't shoot their lightning
At me, for having bred so foul a son.

KING OF CASTILE. So it is thus my favourites behave!

Enter CATALINÓN.

CATALINÓN. My lords, all listen to the greatest wonder
That ever happened in this world, and kill me
If, listening, you don't believe it's true.
Don Juan, making fun of the commander,
Having divested him of life and honour,
And all the gems and ornaments of life,
Pulling the beard upon his granite statue,
Insulted him by asking him to dine.
Oh, that he'd never done so! Then the statue
Went to his house, inviting him in turn,
And then (to make it short, and not to tire you)
When they had finished supper, took his hand
And squeezed it till he squeezed his life out, saying:
"God ordered me to kill you thus, and punish
Your monstrous crimes. For what you've done, you pay."

KING OF CASTILE. What are you saying?

CATALINÓN.   It's the gospel truth.
Don Juan pleaded, first, that he had not
Seduced the Lady Ana: she discovered
The fraud in time.

MARQUIS.   For this delightful news
A thousand gifts I wish to give you.

KING OF CASTILE. Just punishment from Heaven has been dealt.
Now let them all be married, since the cause
Of all their harm is dead.

OCTAVIO.   Since Isabela's
A widow now, I wish to marry her.

MARQUIS. And I to wed my cousin.

BATRICIO.   And us others
With our own girls. For now THE GUEST OF STONE
Is ended.

KING OF CASTILE. Take the tomb to San Francisco,
The great church in Madrid, and there install it
And so preserve this memory through all time.

LIFE IS A DREAM

.

Calderón de la Barca

English Version by Roy Campbell

DRAMATIS PERSONAE

BASIL, *King of Poland*
SEGISMUND, *Prince*
ASTOLFO, *Duke of Muscovy*
CLOTALDO, *old man*
CLARION, *a comical servant*
ROSAURA, *a lady*
STELLA, *a princess*
Soldiers, guards, musicians, servants, retinues, women

The scene is laid in the court of Poland, a nearby fortress, and the open country.

ACT I

On one side a craggy mountain: on the other a rude tower
whose base serves as a prison for SEGISMUND. *The door facing*
the spectators is open. The action begins at nightfall.

ROSAURA, *dressed as a man, appears on the rocks climbing*
down to the plain: behind her comes CLARION.

ROSAURA. You headlong hippogriff who match the gale
   In rushing to and fro, you lightning-flicker
   Who give no light, you scaleless fish, you bird
   Who have no coloured plumes, you animal
   Who have no natural instinct, tell me whither
   You lead me stumbling through this labyrinth
   Of naked crags! Stay here upon this peak
   And be a Phaëthon to the brute-creation!
   For I, pathless save only for the track
   The laws of destiny dictate for me,
   Shall, blind and desperate, descend this height
   Whose furrowed brows are frowning at the sun.
   How rudely, Poland, you receive a stranger
   (Hardly arrived, but to be treated hardly)
   And write her entry down in blood with thorns.
   My plight attests this well, but after all,
   Where did the wretchèd ever pity find?

CLARION. Say *two* so wretchèd. Don't you leave me out
   When you complain! If we two sallied out
   From our own country, questing high adventure,
   And after so much madness and misfortune
   Are still two here, and were two when we fell
   Down those rough crags—shall I not be offended
   To share the trouble yet forego the credit?

ROSAURA. I did not give you shares in my complaint
   So as not to rob you of the right to sorrow
   Upon your own account. There's such relief
   In venting grief that a philosopher

Once said that sorrows should not be bemoaned
But sought for pleasure.

CLARION.   Philosopher?
I call him a long-bearded, drunken sot
And would they'd cudgelled him a thousand blows
To give him something worth his while lamenting!
But, madam, what should we do, by ourselves,
On foot and lost at this late hour of day,
Here on this desert mountain far away—
The sun departing after fresh horizons?

ROSAURA. Clarion, how can I answer, being both
The partner of your plight and your dilemma?

CLARION. Would anyone believe such strange events?

ROSAURA. If there my sight is not deceived by fancy,
In the last timid light that yet remains
I seem to see a building.

CLARION.   Either my hopes
Are lying or I see the signs myself.

ROSAURA. Between the towering crags, there stands so small
A royal palace that the lynx-eyed sun
Could scarce perceive it at midday, so rude
In architecture that it seems but one
Rock more down-toppled from the sun-kissed crags
That form the jaggèd crest.

CLARION.   Let's go closer,
For we have stared enough: it would be better
To let the inmates make us welcome.

ROSAURA.   See:
The door, or, rather, that funereal gap,
Is yawning wide—whence night itself seems born,
Flowing out from its black, rugged centre.

A sound of chains is heard.

CLARION. Heavens! What's that I hear?

ROSAURA.   I have become
A block immovable of ice and fire.

CLARION. Was that a little chain? Why, I'll be hanged
If that is not the clanking ghost of some
Past galley-slave—my terror proves it is!

SEGISMUND. Oh, miserable me! Unhappy me!

ROSAURA. How sad a cry that is! I fear new trials
And torments.

CLARION.   It's a fearful sound.

ROSAURA.   Oh, come,
My Clarion, let us fly from suffering!

CLARION. I'm in such sorry trim, I've not the spirit
Even to run away.

ROSAURA.   And if you had,
You'd not have seen that door, not known of it.
When one's in doubt, the common saying goes
One walks between two lights.

CLARION.   I'm the reverse.
It's not that way with me.

ROSAURA.   What then disturbs you?

CLARION. I walk in doubt between two darknesses.

ROSAURA. Is not that feeble exhalation there
A light? That pallid star whose fainting tremors,
Pulsing a doubtful warmth of glimmering rays,
Make even darker with its spectral glow
That gloomy habitation? Yes! because
By its reflection (though so far away)
I recognise a prison, grim and sombre,
The sepulchre of some poor living carcase.
And, more to wonder at, a man lies there
Clothed in the hides of savage beasts, with limbs
Loaded with fetters, and a single lamp
For company. So, since we cannot flee,
Let us stay here and listen to his plaint
And what his sorrows are.

SEGISMUND.   Unhappy me!
Oh, miserable me! You heavens above,
I try to think what crime I've done against you
By being born. Although to have been born,
I know, is an offence, and with just cause
I bear the rigours of your punishment:
Since to be born is man's worst crime. But yet
I long to know (to clarify my doubts)

What greater crime, apart from being born,
Can thus have earned my greater chastisement.
Aren't others born like me? And yet they seem
To boast a freedom that I've never known.
The bird is born, and in the hues of beauty
Clothed with its plumes, yet scarce has it become
A feathered posy—or a flower with wings—
When through ethereal halls it cuts its way,
Refusing the kind shelter of its nest.
And I, who have more soul than any bird,
Must have less liberty?
The beast is born, and with its hide bright-painted,
In lovely tints, has scarce become a spangled
And starry constellation (thanks to the skilful
Brush of the Painter) than its earthly needs
Teach it the cruelty to prowl and kill,
The monster of its labyrinth of flowers.
Yet I, with better instincts than a beast,
Must have less liberty?
The fish is born, the birth of spawn and slime,
That does not even live by breathing air.
No sooner does it feel itself a skiff
Of silver scales upon the wave than swiftly
It roves about in all directions taking
The measure of immensity as far
As its cold blood's capacity allows.
Yet I, with greater freedom of the will,
Must have less liberty?
The brook is born, and like a snake unwinds
Among the flowers. No sooner, silver serpent,
Does it break through the blooms than it regales
And thanks them with its music for their kindness,
Which opens to its course the majesty
Of the wide plain. Yet I, with far more life,
Must have less liberty?
This fills me with such passion, I become
Like the volcano Etna, and could tear
Pieces of my own heart out of my breast!
What law, justice, or reason can decree
That man alone should never know the joys

And be alone excepted from the rights
God grants a fish, a bird, a beast, a brook?

ROSAURA. His words have filled me full of fear and pity.

SEGISMUND. Who is it overheard my speech? Clotaldo?

CLARION. Say "yes!"

ROSAURA.   It's only a poor wretch, alas,
Who in these cold ravines has overheard
Your sorrows.

SEGISMUND.   Then I'll kill you

Seizes her.

So as to leave no witness of my frailty.
I'll tear you into bits with these strong arms!

CLARION. I'm deaf. I wasn't able to hear that.

ROSAURA. If you were human born, it is enough
That I should kneel to you for you to spare me.

SEGISMUND. Your voice has softened me, your presence halted
      me,
And now, confusingly, I feel respect
For you. Who are you? Though here I have learned
So little of the world, since this grim tower
Has been my cradle and my sepulchre;
And though since I was born (if you can say
I really have been born) I've only seen
This rustic desert where in misery
I dwell alone, a living skeleton,
An animated corpse; and though till now,
I never spoke, save to one man who hears
My griefs and through whose converse I have heard
News of the earth and of the sky; and though,
To astound you more, and make you call me
A human monster, I dwell here, and am
A man of the wild animals, a beast
Among the race of men; and though in such
Misfortune, I have studied human laws,
Instructed by the birds, and learned to measure
The circles of the gentle stars, you only
Have curbed my furious rage, amazed my vision,
And filled with wonderment my sense of hearing.

Each time I look at you, I feel new wonder!
The more I see of you, the more I long
To go on seeing more of you. I think
My eyes are dropsical, to go on drinking
What it is death for them to drink, because
They go on drinking that which I am dying
To see and that which, seen, will deal me death.
Yet let me gaze on you and die, since I
Am so bewitched I can no longer think
What not seeing you would do to me—the sight
Itself being fatal! that would be more hard
Than dying, madness, rage, and fiercest grief:
It would be life—worst fate of all because
The gift of life to such a wretchèd man
Would be the gift of death to happiness!

ROSAURA. Astonished as I look, amazed to hear,
I know not what to say nor what to ask.
All I can say is that heaven guided me
Here to be comforted, if it is comfort
To see another sadder than oneself.
They say a sage philosopher of old,
Being so poor and miserable that he
Lived on the few plain herbs he could collect,
One day exclaimed: "Could any man be poorer
Or sadder than myself?"—when, turning round,
He saw the very answer to his words.
For there another sage philosopher
Was picking up the scraps he'd thrown away.
I lived cursing my fortune in this world
And asked within me: "Is there any other
Suffers so hard a fate?" Now out of pity
You've given me the answer. For within me
I find upon reflection that my griefs
Would be as joys to you and you'd receive them
To give you pleasure. So if they perchance
In any measure may afford relief,
Listen attentively to my misfortune
And take what is left over for yourself.
I am . . .

CLOTALDO, *within.* Guards of the tower! You sluggards
   Or cowards, you have let two people pass
   Into the prison bounds . . .

ROSAURA.   Here's more confusion!

SEGISMUND. That is Clotaldo, keeper of my prison.
   Are my misfortunes still not at an end?

CLOTALDO. Come. Be alert, and either seize or slay them
   Before they can resist!

VOICES, *within.*   Treason! Betrayal!

CLARION. Guards of the tower who let us pass unhindered,
   Since there's a choice, to seize us would be simpler.

   Enter CLOTALDO *with soldiers. He holds a pistol and they
   all wear masks.*

CLOTALDO, *aside to the soldiers.*
   Cover your faces, all! It's a precaution
   Imperative that nobody should know us
   While we are here.

CLARION.   What's this? A masquerade?

CLOTALDO. O you, who ignorantly passed the bounds
   And limits of this region, banned to all—
   Against the king's decree which has forbidden
   That any should find out the prodigy
   Hidden in these ravines—yield up your weapons
   Or else this pistol, like a snake of metal,
   Will spit the piercing venom of two shots
   With scandalous assault upon the air.

SEGISMUND. Tyrannic master, ere you harm these people
   Let my life be the spoil of these sad bonds
   In which (I swear it by Almighty God)
   I'll sooner rend myself with hands and teeth
   Amid these rocks than see them harmed and mourn
   Their suffering.

CLOTALDO.   Since you know, Segismund,
   That your misfortunes are so huge that, even
   Before your birth, you died by heaven's decree,
   And since you know these walls and binding chains
   Are but the brakes and curbs to your proud frenzies,
   What use is it to bluster?

To the guards.

                  Shut the door
Of this close prison! Hide him in its depths!

SEGISMUND. Ah, heavens, how justly you denied me freedom!
  For like a Titan I would rise against you,
  Pile jasper mountains high on stone foundations
  And climb to burst the windows of the sun!

CLOTALDO. Perhaps you suffer so much pain today
  Just to forestall that feat.

ROSAURA.   Now that I see
  How angry pride offends you, I'd be foolish
  Not to plead humbly at your feet for life.
  Be moved by me to pity. It would be
  Notoriously harsh that neither pride
  Nor humbleness found favour in your eyes!

CLARION. And if neither Humility nor Pride
  Impress you (characters of note who act
  And motivate a thousand mystery plays)
  Let me, here, who am neither proud nor humble,
  But merely something halfway in between,
  Plead to you both for shelter and for aid.

CLOTALDO. Ho, there!

SOLDIER.   Sir?

CLOTALDO.   Take their weapons. Bind their eyes
  So that they cannot see the way they're led.

ROSAURA. This is my sword. To nobody but you
  I yield it, since you're, after all, the chief.
  I cannot yield to one of meaner rank.

CLARION. My sword is such that I will freely give it
  To the most mean and wretched.

To one soldier.

                  Take it, you!

ROSAURA. And if I have to die, I'll leave it to you
  In witness of your mercy. It's a pledge
  Of great worth and may justly be esteemed
  For someone's sake who wore it long ago.

CLOTALDO, *apart*. Each moment seems to bring me new
    misfortune!

ROSAURA. Because of that, I ask you to preserve
    This sword with care. Since if inconstant Fate
    Consents to the remission of my sentence,
    It has to win me honour. Though I know not
    The secret that it carries, I do know
    It has got one—unless I trick myself—
    And prize it just as the sole legacy
    My father left me.

CLOTALDO.   Who then was your father?

ROSAURA. I never knew.

CLOTALDO.   And why have you come here?

ROSAURA. I came to Poland to avenge a wrong.

CLOTALDO, *apart*.
    Sacred heavens!

    On taking the sword he becomes very perturbed.
            What's this? Still worse and worse.
    I am perplexed and troubled with more fears.
    Aloud.
    Tell me: who gave that sword to you?

ROSAURA.   A woman.

CLOTALDO. Her name?

ROSAURA.   A secret I am forced to keep.

CLOTALDO. What makes you think this sword contains a secret?

ROSAURA. That she who gave it to me said: "Depart
    To Poland. There with subtlety and art
    Display it so that all the leading people
    And noblemen can see you wearing it,
    And I know well that there's a lord among them
    Who will both shelter you and grant you favour."
    But, lest he should be dead, she did not name him.

CLOTALDO, *aside*. Protect me, heavens! What is this I hear?
    I cannot say if real or imagined
    But here's the sword I gave fair Violante
    In token that, whoever in the future
    Should come from her to me wearing this sword,

Would find in me a tender father's love.
Alas, what can I do in such a pass,
When he who brings the sword to win my favour
Brings it to find his own red death instead
Arriving at my feet condemned already?
What strange perplexity! How hard a fate!
What an inconstant fortune to be plagued with!
This is my son not only by all signs
But also by the promptings of my heart,
Since, seeing him, my heart seems to cry out
To him, and beat its wings, and, though unable
To break the locks, behaves as one shut in,
Who, hearing noises in the street outside,
Cranes from the window-ledge. Just so, not knowing
What's really happening, but hearing sounds,
My heart runs to my eyes which are its windows
And out of them flows into bitter tears.
Protect me, heaven! What am I to do?
To take him to the king is certain death.
To hide him is to break my sacred oath
And the strong law of homage. From one side
Love of one's own, and from the other loyalty—
Call me to yield. Loyalty to my king
(Why do I doubt?) comes before life and honour.
Then live my loyalty, and let him die!
When I remember, furthermore, he came
To avenge an injury—a man insulted
And unavenged is in disgrace. My son
Therefore he is not, nor of noble blood.
But if some danger has mischanced, from which
No one escapes, since honour is so fragile
That any act can smash it, and it takes
A stain from any breath of air, what more
Could any nobleman have done than he,
Who, at the cost of so much risk and danger,
Comes to avenge his honour? Since he's so brave
He is my son, and my blood's in his veins.
And so betwixt the one doubt and the other,
The most important mean between extremes
Is to go to the king and tell the truth—

That he's my son, to kill, if so he wishes.
Perhaps my loyalty thus will move his mercy
And if I thus can merit a live son
I'll help him to avenge his injury.
But if the king prove constant in his rigour
And deal him death, he'll die in ignorance
That I'm his father.

Aloud to ROSAURA *and* CLARION.

                    Come then, strangers, come!
And do not fear that you have no companions
In your misfortunes, since, in equal doubt,
Tossed between life and death, I cannot guess
Which is the greater evil or the less.

A hall at the royal palace, in court

Enter ASTOLFO *and soldiers at one side: from the other side*
PRINCESS STELLA *and ladies. Military music and salvos.*

ASTOLFO. To greet your excellent bright beams
As brilliant as a comet's rays,
The drums and brasses mix their praise
With those of fountains, birds, and streams.
With sounds alike, in like amaze,
Your heavenly face each voice salutes,
Which puts them in such lively fettle,
The trumpets sound like birds of metal,
The songbirds play like feathered flutes.
And thus they greet you, fair señora—
The salvos, as their queen, the brasses,
As to Minerva when she passes,
The songbirds to the bright Aurora,
And all the flowers and leaves and grasses
As doing homage unto Flora,
Because you come to cheat the day
Which now the night has covered o'er—
Aurora in your spruce array,

Flora in peace, Pallas in war,
But in my heart the queen of May.

STELLA. If human voice could match with acts
You would have been unwise to say
Hyperboles that a few facts
May well refute some other day
Confounding all this martial fuss
With which I struggle daringly,
Since flatteries you proffer thus
Do not accord with what I see.
Take heed that it's an evil thing
And worthy of a brute accursed,
Loud praises with your mouth to sing
When in your heart you wish the worst.

ASTOLFO. Stella, you have been badly misinformed
If you doubt my good faith. Here let me beg you
To listen to my plea and hear me out.
The third Eugtorgius died, the King of Poland.
Basil, his heir, had two fair sisters who
Bore you, my cousin, and myself. I would not
Tire you with all that happened here. You know
Clorilene was your mother who enjoys,
Under a better reign, her starry throne.
She was the elder. Lovely Recisunda
(Whom may God cherish for a thousand years!)
The younger one, my mother and your aunt,
Was wed in Muscovy. Now to return:
Basil has yielded to the feebleness
Of age, loves learnèd study more than women,
Has lost his wife, is childless, will not marry.
And so it comes that you and I both claim
The heirdom of the realm. You claim that you
Were daughter to the elder daughter. I
Say that my being born a man, although
Son of the younger daughter, gives me title
To be preferred. We've told the king, our uncle,
Of both of our intentions. And he answered
That he would judge between our rival claims,
For which the time and place appointed was

Today and here. For that same reason I
Have left my native Muscovy. With that
Intent I come—not seeking to wage war
But so that you might thus wage war on me!
May Love, wise god, make true what people say
(Your "people" is a wise astrologer)
By settling this through your being chosen queen—
Queen and my consort, sovereign of my will;
My uncle crowning you, for greater honour;
Your courage conquering, as it deserves;
My love applauding you, its emperor!

STELLA. To such chivalrous gallantry, my breast
Cannot hold out. The imperial monarchy
I wish were mine only to make it yours—
Although my love is not quite satisfied
That you are to be trusted since your speech
Is somewhat contradicted by that portrait
You carry in the locket round your neck.

ASTOLFO. I'll give you satisfaction as to that.

Drums.

But these loud instruments will not permit it
That sound the arrival of the king and council.

Enter KING BASIL *with his following.*

STELLA. Wise Thales . . .

ASTOLFO.   Learned Euclid . . .

STELLA. Among the signs . . .

ASTOLFO.   Among the stars . . .

STELLA. Where you preside in power . . .

ASTOLFO.   Where you reside . . .

STELLA. And plot their paths . . .

ASTOLFO.   And trace their fiery trails . . .

STELLA. Describing . . .

ASTOLFO.   . . . Measuring and judging them . . .

STELLA. Please read my stars that I, in humble bonds . . .

ASTOLFO. Please read them, so that I in soft embraces . . .

STELLA. May twine as ivy to this tree!

ASTOLFO.   May find
Myself upon my knees before these feet!

BASIL. Come and embrace me, niece and nephew. Trust me,
Since you're both loyal to my loving precepts,
And come here so affectionately both—
In nothing shall I leave you cause to cavil,
And both of you as equals will be treated.
The gravity of what I have to tell
Oppresses me, and all I ask of you
Is silence: the event itself will claim
Your wonderment. So be attentive now,
Belovèd niece and nephew, illustrious courtiers,
Relatives, friends, and subjects! You all know
That for my learning I have merited
The surname of The Learnèd, since the brush
Of great Timanthes, and Lisippus' marbles—
Stemming oblivion (consequence of time)—
Proclaimed me to mankind Basil the Great.
You know the science that I most affect
And most esteem is subtle mathematics
(By which I forestall time, cheat fame itself)
Whose office is to show things gradually.
For when I look my tables up and see,
Present before me, all the news and actions
Of centuries to come, I gain on Time—
Since Time recounts whatever I have said
After I say it. Those snowflaking haloes,
Those canopies of crystal spread on high,
Lit by the sun, cut by the circling moon,
Those diamond orbs, those globes of radiant crystal
Which the bright stars adorn, on which the signs
Parade in blazing excellence, have been
My chiefest study all through my long years.
They are the volumes on whose adamantine
Pages, bound up in sapphire, heaven writes,
In lines of burnished gold and vivid letters,
All that is due to happen, whether adverse
Or else benign. I read them in a flash,
So quickly that my spirit tracks their movements—
Whatever road they take, whatever goal

They aim at. Would to heaven that before
My genius had been the commentary
Writ in their margins, or the index to
Their pages, that my life had been the rubble,
The ruin, and destruction of their wrath,
And that my tragedy in them had ended,
Because, to the unlucky, even their merit
Is like a hostile knife, and he whom knowledge
Injures is but a murderer to himself.
And this I say myself, though my misfortunes
Say it far better, which, to marvel at,
I beg once more for silence from you all.
With my late wife, the queen, I had a son,
Unhappy son, to greet whose birth the heavens
Wore themselves out in prodigies and portents.
Ere the sun's light brought him live burial
Out of the womb (for birth resembles death)
His mother many times, in the delirium
And fancies of her sleep, saw a fierce monster
Bursting her entrails in a human form,
Born spattered with her lifeblood, dealing death,
The human viper of this century!
The day came for his birth, and every presage
Was then fulfilled, for tardily or never
Do the more cruel ones prove false. At birth
His horoscope was such that the bright sun,
Stained in its blood, entered ferociously
Into a duel with the moon above.
The whole earth seemed a rampart for the strife
Of heaven's two lights, who—though not hand-to-hand—
Fought light-to-light to gain the mastery!
The worst eclipse the sun has ever suffered
Since Christ's own death horrified earth and sky.
The whole earth overflowed with conflagrations
So that it seemed the final paroxysm
Of existence. The skies grew dark. Buildings shook.
The clouds rained stones. The rivers ran with blood.
In this delirious frenzy of the sun,
Thus, Segismund was born into the world,
Giving a foretaste of his character

By killing his own mother, seeming to speak thus
By his ferocity: "I am a man,
Because I have begun now to repay
All kindnesses with evil." To my studies
I went forthwith, and saw in all I studied
That Segismund would be the most outrageous
Of all men, the most cruel of all princes,
And impious of all monarchs, by whose acts
The kingdom would be torn up and divided
So as to be a school of treachery
And an academy of vices. He,
Risen in fury, amidst crimes and horrors,
Was born to trample me (with shame I say it)
And make of my grey hairs his very carpet.
Who is there but believes an evil Fate?
And more if he discovers it himself,
For self-love lends its credit to our studies.
So I, believing in the Fates, and in
The havoc that their prophecies predestined,
Determined to cage up this newborn tiger
To see if on the stars we sages have
Some power. I gave out that the prince had died
Stillborn, and, well-forewarned, I built a tower
Amidst the cliffs and boulders of yon mountains
Over whose tops the light scarce finds its way,
So stubbornly their obelisks and crags
Defend the entry to them. The strict laws
And edicts that I published then (declaring
That nobody might enter the forbidden
Part of the range) were passed on that account.
There Segismund lives to this day, a captive,
Poor and in misery, where, save Clotaldo,
His guardian, none have seen or talked to him.
The latter has instructed him in all
Branches of knowledge and in the Catholic faith,
Alone the witness of his misery.
There are three things to be considered now:
Firstly, Poland, that I love you greatly,
So much that I would free you from the oppression
And servitude of such a tyrant king.

He would not be a kindly ruler who
Would put his realm and homeland in such danger.
The second fact that I must bear in mind
Is this: that to deny my flesh and blood
The rights which law, both human and divine,
Concedes, would not accord with Christian charity,
For no law says that, to prevent another
Being a tyrant, I may be one myself,
And if my son's a tyrant, to prevent him
From doing outrage, I myself should do it.
Now here's the third and last point I would speak of,
Namely, how great an error it has been
To give too much belief to things predicted,
Because, even if his inclination should
Dictate some headlong, rash precipitancies,
They may perhaps not conquer him entirely,
For the most accursèd destiny, the most
Violent inclination, the most impious
Planet—all can but influence, not force,
The free will which man holds direct from God.
And so, between one motive and another
Vacillating discursively, I hit
On a solution that will stun you all.
I shall tomorrow, but without his knowing
He is my son—your king—place Segismund
(For that's the name with which he was baptised)
Here on my throne, beneath my canopy,
Yes, in my very place, that he may govern you
And take command. And you must all be here
To swear him fealty as his loyal subjects.
Three things may follow from this test, and these
I'll set against the three which I proposed.
The first is that should the prince prove prudent,
Stable, and benign—thus giving the lie
To all that prophecy reports of him—
Then you'll enjoy in him your rightful ruler
Who was so long a courtier of the mountains
And neighbour to the beasts. Here is the second:
If he prove proud, rash, cruel, and outrageous,
And with a loosened rein gallop unheeding

Across the plains of vice, I shall have done
My duty, and fulfilled my obligation
Of mercy. If I then re-imprison him,
That's incontestably a kingly deed—
Not cruelty but merited chastisement.
The third thing's this: that if the prince should be
As I've described him, then—by the love I feel
For you, my vassals—I shall give you worthier
Rulers to wear the sceptre and the crown;
Because your king and queen will be my nephew
And niece, each with an equal right to rule,
Each gaining the inheritance he merits,
And joined in faith of holy matrimony.
This I command you as a king, I ask you
As a kind father, as a sage I pray you,
As an experienced old man I tell you,
And (if it's true, as Spanish Seneca
Says, that the king is slave unto his nation)
This, as a humble slave, I beg of you.

ASTOLFO. If it behoves me to reply (being
The person most involved in this affair)
Then, in the name of all, let Segismund
Appear! It is enough that he's your son!

ALL. Give us our prince: we want him for our king!

BASIL. Subjects, I thank you for your kindly favour.
Accompany these, my two Atlases,
Back to their rooms. Tomorrow you shall see him.

ALL. Long live the great King Basil! Long live Basil!

Exeunt all, accompanying STELLA *and* ASTOLFO. *The* KING
remains.

Enter CLOTALDO *with* ROSAURA *and* CLARION.

CLOTALDO. May I have leave to speak, sire?

BASIL.   Oh, Clotaldo!
You're very welcome.

CLOTALDO.   Thus to kneel before you
Is always welcome, sire—yet not today
When sad and evil Fate destroys the joy
Your presence normally concedes.

BASIL.   What's wrong?

CLOTALDO. A great misfortune, sire, has come upon me
  Just when I should have met it with rejoicing.

BASIL. Continue.

CLOTALDO.   Sire, this beautiful young man
  Who inadvertently and daringly
  Came to the tower, wherein he saw the prince,
  Is my . . .

BASIL.   Do not afflict yourself, Clotaldo.
  Had it not been just now, I should have minded,
  I must confess. But I've revealed the secret,
  And now it does not matter if he knows it.
  Attend me afterwards. I've many things
  To tell you. You in turn have many things
  To do for me. You'll be my minister,
  I warn you, in the most momentous action
  The world has ever seen. These prisoners, lest you
  Should think I blame your oversight, I'll pardon.

  Exit.

CLOTALDO. Long may you live, great sire! A thousand years!

  Aside.

  Heaven improves our fates. I shall not tell him
  Now that he is my son, since it's not needed
  Till he's avenged.

  Aloud.

  Strangers, you may go free.

ROSAURA. Humbly I kiss your feet.

CLARION.   Whilst I'll just *miss* them—
  Old friends will hardly quibble at one letter.

ROSAURA. You've granted me my life, sir. I remain
  Your servant and eternally your debtor.

CLOTALDO. No! It was not your life I gave you. No!
  Since any wellborn man who, unavenged,
  Nurses an insult does not live at all.
  And seeing you have told me that you came
  For that sole reason, it was not life I spared—
  Life in disgrace is not a life at all.

Aside.

I see this spurs him.

ROSAURA.   Freely I confess it—
Although you spared my life, it was no life.
But I will wipe my honour's stain so spotless
That after I have vanquished all my dangers
Life well may seem a shining gift from you.

CLOTALDO. Take here your burnished steel: 'twill be enough,
Bathed in your enemies' red blood, to right you.
For steel that once was mine (I mean of course
Just for the time I've had it in my keeping)
Should know how to avenge you.

ROSAURA. Now, in your name I gird it on once more
And on it I will swear to take revenge
Although my foe were even mightier.

CLOTALDO. Is he so powerful?

ROSAURA.   So much so that . . .
Although I have no doubt in your discretion . . .
I say no more because I'd not estrange
Your clemency.

CLOTALDO. You would have won me had you told me, since
That would prevent me helping him.

Aside.

If only I could discover who he is!

ROSAURA. So that you'll not think that I value lightly
Such confidence, know that my adversary
Is no less than Astolfo, Duke of Muscovy.

CLOTALDO, *aside.* (I hardly can withstand the grief it gives me
For it is worse than aught I could imagine!
Let us inquire of him some further facts.)

Aloud.

If you were born a Muscovite, your ruler
Could never have affronted you. Go back
Home to your country. Leave this headstrong valour.
It will destroy you.

ROSAURA.   Though he's been my prince,
I know that he has done me an affront.

CLOTALDO. Even though he slapped your face, that's no affront.
Aside.

O heavens!

ROSAURA.   My insult was far deeper!

CLOTALDO.   Tell it:
Since nothing I imagine could be deeper.

ROSAURA. Yes. I will tell it, yet, I know not why,
With such respect I look upon your face,
I venerate you with such true affection,
With such high estimation do I weigh you,
That I scarce dare to tell you—these men's clothes
Are an enigma, not what they appear.
So now you know. Judge if it's no affront
That here Astolfo comes to wed with Stella
Although betrothed to me. I've said enough.
Exeunt ROSAURA *and* CLARION.

CLOTALDO. Here! Listen! Wait! What mazed confusion!
It is a labyrinth wherein the reason
Can find no clue. My family honour's injured.
The enemy's all powerful. I'm a vassal
And she's a woman. Heavens! Show a path
Although I don't believe there is a way!
There's nought but evil bodings in the sky.
The whole world is a prodigy, say I.

ACT II

A Hall in the Royal Palace

Enter BASIL *and* CLOTALDO.

CLOTALDO. All has been done according to your orders.

BASIL. Tell me, Clotaldo, how it went?

CLOTALDO.   Why, thus:
    I took to Segismund a calming drug
    Wherein are mixed herbs of especial virtue,
    Tyrannous in their overpowering strength,
    Which seize and steal and alienate man's gift
    Of reasoning, thus making a live corpse
    Of him. His violence evaporated
    With all his faculties and senses too.
    There is no need to prove it's possible
    Because experience teaches us that medicine
    Is full of natural secrets, that there is no
    Animal, plant, or stone that has not got
    Appointed properties. If human malice
    Explores a thousand poisons which deal death,
    Who then can doubt, that being so, that other
    Poisons, less violent, cause only sleep?
    But (leaving that doubt aside, as proven false
    By every evidence) hear then the sequel:
    I went down into Segismund's close prison
    Bearing the drink wherein, with opium,
    Henbane and poppies had been mixed. With him
    I talked a little while of the humanities,
    In which dumb Nature has instructed him,
    The mountains and the heavens and the stars,
    In whose divine academies he learned
    Rhetoric from the birds and the wild creatures.
    To lift his spirit to the enterprise
    Which you require of him, I chose for subject
    The swiftness of a stalwart eagle, who,

Deriding the base region of the wind,
Rises into the sphere reserved for fire,
A feathered lightning, an untethered comet.
Then I extolled such lofty flight and said:
"After all, he's the king of birds, and so
Takes precedence, by right, over the rest."
No more was needful for, in taking up
Majesty for his subject, he discoursed
With pride and high ambition, as his blood
Naturally moves, incites, and spurs him on
To grand and lofty things, and so he said
That in the restless kingdom of the birds
There should be those who swear obedience, too!
"In this, my miseries console me greatly,
Because if I'm a vassal here, it's only
By force, and not by choice. Of my own will
I would not yield in rank to any man."
Seeing that he grew furious—since this touched
The theme of his own griefs—I gave the potion
And scarcely had it passed from cup to breast
Before he yielded all his strength to slumber.
A chill sweat ran through all his limbs and veins.
Had I not known that this was mere feigned death
I would have thought him dead. Then came the men
To whom you've trusted this experiment,
Who placed him in a coach and brought him here
To your own rooms, where all things were prepared
In royalty and grandeur as befitting
His person. In your own bed they have laid him
Where, when the torpor wanes, they'll do him service
As if he were Your Majesty himself.
All has been done as you have ordered it,
And if I have obeyed you well, my lord,
I'd beg a favour (pardon me this freedom)—
To know what your intention is in thus
Transporting Segismund here to the palace.

BASIL. Your curiosity is just, Clotaldo,
And yours alone I'll satisfy. The star
Which governs Segismund, my son, in life,
Threatens a thousand tragedies and woes.

And now I wish to see whether the stars
(Which never lie—and having shown to us
So many cruel signs seem yet more certain)
May yet be brought to moderate their sentence,
Whether by prudence charmed or valour won,
For man does have the power to rule his stars.
I would examine this, bringing him here
Where he may know he is my son, and make
Trial of his talent. If magnanimously
He conquers and controls himself, he'll reign,
But if he proves a tyrant and is cruel,
Back to his chains he'll go. Now, you will ask,
Why did we bring him sleeping in this manner
For the experiment? I'll satisfy you,
Down to the smallest detail, with my answer.
If he knows that he is my son today,
And if tomorrow he should find himself
Once more reduced to prison, to misery,
He would despair entirely, knowing truly
Who, and whose son, he is. What consolation
Could he derive, then, from his lot? So I
Contrive to leave an exit for such grief,
By making him believe it was a dream.
By these means we may learn two things at once:
First, his character—for he will really be
Awake in all he thinks and all his actions;
Second, his consolation—which would be
(If he should wake in prison on the morrow,
Although he saw himself obeyed today)
That he might understand he had been dreaming,
And he will not be wrong, for in this world,
Clotaldo, all who live are only dreaming.

CLOTALDO. I've proofs enough to doubt of your success,
But now it is too late to remedy it.
From what I can make out, I think he's wakened
And that he's coming this way, by the sound.

BASIL. I shall withdraw. You, as his tutor, go
And guide him through his new bewilderments
By answering his queries with the truth.

CLOTALDO. You give me leave to tell the truth of it?

BASIL. Yes, because knowing all things, he may find
   Known perils are the easiest to conquer.

Exit BASIL.

Enter CLARION.

CLARION. It cost me four whacks to get here so quickly.
   I caught them from a red-haired halberdier
   Sprouting a ginger beard over his livery,
   And I've come to see what's going on.
   No windows give a better view than those
   A man brings with him in his head, not asking
   For tickets of admission or paid seats,
   Since at all functions, festivals, or feasts
   He looks out with the same nice self-composure.

CLOTALDO, *aside*. Here's Clarion who's the servant of that
         person—
   That trader in woes, importer from Poland
   Of my disgrace.

Aloud.

                Come, Clarion, what news?

CLARION. Item the first: encouraged by the fact
   Your clemency's disposed to venge her insult,
   Rosaura has resumed her proper clothing.

CLOTALDO. That's right: it's less indecorous and bold.

CLARION. Item: she's changed her name, and given out
   That she's your niece. And now they've made so much
   Of her that she's been raised to maid of honour
   To the unique and only princess, Stella.

CLOTALDO. That's right: her honour stands to my account.

CLARION. Indeed she merely bides the time till you
   Will settle all accounts about her honour.

CLOTALDO. Biding the time is wise, for in the end
   It's Time that's going to settle all accounts!

CLARION. Item: that she's attended like a queen,
   Because they take her for your niece. Item:
   That I, who trudged along with her, am dying
   Of hunger. Nobody remembers me,

Nor yet remembers that I'm like my name
And (should I sound my Clarion) could tell
All to the king and Stella and Astolfo.
For I am both a Clarion and a servant—
Two things which ill-accord with secrecy.
If silence should, by chance, let slip my hand,
Then there's a chorus which would fit me well:
"Dawn-breaking Clarion plays no better tune!"

CLOTALDO. You've reason for complaint. I'll satisfy it
If you'll but serve me . . .

CLARION.   Hush, here's Segismund!

Enter musicians, singing, and servants arraying SEGISMUND,
who seems amazed.

SEGISMUND. Heavens above! What's this that I am seeing?
I wonder at it all, with naught of fear!
But with a mighty doubt, I disbelieve it!
I?—in a sumptuous palace? I—encircled
With rich brocades and silks? I—overwhelmed
With servants in such brilliant liveries?
I—to awake in such a gorgeous bed?
I—in the middle of so many footmen
Who clothe me in rich garments? I'm awake:
It would be false to take this for a dream.
Am I not Segismund? Heavens! disabuse me
If I'm mistaken. Say, what could have happened
In my imagination while I slept—
That I should find myself in such a place?
But why should I worry, whatever it was?
I'll let myself be served and entertained—
Befall what may.

FIRST SERVANT, *aside to* SECOND SERVANT *and* CLARION.
                            He's very melancholy!

SECOND SERVANT. Who would not be, considering all that's
        happened
To him?

CLARION. I would not be!

SECOND SERVANT.   You, speak to him.

FIRST SERVANT. Shall they begin to sing again?

SEGISMUND.   Why, no,
  I would not have them sing.
SECOND SERVANT.   You're so distraught,
  I wish you entertained.
SEGISMUND.   My griefs are such
  That no mere voices can amuse me now—
  Only the martial music pleased my mind.
CLOTALDO. Your Highness, mighty prince, give me your hand
  To kiss. I'm glad to be the first to offer
  Obedience at your feet.
SEGISMUND, *aside*.   This is Clotaldo.
  How is it he, that tyrannised my thralldom,
  Should now be treating me with such respect?
  Aloud.
  Tell me what's happening all round me here.
CLOTALDO. With the perplexities of your new state,
  Your reason will encounter many doubts,
  But I shall try to free you from them all
  (If that may be) because you now must know
  You are hereditary Prince of Poland.
  If you have been withdrawn from public sight
  Under restraint, it was in strict obedience
  To Fate's inclemency, which will permit
  A thousand woes to fall upon this empire
  The moment that you wear the sovereign's crown.
  But trusting that you'll prudently defeat
  Your own malignant stars (since they can be
  Controlled by magnanimity) you've been
  Brought to this palace from the tower you knew
  Even while your soul was yielded up to sleep.
  My lord the king, your father, will be coming
  To see you, and from him you'll learn the rest.
SEGISMUND. Then, vile, infamous traitor, what have I
  To know more than this fact of who I am,
  To show my pride and power from this day onward?
  How have you played your country such a treason
  As to deny me, against law and right,
  The rank which is my own?

CLOTALDO. Unhappy me!

SEGISMUND. You were a traitor to the law, a flattering liar
To your own king, and cruel to myself.
And so the king, the law, and I condemn you,
After such fierce misfortunes as I've borne,
To die here by my hands.

SECOND SERVANT. My lord!

SEGISMUND. Let none
Get in the way. It is in vain. By God!
If you intrude, I'll throw you through the window.

SECOND SERVANT. Clotaldo, fly!

CLOTALDO. Alas, poor Segismund!
That you should show such pride, all unaware
That you are dreaming this.
Exit.

SECOND SERVANT. Take care! Take care!

SEGISMUND. Get out!

SECOND SERVANT. He was obeying the king's orders.

SEGISMUND. In an injustice, no one should obey
The king, and I'm his prince.

SECOND SERVANT. He had no right
To look into the rights and wrongs of it.

SEGISMUND. You must be mad to answer back at me.

CLARION. The prince is right. It's you who're in the wrong!

SECOND SERVANT. Who gave you right to speak?

CLARION. I simply took it.

SEGISMUND. And who are you?

CLARION. I am the go-between,
And in this art I think I am a master—
Since I'm the greatest jackanapes alive.

SEGISMUND, *to* CLARION.
In all this new world, you're the only one
Of the whole crowd who pleases me.

CLARION. Why, my lord,
I am the best pleaser of Segismunds
That ever was: ask anybody here!

Enter ASTOLFO.

ASTOLFO. Blessèd the day, a thousand times, my prince,
On which you landed here on Polish soil
To fill with so much splendour and delight
Our wide horizons, like the break of day!
For you arise as does the rising sun
Out of the rugged mountains, far away.
Shine forth then! And although so tardily
You bind the glittering laurels on your brows,
The longer may they last you still unwithered.

SEGISMUND. God save you.

ASTOLFO.   That you do not know me, sir,
Is some excuse for greeting me without
The honour due to me. I am Astolfo
The Duke of Muscovy. You are my cousin.
We are of equal rank.

SEGISMUND.   Then if I say,
"God save you," do I not display good feeling?
But since you take such note of who you are,
The next time that I see you, I shall say
"God save you *not*," if you would like that better.

SECOND SERVANT, *to* ASTOLFO.
Your Highness, make allowance for his breeding
Amongst the mountains. So he deals with all.

To SEGISMUND.

Astolfo does take precedence, Your Highness—

SEGISMUND. I have no patience with the way he came
To make his solemn speech, then put his hat on!

SECOND SERVANT. He's a grandee!

SEGISMUND.   I'm grander than grandees!

SECOND SERVANT. For all that, there should be respect between
      you,
More than among the rest.

SEGISMUND.   And who told you
To mix in my affairs?

Enter STELLA.

STELLA. Many times welcome to Your Royal Highness,

Now come to grace the dais that receives him
With gratitude and love. Long may you live
August and eminent, despite all snares,
And count your life by centuries, not years!

SEGISMUND, *aside to* CLARION.

Now tell me, who's this sovereign deity
At whose divinest feet Heaven lays down
The fleece of its aurora in the east?

CLARION. Sir, it's your cousin Stella.

SEGISMUND.   She were better
Named "sun" than "star"!

To STELLA.

                              Though your speech was fair,
Just to have seen you and been conquered by you
Suffices for a welcome in itself.
To find myself so blessed beyond my merit
What can I do but thank you, lovely Stella,
For you could add more brilliance and delight
To the most blazing star? When you get up
What work is left the sun to do? O give me
Your hand to kiss, from out whose cup of snow
The solar horses drink the fires of day!

STELLA. Be a more gentle courtier.

ASTOLFO.   I am lost.

SECOND SERVANT. I know Astolfo's hurt. I must divert him.

To SEGISMUND.

Sir, you should know that thus to woo so boldly
Is most improper. And, besides, Astolfo . . .

SEGISMUND. Did I not tell you not to meddle with me?

SECOND SERVANT. I only say what's just.

SEGISMUND.   All this annoys me.
Nothing seems just to me but what I want.

SECOND SERVANT. Why, sir, I heard you say that no obedience
Or service should be lent to what's unjust.

SEGISMUND. You also heard me say that I would throw
Anyone who annoys me from that balcony.

SECOND SERVANT. With men like me you cannot do such things.

SEGISMUND. No? Well, by God, I'll have to prove it then!
He takes him in his arms and rushes out, followed by many,
to return soon after.

ASTOLFO. What on earth have I seen? Can it be true?

STELLA. Go, all, and stop him!

SEGISMUND, *returning.*   From the balcony
He's fallen in the sea. How strange it seems!

ASTOLFO. Measure your acts of violence, my lord:
From crags to palaces, the distance is
As great as that between man and the beasts.

SEGISMUND. Well, since you are for speaking out so boldly,
Perhaps one day you'll find that on your shoulders
You have no head to place your hat upon.
Exit ASTOLFO.
Enter BASIL.

BASIL. What's happened here?

SEGISMUND.   Nothing at all. A man
Wearied me, so I threw him in the sea.

CLARION, *to* SEGISMUND. Be warned. That is the king.

BASIL.   On the first day,
So soon, your coming here has cost a life?

SEGISMUND. He said I couldn't: so I won the bet.

BASIL. It grieves me, Prince, that, when I hoped to see you
Forewarned, and overriding Fate, in triumph
Over your stars, the first thing I should see
Should be such rigour—that your first deed here
Should be a grievous homicide. Alas!
With what love, now, can I offer my arms,
Knowing your own have learned to kill already?
Who sees a dirk, red from a mortal wound,
But does not fear it? Who can see the place
Soaking in blood, where late a man was murdered,
But even the strongest must respond to nature?
So in your arms seeing the instrument
Of death, and looking on a blood-soaked place,
I must withdraw myself from your embrace,
And though I thought in loving bonds to bind
Your neck, yet fear withholds me from your arms.

SEGISMUND. Without your loving arms I can sustain
     Myself as usual. That such a loving father
     Could treat me with such cruelty, could thrust me
     From his side ungratefully, could rear me
     As a wild beast, could hold me for a monster,
     And pray that I were dead, that such a father
     Withholds his arms from winding round my neck,
     Seems unimportant, seeing that he deprives
     Me of my very being as a man.

BASIL. Would to heaven I had never granted it,
     For then I never would have heard your voice,
     Nor seen your outrages.

SEGISMUND.   Had you denied
     Me being, then I would not have complained,
     But that you took it from me when you gave it—
     That is my quarrel with you. Though to give
     Is the most singular and noble action,
     It is the basest action if one gives
     Only to take away.

BASIL.   How well you thank me
     For being raised from pauper to a prince!

SEGISMUND. In this what is there I should thank you for?
     You tyrant of my will! If you are old
     And feeble, and you die, what can you give me
     More than what is my own by right of birth?
     You are my father and my king, therefore
     This grandeur comes to me by natural law.
     Therefore, despite my present state, I'm not
     Indebted to you, rather can I claim
     Account of all those years in which you robbed me
     Of life and being, liberty, and honour.
     You ought to thank me that I press no claim
     Since you're my debtor, even to bankruptcy.

BASIL. Barbarous and outrageous brute! The heavens
     Have now fulfilled their prophecy: I call
     Them to bear witness to your pride. Although
     You know now, disillusioned, who you are,
     And see yourself where you take precedence,
     Take heed of this I say: be kind and humble

Since it may be that you are only dreaming,
Although it seems to you you're wide-awake.

Exit BASIL.

SEGISMUND. Can I perhaps be dreaming, though I seem
So wide-awake? No: I am not asleep,
Since I can touch, and realise what I
Have been before, and what I am today.
And if you even now relented, Father,
There'd be no cure since I know who I am
And you cannot, for all your sighs and groans,
Cheat me of my hereditary crown.
And if I was submissive in my chains
Before, then I was ignorant of what I am,
Which I now know (and likewise know that I
Am partly man but partly beast as well).

Enter ROSAURA *in woman's clothing.*

ROSAURA, *aside.* I came in Stella's train. I am afraid
Of meeting with Astolfo, since Clotaldo
Says he must not know who I am, not see me,
Because (he says) it touches on my honour.
And well I trust Clotaldo since I owe him
The safety of my life and honour both.

CLARION. What pleases you, and what do you admire
Most, of the things you've seen here in the world?

SEGISMUND. Why, nothing that I could not have foreseen—
Except the loveliness of women! Once,
I read among the books I had out there
That who owes God most grateful contemplation
Is Man: who is himself a tiny world.
But I think who owes God more grateful study
Is Woman—since she is a tiny heaven,
Having as much more beauty than a man
As heaven than earth. And even more, I say,
If she's the one that I am looking at.

ROSAURA, *aside.* That is the prince. I'll go.

SEGISMUND.   Stop! Woman! Wait!
Don't join the sunset with the breaking day
By fading out so fast. If east and west

Should clash like that, the day would surely suffer
A syncope. But what is this I see?

ROSAURA. What I am looking at I doubt, and yet
Believe.

SEGISMUND, *aside*. This beauty I have seen before.

ROSAURA, *aside*. This pomp and grandeur I have seen before
Cooped in a narrow dungeon.

SEGISMUND, *aside*.   I have found
My life at last.

Aloud.

                    Woman (for that sole word
Outsoars all wooing flattery of speech
From one that is a man), woman, who are you?
If even long before I ever saw you
You owed me adoration as your prince,
How much the more should you be conquered by me
Now I recall I've seen you once before!
Who are you, beauteous woman?

ROSAURA, *aside*.   I'll pretend.

Aloud.

In Stella's train, I am a luckless lady.

SEGISMUND. Say no such thing. You are the sun from which
The minor star that's Stella draws its life,
Since she receives the splendour of your rays.
I've seen how in the kingdom of sweet odours,
Commander of the squadrons of the flowers,
The rose's deity presides, and is
Their empress by divine right of her beauty.
Among the precious stones which can be listed
In the academy of mines, I've seen
The diamond much preferred above the rest,
And crowned their emperor, for shining brightest.
In the revolving empire of the stars
The morning star takes pride among the others.
In their perfected spheres, when the sun calls
The planets to his council, he presides
And is the very oracle of day.
Then if among stars, gems, planet, and flowers

The fairest are exalted, why do you
Wait on a lesser beauty than yourself
Who are, in greater excellence and beauty,
The sun, the morning star, the diamond, and the rose!

Enter CLOTALDO, *who remains by the stage-curtain.*

CLOTALDO, *aside.*

I wish to curb him, since I brought him up.
But, what is this?

ROSAURA.   I reverence your favour,
And yet reply, rhetorical, with silence,
For when one's mind is clumsy and untaught,
He answers best who does not speak at all.

SEGISMUND. Stay! Do not go! How can you wish to go
And leave me darkened by my doubts?

ROSAURA.   Your Highness,
I beg your leave to go.

SEGISMUND.   To go so rudely
Is not to beg my leave but just to take it.

ROSAURA. But if you will not grant it, I must take it.

SEGISMUND. That were to change my courtesy to rudeness.
Resistance is like venom to my patience.

ROSAURA. But even if this deadly, raging venom
Should overcome your patience, yet you dare not
And could not treat me with dishonour, sir.

SEGISMUND. Why, just to see then if I can, and dare to—
You'll make me lose the fear I bear your beauty,
Since the impossible is always tempting
To me. Why, only now I threw a man
Over this balcony who said I couldn't:
And so to find out if I can or not
I'll throw your honour through the window too.

CLOTALDO, *aside.*

He seems determined in this course. Oh, heavens!
What's to be done that for a second time
My honour's threatened by a mad desire?

ROSAURA. Then with good reason it was prophesied
Your tyranny would wreak this kingdom

Outrageous scandals, treasons, crimes, and deaths.
But what can such a creature do as you
Who are not even a man, save in the name—
Inhuman, barbarous, cruel, and unbending
As the wild beasts amongst whom you were nursed?

SEGISMUND. That you should not insult me in this way
I spoke to you most courteously, and thought
I'd thereby get my way; but if you curse me thus
Even when I am speaking gently, why,
By the living God, I'll really give you cause.
Ho there! Clear out, the lot of you, at once!
Leave her to me! Close all the doors upon us.
Let no one enter!

Exeunt CLARION *and other attendants.*

ROSAURA.   I am lost . . . I warn you . . .

SEGISMUND. I am a tyrant and you plead in vain.

CLOTALDO, *aside.*
Oh, what a monstrous thing! I must restrain him
Even if I die for it.
Aloud.
                Sir! Wait! Look here!

SEGISMUND. A second time you have provoked my anger,
You feeble, mad old man! Do you prize lightly
My wrath and rigour that you've gone so far?

CLOTALDO. Brought by the accents of her voice, I came
To tell you you must be more peaceful
If still you hope to reign, and warn you that
You should not be so cruel, though you rule—
Since this, perhaps, is nothing but a dream.

SEGISMUND. When you refer to disillusionment
You rouse me near to madness. Now you'll see,
Here as I kill you, if it's truth or dreaming!
As he tries to pull out his dagger, CLOTALDO *restrains him
and throws himself on his knees before him.*

CLOTALDO. It's thus I'd save my life: and hope to do so—

SEGISMUND. Take your presumptuous hand from off this steel.

CLOTALDO. Till people come to hold your rage and fury
I shall not let you go.

ROSAURA.   O heavens!

SEGISMUND.   Loose it,

They struggle.

I say, or else—you interfering fool—
I'll crush you to your death in my strong arms!

ROSAURA. Come quickly! Here's Clotaldo being killed!

Exit.

ASTOLFO *appears as* CLOTALDO *falls on the floor, and the
former stands between* SEGISMUND *and* CLOTALDO.

ASTOLFO. Why, what is this, most valiant prince? What?
    Staining
Your doughty steel in such old, frozen blood?
For shame! For shame! Sheathe your illustrious weapon!

SEGISMUND. When it is stained in his infamous blood!

ASTOLFO. At my feet here he has found sanctuary
And there he's safe, for it will serve him well.

SEGISMUND. Then serve me well by dying, for like this
I will avenge myself for your behaviour
In trying to annoy me first of all.

ASTOLFO. To draw in self-defence offends no king,
Though in his palace.

    ASTOLFO *draws his sword and they fight.*

CLOTALDO, *to* ASTOLFO. Do not anger him!

    Enter BASIL, STELLA, *and attendants.*

BASIL. Hold! Hold! What's this? Fighting with naked swords?

STELLA, *aside.* It is Astolfo! How my heart misgives me!

BASIL. Why, what has happened here?

ASTOLFO.   Nothing, my Lord,
    Since you've arrived.

    Both sheathe their swords.

SEGISMUND.   Much, though you *have* arrived.
    I tried to kill the old man.

BASIL.   Had you no
    Respect for those white hairs?

CLOTALDO.   Sire, since they're only
    Mine, as you well can see, it does not matter!

SEGISMUND. It is in vain you'd have me hold white hairs
In such respect, since one day you may find
Your own white locks prostrated at my feet
For still I have not taken vengeance on you
For the foul way in which you had me reared.
Exit.

BASIL. Before that happens you will sleep once more
Where you were reared, and where what's happened may
Seem just a dream (being mere earthly glory).
All save ASTOLFO *and* STELLA *leave.*

ASTOLFO. How seldom does prediction fail, when evil!
How oft, foretelling good! Exact in harm,
Doubtful in benefit! Oh, what a great
Astrologer would be one who foretold
Nothing but harms, since there's no doubt at all
That they are always due! In Segismund
And me the case is illustrated clearly.
In him, crimes, cruelties, deaths, and disasters
Were well predicted, since they all came true.
But in my own case, to predict for me
(As I foresaw beholding rays which cast
The sun into the shade and outface heaven)
Triumphs and trophies, happiness and praise,
Was false—and yet was true: it's only just
That when predictions start with promised favours
They should end in disdain.

STELLA.   I do not doubt
Your protestations are most heartfelt; only
They're not for me, but for another lady
Whose portrait you were wearing round your neck
Slung in a locket when you first arrived.
Since it is so, she only can deserve
These wooing flatteries. Let her repay you
For in affairs of love, flatteries and vows
Made for another are mere forged credentials.
ROSAURA enters but waits by the curtain.

ROSAURA, *aside.* Thanks be to God, my troubles are near ended!
To judge from what I see, I've naught to fear.

ASTOLFO. I will expel that portrait from my breast
  To make room for the image of your beauty
  And keep it there. For there where Stella is
  Can be no room for shade, and where the sun is
  No place for any star. I'll fetch the portrait.
  Aside.
  Forgive me, beautiful Rosaura, that,
  When absent, men and women seldom keep
  More faith than this.
  Exit.
  ROSAURA *comes forward.*

ROSAURA, *aside.* I could not hear a word. I was afraid
  That they would see me.

STELLA.   Oh, Astrea!

ROSAURA.   My lady!

STELLA. I am delighted that you came. Because
  To you alone would I confide a secret.

ROSAURA. Thereby you greatly honour me, your servant.

STELLA. Astrea, in the brief time I have known you
  I've given you the latchkey of my will.
  For that, and being who you are, I'll tell you
  A secret which I've very often hidden
  Even from myself.

ROSAURA.   I am your slave.

STELLA.   Then, briefly:
  Astolfo, who's my cousin (the word cousin
  Suffices, since some things are plainly said
  Even by thinking them), is to wed me
  If Fortune thus can wipe so many cares
  Away with one great joy. But I am troubled
  In that, the day he first came here, he carried
  A portrait of a lady round his neck.
  I spoke to him about it courteously.
  He was most amiable, he loves me well,
  And now he's gone for it. I am embarrassed
  That he should give it me himself. Wait here,
  And tell him to deliver it to you.

Do not say more. Since you're discreet and fair:
You'll surely know just what love is.
Exit.

ROSAURA.   Great heavens!
How I wish that I did not! For who could be
So prudent or so skilful as would know
What to advise herself in such a case?
Lives there a person on this earth today
Who's more beset by the inclement stars,
Who has more cares besieging him, or fights
So many dire calamities at once?
What can I do in such bewilderment
Wherein it seems impossible to find
Relief or comfort? Since my first misfortune
No other thing has chanced or happened to me
But was a new misfortune. In succession
Inheritors and heirs of their own selves
(Just like the Phoenix, his own son and father)
Misfortunes reproduce themselves, are born,
And live by dying. In their sepulchre
The ashes they consume are hot forever.
A sage once said misfortunes must be cowards
Because they never dare to walk alone
But come in crowds. I say they are most valiant
Because they always charge so bravely on
And never turn their backs. Who charges with them
May dare all things because there is no fear
That they'll ever desert him; and I say it
Because in all my life I never once
Knew them to leave me, nor will they grow tired
Of me till, wounded and shot through and through
By Fate, I fall into the arms of death.
Alas, what can I do in this dilemma?
If I reveal myself, then old Clotaldo,
To whom I owe my life, may take offence,
Because he told me to await the cure
And mending of my honour in concealment.
If I don't tell Astolfo who I am
And he detects me, how can I dissimulate?

Since even if I say I am not I,
The voice, the language, and the eyes will falter,
Because the soul will tell them that they lie.
What shall I do? It is in vain to study
What I should do, when I know very well
That, whatsoever way I choose to act,
When the time comes I'll do as sorrow bids,
For no one has control over his sorrows.
Then since my soul dares not decide its actions
Let sorrow fill my cup and let my grief
Reach its extremity and, out of doubts
And vain appearances, once and for all
Come out into the light—and Heaven shield me!

Enter ASTOLFO.

ASTOLFO. Here, lady, is the portrait . . . but . . . great God!

ROSAURA. Why does Your Highness halt, and stare astonished?

ASTOLFO. Rosaura! Why, to see you here!

ROSAURA.   Rosaura?
Sir, you mistake me for some other lady.
I am Astrea, and my humble station
Deserves no perturbation such as yours.

ASTOLFO. Enough of this pretence, Rosaura, since
The soul can never lie. Though as Astrea
I see you now, I love you as Rosaura.

ROSAURA. Not having understood Your Highness' meaning
I can make no reply except to say
That Stella (who might be the star of Venus)
Told me to wait here and to tell you from her
To give to me the portrait you were fetching
(Which seems a very logical request)
And I myself will take it to my lady.
Thus Stella bids: even the slightest things
Which do me harm are governed by some star.

ASTOLFO. Even if you could make a greater effort
How poorly you dissimulate, Rosaura!
Tell your poor eyes they do not harmonise
With your own voice, because they needs must jangle
When the whole instrument is out of tune.

> You cannot match the falsehood of your words
> With the sincerity of what you're feeling.

ROSAURA. All I can say is—that I want the portrait.

ASTOLFO. As you require a fiction, with a fiction
> I shall reply. Go and tell Stella this:
> That I esteem her so, it seems unworthy
> Only to send the counterfeit to her
> And that I'm sending her the original.
> And you, take the original along with you,
> Taking yourself to her.

ROSAURA.   When a man starts
> Forth on a definite task, resolved and valiant,
> Though he be offered a far greater prize
> Than what he seeks, yet he returns with failure
> If he returns without his task performed.
> I came to get that portrait. Though I bear
> The original with me, of greater value,
> I would return in failure and contempt
> Without the copy. Give it me, Your Highness,
> Since I cannot return without it.

ASTOLFO.   But
> If I don't give it you, how can you do so?

ROSAURA. Like this, ungrateful man! I'll take it from you.

She tries to wrest it from him.

ASTOLFO. It is in vain.

ROSAURA.   By God, it shall not come
> Into another woman's hands!

ASTOLFO.   You're terrifying!

ROSAURA. And you're perfidious!

ASTOLFO.   Enough, my dear
> Rosaura!

ROSAURA.   I, your dear? You lie, you villain!

They are both clutching the portrait.

Enter STELLA.

STELLA. Astrea and Astolfo, what does this mean?

ASTOLFO, *aside.* Here's Stella.

ROSAURA, *aside.*   Love, grant me the strength to win
My portrait.

To STELLA.

If you want to know, my lady,
What this is all about, I will explain.

ASTOLFO, *to* ROSAURA, *aside.* What do you mean?

ROSAURA.   You told me to await
Astolfo here and ask him for a portrait
On your behalf. I waited here alone
And as one thought suggests another thought,
Thinking of portraits, I recalled my own
Was here inside my sleeve. When one's alone,
One is diverted by a foolish trifle
And so I took it out to look at it.
It slipped and fell, just as Astolfo here,
Bringing the portrait of the other lady,
Came to deliver it to you as promised.
He picked my portrait up, and so unwilling
Is he to give away the one you asked for,
Instead of doing so, he seized upon
The other portrait which is mine alone
And will not give it back though I entreated
And begged him to return it. I was angry
And tried to snatch it back. That's it he's holding,
And you can see yourself if it's not mine.

STELLA. Let go the portrait.

She snatches it from him.

ASTOLFO.   Madam!

STELLA.   The draughtsman
Was not unkind to truth.

ROSAURA.   Is it not mine?

STELLA. Why, who could doubt it?

ROSAURA.   Ask him for the other.

STELLA. Here, take your own, Astrea. You may leave us.

ROSAURA, *aside.* Now I have got my portrait, come what will.

Exit.

STELLA. Now give me up the portrait that I asked for

Although I'll see and speak to you no more.
I do not wish to leave it in your power
Having been once so foolish as to beg it.

ASTOLFO, *aside.* Now how can I get out of this foul trap?
To STELLA.

Beautiful Stella, though I would obey you,
And serve you in all ways, I cannot give you
The portrait, since . . .

STELLA.   You are a crude, coarse villain
And ruffian of a wooer. For the portrait—
I do not want it now, since, if I had it,
It would remind me I had asked you for it.
Exit.

ASTOLFO. Listen! Look! Wait! Let me explain!
Aside.

                                        Oh, damn

Rosaura! How the devil did she get
To Poland for my ruin and her own?

The prison of Segismund in the tower

SEGISMUND *lying on the ground loaded with fetters and clothed
in skins as before.* CLOTALDO, *two attendants, and* CLARION

CLOTALDO. Here you must leave him—since his reckless pride
Ends here today where it began.

ATTENDANT.   His chain
I'll rivet as it used to be before.

CLARION. O Prince, you'd better not awake too soon
To find how lost you are, how changed your fate,
And that your fancied glory of an hour
Was but a shade of life, a flame of death!

CLOTALDO. For one who knows so well to wield his tongue
It's fit a worthy place should be provided
With lots of room and lots of time to argue.

This is the fellow that you have to seize
To the attendants.
And that's the room in which you are to lock him.
Points to the nearest cell.

CLARION. Why me?

CLOTALDO.   Because a Clarion who knows
Too many secrets must be kept in gaol—
A place where even clarions are silent.

CLARION. Have I, by chance, wanted to kill my father
Or thrown an Icarus from a balcony?
Am I asleep or dreaming? To what end
Do you imprison me?

CLOTALDO.   You're Clarion.

CLARION. Well, say I swear to be a cornet now,
A silent one, a wretched instrument . . . ?

They hustle him off.

CLOTALDO *remains.*

Enter BASIL, *wearing a mask.*

BASIL. Clotaldo.

CLOTALDO.   Sire . . . and is it thus alone
Your Majesty has come?

BASIL.   Vain curiosity
To see what happens here to Segismund.

CLOTALDO. See where he lies, reduced to misery!

BASIL. Unhappy prince! Born at a fatal moment!
Come waken him, now he has lost his strength
With all the opium he's drunk.

CLOTALDO.   He's stirring
And talking to himself.

BASIL.   What is he dreaming?
Let's listen now.

SEGISMUND.   He who chastises tyrants
Is a most pious prince . . . Now let Clotaldo
Die by my hand . . . my father kiss my feet . . .

CLOTALDO. He threatens me with death!

BASIL.   And me with insult
And cruelty.

CLOTALDO.   He'd take my life away.

BASIL. And he'd humiliate me at his feet.

SEGISMUND, *still in a dream.*
Throughout the expanse of this world's theatre
I'll show my peerless valour, let my vengeance
Be wreaked, and the Prince Segismund be seen
To triumph—over his father . . . but, alas!
Awakening.
Where am I?

BASIL, *to* CLOTALDO. Since he must not see me here,
I'll listen further off. You know your cue.
Retires to one side.

SEGISMUND. Can this be I? Am I the same who, chained
And long imprisoned, rose to such a state?
Are you not still my sepulchre and grave,
You dismal tower? God! What things I have dreamed!

CLOTALDO, *aside.* Now I must go to him to disenchant him.
Aloud.
Awake already?

SEGISMUND.   Yes: it was high time.

CLOTALDO. What? Do you have to spend all day asleep?
Since I was following the eagle's flight
With tardy discourse, have you still lain here
Without awaking?

SEGISMUND.   No. Nor even now
Am I awake. It seems I've always slept,
Since, if I've dreamed what I've just seen and heard
Palpably and for certain, then I am dreaming
What I see now—nor is it strange I'm tired,
Since what I, sleeping, see, tells me that I
Was dreaming when I thought I was awake.

CLOTALDO. Tell me your dream.

SEGISMUND.   That's if it *was* a dream!
No, I'll not tell you what I dreamed; but what
I lived and saw, Clotaldo, I *will* tell you.

I woke up in a bed that might have been
The cradle of the flowers, woven by Spring.
A thousand nobles, bowing, called me Prince,
Attiring me in jewels, pomp, and splendour.
My equanimity you turned to rapture
Telling me that I was the Prince of Poland.

CLOTALDO. I must have got a fine reward!

SEGISMUND.   Not so:
For as a traitor, twice, with rage and fury,
I tried to kill you.

CLOTALDO.   Such cruelty to me?

SEGISMUND. I was the lord of all, on all I took revenge,
Except I loved one woman . . . I believe
That *that* was true, though all the rest has faded.
Exit BASIL.

CLOTALDO, *aside*. I see the king was moved, to hear him speak.
Aloud.

Talking of eagles made you dream of empires,
But even in your dreams it's good to honour
Those who have cared for you and brought you up.
For Segismund, even in dreams, I warn you
Nothing is lost by trying to do good.
Exit.

SEGISMUND. That's true, and therefore let us subjugate
The bestial side, this fury and ambition,
Against the time when we may dream once more,
As certainly we shall, for this strange world
Is such that but to live here is to dream.
And now experience shows me that each man
Dreams what he is until he is awakened.
The king dreams he's a king and in this fiction
Lives, rules, administers with royal pomp.
Yet all the borrowed praises that he earns
Are written in the wind, and he is changed
(How sad a fate!) by death to dust and ashes.
What man is there alive who'd seek to reign
Since he must wake into the dream that's death.
The rich man dreams his wealth which is his care

And woe. The poor man dreams his sufferings.
He dreams who thrives and prospers in this life.
He dreams who toils and strives. He dreams who injures,
Offends, and insults. So that in this world
Everyone dreams the thing he is, though no one
Can understand it. I dream I am here,
Chained in these fetters. Yet I dreamed just now
I was in a more flattering, lofty station.
What is this life? A frenzy, an illusion,
A shadow, a delirium, a fiction.
The greatest good's but little, and this life
Is but a dream, and dreams are only dreams.

ACT III

The tower

Enter CLARION.

CLARION. I'm held in an enchanted tower, because
Of all I know. What would they do to me
For all I don't know, since—for all I know—
They're killing me by starving me to death.
O that a man so hungry as myself
Should live to die of hunger while alive!
I am so sorry for myself that others
May well say "I can well believe it," since
This silence ill accords with my name "Clarion",
And I just can't shut up. My fellows here?
Spiders and rats—fine feathered songsters those!
My head's still ringing with a dream of fifes
And trumpets and a lot of noisy humbug
And long processions as of penitents
With crosses, winding up and down, while some
Faint at the sight of blood besmirching others.
But now to tell the truth, I am in prison.
For knowing secrets, I am kept shut in,
Strictly observed as if I were a Sunday,
And feeling sadder than a Tuesday, where
I neither eat nor drink. They say a secret
Is sacred and should be as strictly kept
As any saint's day on the calendar.
Saint Secret's Day for me's a working day
Because I'm never idle then. The penance
I suffer here is merited, I say:
Because being a lackey, I was silent,
Which, in a servant, is a sacrilege.

A noise of drums and trumpets.

FIRST SOLDIER, *within.*

Here is the tower in which he is imprisoned.
Smash in the door and enter, everybody!

CLARION. Great God! They've come to seek me. That is certain
Because they say I'm here. What can they want?

Enter several soldiers.

FIRST SOLDIER. Go in.

SECOND SOLDIER. He's here!

CLARION. No, he's not here!

ALL THE SOLDIERS. Our lord!

CLARION. What, are they drunk?

FIRST SOLDIER. You are our rightful prince.
We do not want and never shall allow
A stranger to supplant our trueborn prince.
Give us your feet to kiss!

ALL THE SOLDIERS. Long live the prince!

CLARION. Bless me, if it's not real! In this strange kingdom
It seems the custom, everyday, to take
Some fellow and to make him prince and then
Shut him back in this tower. That *must* be it!
So I must play my role.

ALL THE SOLDIERS. Give us your feet.

CLARION. I can't. They're necessary. After all
What sort of use would be a footless prince?

SECOND SOLDIER. All of us told your father, as one man,
We want no prince of Muscovy but you!

CLARION. You weren't respectful to my father? Shame!

FIRST SOLDIER. It was our loyalty that made us tell him.

CLARION. If it was loyalty, you have my pardon.

SECOND SOLDIER. Restore your empire. Long live Segismund!

CLARION, *aside.* That is the name they seem to give to all
These counterfeited princes.

Enter SEGISMUND.

SEGISMUND. Who called Segismund?

CLARION, *aside.* I seem to be a hollow sort of prince.

FIRST SOLDIER. Which of you's Segismund?

SEGISMUND. I am.

SECOND SOLDIER, *to* CLARION. Then, why,

Rash fool, did you impersonate the prince
Segismund?

CLARION.   What? I, Segismund? Yourselves
Be-Segismunded me without request.
All yours was both the rashness and the folly.

FIRST SOLDIER. Prince Segismund, whom we acclaim our lord,
Your father, great King Basil, in his fear
That heaven would fulfil a prophecy
That one day he would kneel before your feet
Wishes now to deprive you of the throne
And give it to the Duke of Muscovy.
For this he called a council, but the people
Discovered his design and knowing, now,
They have a native king, will have no stranger.
So scorning the fierce threats of destiny,
We've come to seek you in your very prison,
That aided by the arms of the whole people,
We may restore you to the crown and sceptre,
Taking them from the tyrant's grasp. Come, then:
Assembling here, in this wide desert region,
Hosts of plebeians, bandits, and freebooters,
Acclaim you king. Your liberty awaits you!
Hark to its voice!
Shouts within.

                    Long life to Segismund!

SEGISMUND. Once more, you heavens will that I should dream
Of grandeur, once again, 'twixt doubts and shades,
Behold the majesty of pomp and power
Vanish into the wind, once more you wish
That I should taste the disillusion and
The risk by which all human power is humbled,
Of which all human power should live aware.
It must not be. I'll not be once again
Put through my paces by my fortune's stars.
And since I know this life is all a dream,
Depart, vain shades, who feign, to my dead senses,
That you have voice and body, having neither!
I want no more feigned majesty, fantastic
Display, nor void illusions, that one gust

Can scatter like the almond tree in flower,
Whose rosy buds, without advice or warning,
Dawn in the air too soon and then, as one,
Are all extinguished, fade, and fall, and wither
In the first gust of wind that comes along!
I know you well. I know you well by now.
I know that all that happens in yourselves
Happens as in a sleeping man. For me
There are no more delusions and deceptions
Since I well know this life is all a dream.

SECOND SOLDIER. If you think we are cheating, just sweep
　　Your gaze along these towering peaks, and see
　　The hosts that wait to welcome and obey you.

SEGISMUND. Already once before I've seen such crowds
　　Distinctly, quite as vividly as these:
　　And yet it was a dream.

SECOND SOLDIER.　　　　　No great event
　　Can come without forerunners to announce it
　　And this is the real meaning of your dream.

SEGISMUND. Yes, you say well. It was the fore-announcement
　　And just in case it was correct, my soul,
　　(Since life's so short) let's dream the dream anew!
　　But it must be attentively, aware
　　That we'll awake from pleasure in the end.
　　Forewarned of that, the shock's not so abrupt,
　　The disillusion's less. Evils anticipated
　　Lose half their sting. And armed with this precaution—
　　That power, even when we're sure of it, is borrowed
　　And must be given back to its true owner—
　　We can risk anything and dare the worst.
　　Subjects, I thank you for your loyalty.
　　In me you have a leader who will free you,
　　Bravely and skilfully, from foreign rule.
　　Sound now to arms, you'll soon behold my valour.
　　Against my father I must march and bring
　　Truth from the stars. Yes: he must kneel to me.
　　Aside.
　　But yet, since I may wake before he kneels,
　　Perhaps I'd better not proclaim what may not happen.

ALL. Long live Segismund!

 Enter CLOTALDO.

CLOTALDO.   Gracious heavens! What is
 This riot here?

SEGISMUND. Clotaldo!

CLOTALDO.   Sir!

 Aside.

        He'll prove
 His cruelty on me.

CLARION.   I bet he throws him
 Over the mountain.

CLOTALDO.   At your royal feet
 I kneel, knowing my penalty is death.

SEGISMUND. Rise, rise, my foster father, from the ground,
 For you must be the compass and the guide
 In which I trust. You brought me up, and I
 Know what I owe your loyalty. Embrace me!

CLOTALDO. What's that you say?

SEGISMUND.   I know I'm in a dream,
 But I would like to act well, since good actions,
 Even in a dream, are not entirely lost.

CLOTALDO. Since doing good is now to be your glory,
 You will not be offended that I too
 Should do what's right. You march against your father!
 I cannot give you help against my king.
 Here at your feet, my lord, I plead for death.

SEGISMUND, *aloud.* Villain!

 Aside.

      But let us suffer this annoyance.
 Though my rage would slay him, yet he's loyal.
 A man does not deserve to die for that.
 How many angry passions does this leash
 Restrain in me, this curb of knowing well
 That I must wake and find myself alone!

SECOND SOLDIER. All this fine talk, Clotaldo, is a cruel
 Spurn of the public welfare. We are loyal
 Who wish our own prince to reign over us.

CLOTALDO. Such loyalty, after the king were dead,
Would honour you. But while the king is living
He is our absolute, unquestioned lord.
There's no excuse for subjects who oppose
His sovereignty in arms.

FIRST SOLDIER.   We'll soon see well
Enough, Clotaldo, what this loyalty
Is worth.

CLOTALDO. You would be better if you had some.
It is the greatest prize.

SEGISMUND.   Peace, peace, I pray you.

CLOTALDO. My lord!

SEGISMUND.   Clotaldo, if your feelings
Are truly thus, go you, and serve the king;
That's prudence, loyalty, and common sense.
But do not argue here with anyone
Whether it's right or wrong, for every man
Has his own honour.

CLOTALDO.   Humbly I take my leave.
Exit.

SEGISMUND. Now sound the drums and march in rank and
    order
Straight to the palace.

ALL.   Long live Segismund!

SEGISMUND. Fortune, we go to reign! Do not awake me
If I am dreaming! Do not let me fall
Asleep if it is true! To act with virtue
Is what matters, since if this proves true,
That truth's sufficient reason in itself;
If not, we win us friends against the time
When we at last awake.

A room in the royal palace

Enter BASIL *and* ASTOLFO.

BASIL. Whose prudence can rein in a bolting horse?
　Who can restrain a river's pride, in spate?
　Whose valour can withstand a crag dislodged
　And hurtling downwards from a mountain peak?
　All these are easier by far than to hold back
　A crowd's proud fury, once it has been roused.
　It has two voices, both proclaiming war,
　And you can hear them echoing through the mountains,
　Some shouting "Segismund," others "Astolfo."
　The scene I set for swearing of allegiance
　Lends but an added horror to this strife:
　It has become the back cloth to a stage
　Where Fortune plays out tragedies in blood.

ASTOLFO. My lord, forget the happiness and wealth
　You promised me from your most blessèd hand.
　If Poland, which I hope to rule, refuses
　Obedience to my right, grudging me honour,
　It is because I've got to earn it first.
　Give me a horse, that I with angry pride
　May match the thunder in my voice and ride
　To strike, like lightning, terror far and wide.

Exit ASTOLFO.

BASIL. No remedy for what's infallible!
　What is foreseen is perilous indeed!
　If something has to be, there's no way out;
　In trying to evade it, you but court it.
　This law is pitiless and horrible.
　Thinking one can evade the risk, one meets it:
　My own precautions have been my undoing,
　And I myself have quite destroyed my kingdom.

Enter STELLA.

STELLA. If you, my lord, in person do not try

To curb the vast commotion that has started
In all the streets between the rival factions,
You'll see your kingdom, swamped in waves of crimson,
Swimming in its own blood, with nothing left
But havoc, dire calamity, and woe.
So frightful is the damage to your empire
That, seen, it strikes amazement; heard, despair.
The sun's obscured, the very winds are hindered.
Each stone is a memorial to the dead.
Each flower springs from a grave while every building
Appears a mausoleum, and each soldier
A premature and walking skeleton.

Enter CLOTALDO.

CLOTALDO. Praise be to God, I reach your feet alive!

BASIL. Clotaldo! What's the news of Segismund?

CLOTALDO. The crowd, a headstrong monster blind with rage,
Entered his dungeon tower and set him free.
He, now exalted for the second time,
Conducts himself with valour, boasting how
He will bring down the truth out of the stars.

BASIL. Give me a horse, that I myself, in person,
May vanquish such a base, ungrateful son!
For I, in the defence of my own crown,
Shall do by steel what science failed to do.

Exit.

STELLA. I'll be Bellona to your Sun, and try
To write my name next yours in history.
I'll ride as though I flew on outstretched wings
That I may vie with Pallas.

Exit.

Enter ROSAURA, *holding back* CLOTALDO.

ROSAURA. I know that all is war, Clotaldo, yet
Although your valour calls you to the front,
First hear me out. You know quite well that I
Arrived in Poland poor and miserable,
Where, shielded by your valour, I found mercy.
You told me to conceal myself, and stay
Here in the palace, hiding from Astolfo.

He saw me in the end, and so insulted
My honour that (although he saw me clearly)
He nightly speaks with Stella in the garden.
I have the key to it and I will show you
How you can enter there and end my cares.
Thus bold, resolved, and strong, you can recover
My honour, since you're ready to avenge me
By killing him.

CLOTALDO.   It's true that I intended,
Since first I saw you (having heard your tale)
With my own life to rectify your wrongs.
The first step that I took was bid you dress
According to your sex, for fear Astolfo
Might see you as you were, and deem you wanton.
I was devising how we could recover
Your honour (so much did it weigh on me)
Even though we had to kill him. (A wild plan—
Though since he's not my king, I would not flinch
From killing him.) But then, when suddenly
Segismund tried to kill me, it was he
Who saved my life with his surpassing valour.
Consider: how can I requite Astolfo
With death for giving me my life so bravely,
And when my soul is full of gratitude?
So torn between the two of you I stand—
Rosaura, whose life I saved, and Astolfo,
Who saved my life. What's to be done? Which side
To take, and whom to help, I cannot judge.
What I owe you in that I gave you life
I owe to him in that he gave me life.
And so there is no course that I can take
To satisfy my love. I am a person
Who has to act, yet suffer either way.

ROSAURA. I should not have to tell so brave a man
That if it is nobility to give,
It's baseness to receive. That being so
You owe no gratitude to him, admitting
That it was he who gave you life, and you
Who gave me life, since he forced you to take

A meaner role, and through me you assumed
A generous role. So you should side with me:
My cause is so far worthier than his own
As giving is than taking.

CLOTALDO.   Though nobility
Is with the giver, it is gratitude
That dwells with the receiver. As a giver
I have the name of being generous:
Then grant me that of being grateful too
And let me earn the title and be grateful,
As I am liberal, giving or receiving.

ROSAURA. You granted me my life, at the same time
Telling me it was worthless, since dishonoured,
And therefore was no life. Therefore from you
I have received no life at all. And since
You should be liberal first and grateful after
(Since so you said yourself) I now entreat you
Give me the life, the life you never gave me!
As giving magnifies the most, give first
And then be grateful after, if you will!

CLOTALDO. Won by your argument, I will be liberal.
Rosaura, I shall give you my estate
And you shall seek a convent, there to live.
This measure is a happy thought, for, see,
Fleeing a crime, you find a sanctuary.
For when the empire's threatened with disasters
And is divided thus, I, born a noble,
Am not the man who would augment its woes.
So with this remedy which I have chosen
I remain loyal to the kingdom, generous
To you, and also grateful to Astolfo.
And thus I choose the course that suits you best.
Were I your father, what could I do more?

ROSAURA. Were you my father, then I would accept
The insult. Since you are not, I refuse.

CLOTALDO. What do you hope to do then?

ROSAURA.   Kill the duke!

CLOTALDO. A girl who never even knew her father
Armed with such courage?

ROSAURA.   Yes.

CLOTALDO.   What spurs you on?

ROSAURA. My good name.

CLOTALDO.   In Astolfo you will find . . .

ROSAURA. My honour rides on him and strikes him down!

CLOTALDO. Your king, too, Stella's husband!

ROSAURA.   Never, never
   Shall that be, by almighty God, I swear!

CLOTALDO. Why, this is madness!

ROSAURA.   Yes it is!

CLOTALDO.   Restrain it.

ROSAURA. That I cannot.

CLOTALDO.   Then you are lost forever!

ROSAURA. I know it!

CLOTALDO.   Life and honour both together!

ROSAURA. I well believe it!

CLOTALDO.   What do you intend?

ROSAURA. My death.

CLOTALDO.   This is despair and desperation.

ROSAURA. It's honour.

CLOTALDO.   It is nonsense.

ROSAURA.   It is valour.

CLOTALDO. It's frenzy.

ROSAURA.   Yes, it's anger! Yes, it's fury!

CLOTALDO. In short you cannot moderate your passion?

ROSAURA. No.

CLOTALDO.   Who is there to help you?

ROSAURA.   I, myself.

CLOTALDO. There is no cure?

ROSAURA.   There is no cure!

CLOTALDO.   Think well
   If there's not some way out . . .

ROSAURA.   Some other way
   To do away with me . . .

Exit.

CLOTALDO.   If you are lost,
My daughter, let us both be lost together!

In the country

Enter SEGISMUND *clothed in skins. Soldiers marching.*
CLARION. *Drums beating.*

SEGISMUND. If Rome, today, could see me here, renewing
Her olden triumphs, she might laugh to see
A wild beast in command of mighty armies,
A wild beast, to whose fiery aspirations
The firmament were all too slight a conquest!
But stoop your flight, my spirit. Do not thus
Be puffed to pride by these uncertain plaudits
Which, when I wake, will turn to bitterness
In that I won them only to be lost.
The less I value them, the less I'll miss them.

A trumpet sounds.

CLARION. Upon a rapid courser (pray excuse me,
Since if it comes to mind I must describe it)
In which it seems an atlas was designed
Since if its body is earth, its soul is fire
Within its breast, its foam appears the sea,
The wind its breath, and chaos its condition,
Since in its soul, its foam, its breath and flesh,
It seems a monster of fire, earth, sea, and wind,
Upon the horse, all of a patchwork colour,
Dappled, and rushing forward at the will
Of one who plies the spur, so that it flies
Rather than runs—see how a woman rides
Boldly into your presence.[1]

SEGISMUND.   Her light blinds me.

CLARION. Good God! Why, here's Rosaura!

---

[1] Clarion's speech is a parody of exaggerated style—including
Calderón's. [R.C.]

SEGISMUND.   It is heaven
    That has restored her to my sight once more.
    Enter ROSAURA *with sword and dagger in riding costume.*
ROSAURA. Generous Segismund, whose majesty
    Heroically rises in the lustre
    Of his great deeds out of his night of shadows,
    And as the greatest planet, in the arms
    Of his aurora, lustrously returns
    To plants and roses, over hills and seas,
    When, crowned with gold, he looks abroad, dispersing
    Radiance, flashing his rays, bathing the summits,
    And broidering the fringes of the foam,
    So may you dawn upon the world, bright sun
    Of Poland, that a poor unhappy woman
    May fall before your feet and beg protection
    Both as a woman and unfortunate—
    Two things that must oblige you, sire, as one
    Who prize yourself as valiant, each of them
    More than suffices for your chivalry.
    Three times you have beheld me now, three times
    Been ignorant of who I am, because
    Three times you saw me in a different clothing.
    The first time you mistook me for a man,
    Within that rigorous prison, where your hardships
    Made mine seem pleasure. Next time, as a woman,
    You saw me, when your pomp and majesty
    Were as a dream, a phantasm, a shade.
    The third time is today when, as a monster
    Of both the sexes, in a woman's costume
    I bear a soldier's arms. But to dispose you
    The better to compassion, hear my story.
    My mother was a noble in the court
    Of Moscow, who, since most unfortunate,
    Must have been beautiful. Then came a traitor
    And cast his eyes on her (I do not name him,
    Not knowing who he is). Yet I deduce
    That he was valiant too from my own valour,
    Since he gave form to me—and I could wish
    I had been born in pagan times, that I might

Persuade myself he was some god of those
Who rain in showers of gold, turn into swans
Or bulls, for Danaës, Ledas, or Europas.
That's strange: I thought I was just rambling on
By telling old perfidious myths, yet find
I've told you how my mother was cajoled.
Oh, she was beautiful as no one else
Has been, but was unfortunate like all.
He swore to wed her (that's an old excuse)
And this trick reached so nearly to her heart
That thought must weep, recalling it today.
The tyrant left her only with his sword
As Aeneas left Troy. I sheathed its blade here
Upon my thigh, and I will bare it too
Before the ending of this history.
Out of this union, this poor link which neither
Could bind the marriage nor handcuff the crime,
Myself was born, her image and her portrait,
Not in her beauty, but in her misfortune,
For mine's the same. That's all I need to say.
The most that I can tell you of myself
Is that the man who robbed me of the spoils
And trophies of my honour is Astolfo.
Alas! to name him my heart rages so
(As hearts will do when men name enemies).
Astolfo was my faithless and ungrateful
Lord, who (quite forgetful of our happiness,
Since of a past love even the memory fades)
Came here to claim the throne and marry Stella
For she's the star who rises as I set.
It's hard to credit that a star should sunder
Lovers the stars had made conformable!
So hurt was I, so villainously cheated,
That I became mad, brokenhearted, sick,
Half wild with grief, and like to die, with all
Hell's own confusion ciphered on my mind
Like Babel's incoherence. Mutely I told
My griefs (since woes and griefs declare themselves
Better than can the mouth, by their effects),
When, with my mother (we were by ourselves),

She broke the prison of my pent-up sorrows
And from my breast they all rushed forth in troops.
I felt no shyness, for in knowing surely
That one to whom one's errors are recounted
Has also been an ally in her own,
One finds relief and rest, since bad example
Can sometimes serve for a good purpose too.
She heard my plaint with pity, and she tried
To palliate my sorrows with her own.
How easily do judges pardon error
When they've offended too! An example,
A warning, in herself, she did not trust
To idleness, or the slow cure of time,
Nor try to find a remedy for her honour
In my misfortunes, but, with better counsel,
She bade me follow him to Poland here
And with prodigious gallantry persuade him
To pay the debt to honour that he owes me.
So that it would be easier to travel,
She bade me don male clothing, and took down
This ancient sword which I am wearing now.
Now it is time that I unsheathe the blade
As I was bid, for, trusting in its sign,
She said: "Depart to Poland, show this sword
That all the nobles may behold it well,
And it may be that one of them will take
Pity on you, and counsel you, and shield you."
I came to Poland and, you will remember,
Entered your cave. You looked at me in wonder.
Clotaldo passionately took my part
To plead for mercy to the king, who spared me,
Then, when he heard my story, bade me change
Into my own clothes and attend on Stella,
There to disturb Astolfo's love and stop
Their marriage. Again you saw me in woman's dress
And were confused by the discrepancy.
But let's pass to what's new: Clotaldo, now
Persuaded that Astolfo must, with Stella,
Come to the throne, dissuades me from my purpose,
Against the interests of my name and honour.

But seeing you, O valiant Segismund,
Are claiming your revenge, now that the heavens
Have burst the prison of your rustic tower,
(Wherein you were the tiger of your sorrows,
The rock of sufferings and direful pains)
And sent you forth against your sire and country,
I come to aid you, mingling Dian's silks
With the hard steel of Pallas. Now, strong Captain,
It well behoves us both to stop this marriage—
Me, lest my promised husband should be wed,
You, lest, when their estates are joined, they weigh
More powerfully against your victory.
I come, as a mere woman, to persuade you
To right my shame; but, as a man, I come
To help you battle for your crown. As woman,
To melt your heart, here at your feet I fall;
But, as a man, I come to serve you bravely
Both with my person and my steel, and thus,
If you today should woo me as a woman,
Then I should have to kill you as a man would
In honourable service of my honour;
Since I must be three things today at once—
Passionate, to persuade you: womanly,
To ply you with my woes: manly, to gain
Honour in battle.

SEGISMUND.   Heavens! If it is true I'm dreaming,
Suspend my memory, for in a dream
So many things could not occur. Great heavens!
If I could only come free of them all!
Or never think of any! Who ever felt
Such grievous doubts? If I but dreamed that triumph
In which I found myself, how can this woman
Refer me to such sure and certain facts?
Then all of it was true and not a dream.
But if it be the truth, why does my past life
Call it a dream? This breeds the same confusion.
Are dreams and glories so alike, that fictions
Are held for truths, realities for lies?
Is there so little difference in them both
That one should question whether what one sees

And tastes is true or false? What? Is the copy
So near to the original that doubt
Exists between them? Then if that is so,
And grandeur, power, majesty, and pomp,
Must all evaporate like shades at morning,
Let's profit by it, this time, to enjoy
That which we only can enjoy in dreams.
Rosaura's in my power: my soul adores her beauty.
Let's take the chance. Let love break every law
On which she has relied in coming here
And kneeling, trustful, prostrate at my feet.
This is a dream. If so, dream pleasures now
Since they must turn to sorrows in the end!
But with my own opinions, I begin
Once again to convince myself. Let's think.
If it is but vainglory and a dream,
Who for mere human vainglory would lose
True glory? What past blessing is not merely
A dream? Who has known heroic glories,
That deep within himself, as he recalls them,
Has never doubted that they might be dreams?
But if this all should end in disenchantment,
Seeing that pleasure is a lovely flame
That's soon converted into dust and ashes
By any wind that blows, then let us seek
That which endures in thrifty, lasting fame
In which no pleasures sleep, nor grandeurs dream.
Rosaura's without honour. In a prince
It's worthier to restore it than to steal it.
I shall restore it, by the living God,
Before I win my throne! Let's shun the danger
And fly from the temptation which is strong!
Then sound to arms!

To a soldier.

Today I must give battle before darkness
Buries the rays of gold in green-black waves!

ROSAURA. My lord! Alas, you stand apart, and offer
No word of pity for my plight. How is it

You neither hear nor see me nor even yet
Have turned your face on me?

SEGISMUND.   Rosaura, for your honour's sake
I must be cruel to you, to be kind.
My voice must not reply to you because
My honour must reply to you. I am silent
Because my deeds must speak to you alone.
I do not look at you since, in such straits,
Having to see your honour is requited,
I must not s e your beauty.
Exit with soldiers.

ROSAURA. What strange enigma's this? After such trouble
Still to be treated with more doubtful riddles!
Enter CLARION.

CLARION. Madam, may you be visited just now?

ROSAURA. Why, Clarion, where have you been all this time?

CLARION. Shut in the tower, consulting cards
About my death: "to be or not to be."
And it was a near thing.

ROSAURA.   Why?

CLARION.   Because I know
The secret who you are: in fact, Clotaldo . . .
Drums.
But hush what noise is that?

ROSAURA.   What can it be?

CLARION. From the beleaguered palace a whole squadron
Is charging forth to harry and defeat
That of fierce Segismund.

ROSAURA.   Why, what a coward
Am I, not to be at his side, the terror
And scandal of the world, while such fierce strife
Presses all round in lawless anarchy.
Exit.

VOICES OF SOME. Long live our king!

VOICES OF OTHERS.   Long live our liberty!

CLARION. Long live both king and liberty. Yes, live!
  And welcome to them both! I do not worry.
  In all this pother, I behave like Nero
  Who never grieved at what was going on.
  If I had anything to grieve about
  It would be me, myself. Well hidden here,
  Now, I can watch the sport that's going on.
  This place is safe and hidden between crags,
  And since death cannot find me here, two figs for death!
  He hides. Drums and the clash of arms are heard.

  Enter BASIL, CLOTALDO, *and* ASTOLFO, *fleeing.*

BASIL. Was ever king so hapless as myself
  Or father more ill used?

CLOTALDO.   Your beaten army
  Rush down, in all directions, in disorder.

ASTOLFO. The traitors win!

BASIL.   In battles such as these
  Those on the winning side are ever "loyal,"
  And traitors the defeated. Come, Clotaldo,
  Let's flee from the inhuman cruelty
  Of my fierce son!

  Shots are fired within. CLARION *falls wounded.*

CLARION.   Heavens, save me!

ASTOLFO.   Who is this
  Unhappy soldier bleeding at our feet?

CLARION. I am a most unlucky man who, wishing
  To guard myself from death, have sought it out
  By fleeing from it. Shunning it, I found it,
  Because, to death, no hiding-place is secret.
  So you can argue that whoever shuns it
  Most carefully runs into it the quickest.
  Turn, then, once more into the thick of battle:
  There is more safety there amidst the fire
  And clash of arms than here on this secluded
  Mountain, because no hidden path is safe
  From the inclemency of Fate; and so,
  Although you flee from death, yet you may find it
  Quicker than you expect, if God so wills.

He falls dead.

BASIL. "If God so wills" . . . With what strange eloquence
This corpse persuades our ignorance and error
To better knowledge, speaking from the mouth
Of its fell wound, where the red liquid flowing
Seems like a bloody tongue which teaches us
That the activities of man are vain
When they are pitted against higher powers.
For I, who wished to liberate my country
From murder and sedition, gave it up
To the same ills from which I would have saved it.

CLOTALDO. Though Fate, my lord, knows every path, and finds
Him whom it seeks even in the midst of crags
And thickets, it is not a Christian judgment
To say there is no refuge from its fury.
A prudent man can conquer Fate itself.
Though you are not exempted from misfortune,
Take action to escape it while you can!

ASTOLFO. Clotaldo speaks as one mature in prudence,
And I as one in valour's youthful prime.
Among the thickets of this mount is hidden
A horse, the very birth of the swift wind.
Flee on him, and I'll guard you in the rear.

BASIL. If it is God's will I should die, or if
Death waits here for my coming, I will seek
Him out today, and meet him face to face.

Enter SEGISMUND, STELLA, ROSAURA, *soldiers, and their train.*

A SOLDIER. Amongst the thickets of this mountain
The king is hiding.

SEGISMUND.   Seek him out at once!
Leave no foot of the summit unexplored
But search from stem to stem and branch to branch!

CLOTALDO. Fly, sir!

BASIL.   What for?

ASTOLFO.   What do you mean to do?

BASIL. Astolfo, stand aside!

CLOTALDO.   What is your wish?

BASIL. To take a cure I've needed for sometime.

To SEGISMUND.

If you have come to seek me, here I am.

Kneeling.

Your father, prince, kneels humbly at your feet.
The white snow of my hair is now your carpet.
Tread on my neck and trample on my crown!
Lay low and drag my dignity in dust!
Take vengeance on my honour! Make a slave
Of me and, after all I've done to thwart them,
Let Fate fulfil its edict and claim homage
And Heaven fulfil its oracles at last!

SEGISMUND. Illustrious court of Poland, who have been
The witnesses of such unwonted wonders,
Attend to me, and hear your prince speak out.
What Heaven decrees and God writes with his finger
(Whose prints and ciphers are the azure leaves
Adorned with golden lettering of the stars)
Never deceives nor lies. They only lie
Who seek to penetrate the mystery
And, having reached it, use it to ill purpose.
My father, who is here to evade the fury
Of my proud nature, made me a wild beast:
So, when I, by my birth of gallant stock,
My generous blood, and inbred grace and valour,
Might well have proved both gentle and forbearing,
The very mode of life to which he forced me,
The sort of bringing up I had to bear
Sufficed to make me savage in my passions.
What a strange method of restraining them!
If one were to tell any man: "One day
You will be killed by an inhuman monster,"
Would it be the best method he could choose
To wake that monster when it was asleep?
Or if they told him: "That sword which you're wearing
Will be your death," what sort of cure were it
To draw it forth and aim it at his breast?
Or if they told him: "Deep blue gulfs of water
Will one day be your sepulchre and grave

Beneath a silver monument of foam,"
He would be mad to hurl himself in headlong
When the sea highest heaved its showy mountains
And crystalline sierras plumed with spray.
The same has happened to the king as to him
Who wakes a beast which threatens death, to him
Who draws a naked sword because he fears it,
To him who dives into the stormy breakers.
Though my ferocious nature (hear me now)
Was like a sleeping beast, my inborn rage
A sheathèd sword, my wrath a quiet ripple,
Fate should not be coerced by man's injustice—
This rouses more resentment. So it is
That he who seeks to tame his fortune must
Resort to moderation and to measure.
He who foresees an evil cannot conquer it
Thus in advance, for though humility
Can overcome it, this it can do only
When the occasion's there, for there's no way
To dodge one's fate and thus evade the issue.
Let this strange spectacle serve as example—
This prodigy, this horror, and this wonder,
Because it is no less than one, to see,
After such measures and precautions taken
To thwart it, that a father thus should kneel
At his son's feet, a kingdom thus be shattered.
This was the sentence of the heavens above,
Which he could not evade, much though he tried.
Can I, younger in age, less brave, and less
In science than the king, conquer that fate?

To the KING.

Sire, rise, give me your hand, now that the heavens
Have shown you that you erred as to the method
To vanquish them. Humbly I kneel before you
And offer you my neck to tread upon.

BASIL. Son, such a great and noble act restores you
Straight to my heart. Oh, true and worthy prince!
You have won both the laurel and the palm.
Crown yourself with your deeds! For you *have* conquered!

ALL. Long live Segismund! Long live Segismund!

SEGISMUND. Since I have other victories to win,
  The greatest of them all awaits me now:
  To conquer my own self. Astolfo, give
  Your hand here to Rosaura, for you know
  It is a debt of honour and must be paid.

ASTOLFO. Although, it's true, I owe some obligations—
  She does not know her name or who she is,
  It would be base to wed a woman who . . .

CLOTALDO. Hold! Wait! Rosaura's of as noble stock
  As yours, Astolfo. In the open field
  I'll prove it with my sword. She is my daughter
  And that should be enough.

ASTOLFO.   What do you say?

CLOTALDO. Until I saw her married, righted, honoured,
  I did not wish for it to be discovered.
  It's a long story but she is my daughter.

ASTOLFO. That being so, I'm glad to keep my word.

SEGISMUND. And now, so that the princess Stella here
  Will not remain disconsolate to lose
  A prince of so much valour, here I offer
  My hand to her, no less in birth and rank.
  Give me your hand.

STELLA.   I gain by meriting
  So great a happiness.

SEGISMUND.   And now, Clotaldo,
  So long so loyal to my father, come
  To my arms. Ask me anything you wish.

FIRST SOLDIER. If thus you treat a man who never served you,
  What about me who led the revolution
  And brought you from your dungeon in the tower?
  What will you give me?

SEGISMUND.   That same tower and dungeon
  From which you never shall emerge till death.
  No traitor is of use after his treason.

BASIL. All wonder at your wisdom!

ASTOLFO.   What a change
  Of character!

ROSAURA.   How wise and prudent!

SEGISMUND.   Why
  Do you wonder? Why do you marvel, since
  It was a dream that taught me and I still
  Fear to wake up once more in my close dungeon?
  Though that may never happen, it's enough
  To dream it might, for thus I came to learn
  That all our human happiness must pass
  Away like any dream, and I would here
  Enjoy it fully ere it glide away,
  Asking (for noble hearts are prone to pardon)
  Pardon for faults in the actors or the play.

NOTES

GENERAL. A comprehensive list of Spanish works that have been translated into English has been published under the title: *English Translations from the Spanish, 1484–1943, A Bibliography*, by Remigio Ugo Pane (Rutgers University Press, 1944). A highly readable general history of Spanish literature is now available in paperbacks: *The Literature of the Spanish People* by Gerald Brenan (Meridian Books, 1957). For those who can read a little Spanish, a Spanish collection with English notes is recommended: *Diez Comedias del Siglo de Oro*, edited by Hyman Alpern and José Martel (Harper & Bros., 1939).

Two Victorian translations of THE SIEGE OF NUMANTIA (1585) precede the Campbell version in print. The first was that of G. W. J. Gyll in 1870 (as included in a volume of Cervantes also containing *The Voyage to Parnassus* and *The Commerce of Algiers*), the second that of James Young Gibson (1885), Gibson's translation being dedicated "To the Memory of General Gordon, the Hero of Khartoum, the Modern Paladin," etc. If in the nineteenth century, Cervantes was enlisted in the cause of British Imperialism, in the twentieth he was made to serve Stalinism as represented by Rafael Alberti (who made two different modern versions: one for Madrid in 1937, one for Montevideo in 1943). In the same year as the "realist" Alberti made his first "social" interpretation of the play, a "formalist" of the Paris theatre, Jean-Louis Barrault, used Cervantes' text as the basis for an exploration of the theatrical medium. Today the play is probably better known in Paris than in any other city in the world: when an enterprising publisher started a paperback series called "Répertoire pour un théâtre populaire," *La Numance* was in the first group of plays chosen.

The author of the present translation was a supporter of
General Franco in war and peace: what *The Siege of Numantia* would mean to him can be deduced from his poem *Flowering Rifle*.

In his book *Sentido y Forma del Teatro de Cervantes*
(Madrid, 1951), Joaquín Casalduero advances the view that
the play is essentially unpolitical.

It was in the late eighteenth century that the classic Spanish drama first made a tremendous impact upon European cul-
ture, and from then on, for some decades at least, the most
favored of the Spanish playwrights was Calderón. The Calderón vogue was challenged before the mid-nineteenth century,
however, by George Henry Lewes for one, who preferred Lope
de Vega. If Calderón's *Life is a Dream* remained, in the general mind, the Spanish masterpiece par excellence, its position
was at least endangered in the twentieth century by Lope's
Fuente Ovejuna (1619). The reason for this is evident in
the first important defence of the play in Spanish, that of
Menendez y Pelayo, who wrote: "There is not a more demo-
cratic work in all of Castilian theatre . . ." As such the play
was taken up by the avant-garde Russian theatre before the
Revolution and widely championed by Communists in later
decades. An article on "Revolutionary Staging of the Classics"
by G. Boyadzhiev, "a prominent Soviet critic," in *Theatre
Workshop*, New York, 1938, is all about *Fuente Ovejuna*. In
the forties, Erwin Piscator put the "left-wing" interpretation
of the play on the stage of his Dramatic Workshop in New
York City. And in the late fifties one finds the play recommended for the *théâtre populaire* and *teatro populare* by
French and Italian writers of the Communist ambiance.

The limits of the modern, "left-wing" view of the play have
been defined by Joaquín Casalduero in his essay "Fuente-
ovejuna" in *La Revista de Filologia Hispanica*, 1943.

Two translations into English have preceded Roy Campbell's in print: that of John Garrett Underhill in his *Four Plays
of Lope de Vega* (1936) and that of Angel Flores and Muriel

Kittel in John Gassner's *Treasury of the Theatre* (New York, 1950–51) and in Mr. Flores' *Masterpieces of the Spanish Golden Age* (New York, 1957).

Even if THE TRICKSTER OF SEVILLE (1630) were not a great play, it would still be a great document of European civilisation, and therefore it is no less than amazing that, through the centuries, it was never translated into English. Pane's bibliography lists only one translation: *The Love-Rogue. A Poetic Drama in Three Acts* (New York, 1923). The translator was Harry Kemp, and his book is neither good writing nor faithful translation.

The play marks the entrance into literature of Don Juan. Though even this fact is often overlooked by non-Spanish writers, it has been known to those who wished to know it; for example, to Bernard Shaw, who once answered as follows the present editor's request for the right to reprint *Man and Superman* alongside Molière's *Festin de Pierre*: "*Le Festin de Pierre* should be preceded by Tirso de Molina's *Burlador de Seville* [sic] not followed by *Man and Superman*."

The Don Juan literature is surveyed in *La Légende de Don Juan* by Gendarme de Bévotte, Paris, 1911, 2 volumes, and in *The Metamorphoses of Don Juan* by Leo Weinstein, Stanford, California, 1959. There is one good book on Tirso de Molina in English: *Tirso de Molina: Studies in Dramatic Realism* by I. L. McClelland, Liverpool, 1948.

On Tirso's possible model for the now legendary role, see: "Grandeur and Misery of Don Juan," by Gregorio Marañon, in *Partisan Review*, Summer 1957. Of the many speculations on the legendary figure himself, particularly suggestive, though chiefly based on the Mozart-Da Ponte version, is Otto Rank's *Die Don Juan Gestalt* (Leipzig, 1924).

A radio adaptation of the Campbell version of *Trickster of Seville* has already been printed in *Masterpieces of the Spanish Golden Age*, edited by Angel Flores (New York, 1957). Though the radio is not mentioned in this publication, no attempt has been made to delete interpolations made to identify characters for an audience that cannot see them.

LIFE IS A DREAM (1635), still perhaps the most celebrated of all Spanish plays, has been translated into English a number of times. The earliest attempt recorded by Pane is that of R. C. Trench (an incomplete translation) in 1856. After Trench came Fitzgerald (1865), though earlier he had written: "Such plays as the *Magico Prodigioso* and the *Vida es Sueño* require another translator"; MacCarthy (1873); William E. Colford (1958). (The foregoing have all been inspected by the present editor. Three others are mentioned in Colford's bibliography: Frank Birch and J. B. Trend in collaboration [1925], C. Morgan [1928], and W. F. Stirling [1942].) Of value to anyone wishing to produce the play is the French stage version by Alexandre Arnoux which was the fruit of a collaboration with Charles Dullin (in Calderón: *Trois Comédies*, Paris, 1955).

The most authoritative recent discussion of the play's meaning is, perhaps, "La vida es sueño," by E. M. Wilson, *Revista de la Universidad de Buenos Aires*, 1947. Along with this article, the following are recommended: the same author's "Gerald Brenan's Calderón," *Bulletin of the Comediantes*, 1952, and A. A. Parker's *The Approach to the Spanish Drama of the Golden Age*, a lecture separately published by The Hispanic & Luso-Brazilian Councils, London, 1957, and reprinted in The Tulane Drama Review, Autumn, 1959.

The preceding Notes have been reproduced from The Classic Theatre, Volume III, 1959. The following were added for the present Applause presentation in 1985:—

The bibliography cited in the note on the Trickster is English Translations from the Spanish, 1484-1943, a Bibliography, by Remigio Ugo Pane (1944).

A very good translation of Life is a Dream was published in 1970 by Hill and Wang, New York. The translator is Edwin Honig, who was also translator of Calderón, Four Plays, (Hill and Wang, 1961), and author of Calderón and the Seizures of Honor (Harvard, 1972).

A Roy Campbell item not included in The Classic Theatre was published by the University of Wisconsin Press in 1960: this was his translation of The Surgeon of His Honour by Calderón.

The E.M. Wilson essay cited above became more accessible in 1965 when included by New York University Press in Critical Essays on the Theatre of Calderón, edited by Bruce W. Wardropper.

The A.A. Parker essay re-appeared in Eric Bentley's anthology The Great Playwrights (Doubleday, 1970).